Marlene Vernon

$9 + 3^{95}$

10^{15}

WOMAN

AN ISSUE

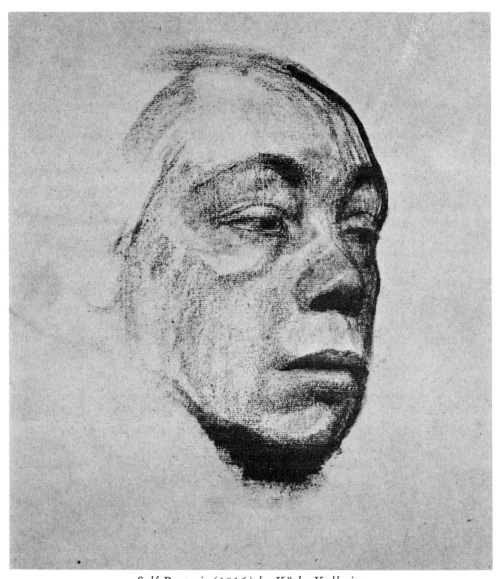

Self-Portrait (1916) by Käthe Kollwitz

WOMAN
AN ISSUE

Edited by Lee R. Edwards, Mary Heath and Lisa Baskin

LITTLE, BROWN AND COMPANY — BOSTON–TORONTO

FIRST EDITION

T 11/72

Library of Congress Cataloging in Publication Data

Edwards, Lee R   comp.
  Woman: an issue.

  (The Massachusetts review, v. 13, nos. 1 & 2)
  Includes bibliographical references.
  1. Woman--History and condition of women.
I. Heath, Mary, 1931-   joint comp. II. Baskin,
Lisa, joint comp. III. Title. IV. Series.
AS30.M3A22 vol. 13, nos. 1-2 [HQ1154] 051s [301.41'2]
ISBN 0-316-21171-0   72-8726
ISBN 0-316-21170-2 (pbk.)

*Published simultaneously in Canada
by Little, Brown & Company (Canada) Limited*

PRINTED IN THE UNITED STATES OF AMERICA

FOREWORD

Woman: An Issue began with a pun: an issue—in fact, a double issue—of *The Massachusetts Review;* a subject of concern; a birth. Now as we publish it as a book, even though the pun is lost, the title remains appropriate: considering women, we are necessarily moved into a world where words and concepts shift and become multiple. In this prismatic universe we discover that those patterns we believed conceptually fixed as both root and mirror of society no longer seem either so permanent or so accurate as they once did. The works in this collection reflect three worlds: the public world of politics and history; the private world of memory, psychology, and meditation; and, if only speculatively, the still unformed world which consciousness creates as we confront aspects of our personal and communal lives previously ignored or, worse, forgotten. Looking at women, we see with many eyes, speak with many voices. As undertone, however, a kind of serious playfulness persists; in exploring and exposing the facts of our existence, irony mediates anger; a hope for comedy is balanced against a necessary acknowledgement of reality's frequent darkness. A pun, a prism, a mysterious face behind a veil, all suggest this complex multivalence.

The essays, poems, fiction, documents, and pictures in this issue constitute only a small fragment of the material received in response to our initial request for contributions. We deeply regret our inability to publish more and wish not merely to acknowledge, but to thank, those whose enthusiasm, energy, and intelligence made our work as editors both so difficult and so rewarding.

L.R.E.
M.H.
L.U.B.

NOTES ON CONTRIBUTORS

Congresswoman BELLA ABZUG was recently battling for reelection to the U.S. House of Representatives. ANNETTE BARNES teaches philosophy at Amherst College. LISA UNGER BASKIN, artist and antique dealer, is active in the Women's movement. BERENICE CARROLL, associate professor of political science at Illinois, is the author of *Design for Total War;* she served as chairwoman of the Coordinating Committee on Women in the Historical Profession. LUCILLE CLIFTON has published children's books as well as poetry. Her newest collection of poems is *Good News About the Earth.* JOHNNETTA COLE is an anthropologist in the W. E. B. Dubois Department of Afro-American Studies, University of Massachusetts, Amherst. MARY DOYLE CURRAN is currently professor of Irish literature, the University of Massachusetts, Boston.

ANGELA DAVIS wrote the essay reprinted in our collection while she was imprisoned in California. ARLYN DIAMOND, medievalist and feminist, raises Irish wolfhounds. She and LEE EDWARDS are currently co-editing a book of feminist criticism and a collection of neglected imaginative writings by women. CYNTHIA EDGAR is an administrative assistant to Representative Bella Abzug. ELLEN DIBBLE's poems have previously appeared in *The Women's Journal.* Winner of the Gold Medal of Jamaica, AMY JACQUES GARVEY is a widely published author, lecturer, and spokesman for Pan-Africanism. At work on theories of the novel, PRISCILLA GIBSON teaches English at the University of Massachusetts, Amherst. PENINA GLAZER lectures at Hampshire College on political women in America. JOAN GOULIANOS writes and teaches in New York City; her most recent book is *By a Woman Writt.*

"The Confessions of Mother Goose" by ANNE HALLEY, poet and translator, is part of a novel in progress. Actress and professor of English, CAROL HEBALD has published her poems in the *Antioch Review, North American Review,* and many other periodicals. MARY HEATH's prize-winning stories have appeared in *The Virginia Quarterly.* SONDRA HERMAN is preparing a study of women in American

Notes on Contributors

history, and the sex roles of women in America. Author of *The Abduction,* and *The Nightmare Factory,* MAXINE KUMIN's new book of poems *Up Country* will be out this fall. AUDRE LORDE's most recent book of poems is *Cables to Rage.*

SUE MULLINS has been active in the Women's movement since 1968. Poet and activist GIULIANA MUTTI was born on Vanzetti's birthday. Long a distinguished voice in modern literature, ANAIS NIN has just published the fourth volume of her diaries. ELIZABETH POCHODA teaches literature at Temple University, Philadelphia. Poet NANCY RAINE is now writing short stories, and a children's book. Ph.D. candidate NANCY RICE has previously published in *The Women's Journal.* LILLIAN ROBINSON appears in *The Politics of Literature;* she teaches a course, "The Sexual Order," at M.I.T. One of the original members of the Black Studies program at San Francisco State College, SONIA SANCHEZ is a poet and the editor of *Three Hundred and Sixty Degrees of Blackness Comin at You.* Former Fulbright fellow MARGARET SHOOK is now at Smith College.

CHRISTINE STANSELL is a student of nineteenth-century feminism. Winner of the Jennie Tane Award for Poetry and director of poetry writing programs in Massachusetts schools, RUTH WHITMAN has just published a new book of translations, *The Selected Poems of Jacob Glatstein.* J. J. WILSON teaches comparative literature at Sonoma State College, Calif. CYNTHIA GRIFFIN WOLFF's new book *Other Lives* is due out shortly.

ACKNOWLEDGMENTS

The editors would like to thank the following people and institutions for special assistance: *Aperture Magazine;* David Batchelder, photographer; Allen Fern, Library of Congress; Harold McGrath, pressman at the Gehenna Press; Howard Hugo and the staff of Meriden Gravure Co.; Ms. Irene Piper and Commonwealth Press of Worcester, Mass.; the Museum of Modern Art, New York; the Philadelphia Museum; the Oakland Museum, Oakland, California; Ms. Dorothy Porter, Founders Library, Howard University; the Sophia Smith Collection at Smith College; Michael Thelwell and the editors of *The Black Scholar;* and, especially, Leonard Baskin, Jules Chametzky, John Hicks, and Sidney Kaplan, who for purposes of this issue have been declared honorary women.

L.R.E.
M.H.
L.U.B.

CONTENTS

Contents

WOMAN
AN ISSUE

*Medal by Patrick Reason (1837). Collection of Emma and
Sidney Kaplan*

WOMEN AND POLITICS:
THE STRUGGLE FOR REPRESENTATION

Bella S. Abzug and Cynthia Edgar

FOR MOST OF THIS country's history, women's place has been in the home, in the fields, in the factories, in the sweatshops, or any place except where the power is. Women have been excluded from the decision-making levels of political parties, and from all levels of government of American society. In the world's greatest democracy, women have been in a worse position than the children who have been entrusted to them, for women have been neither seen nor heard.

How strange that a young revolutionary nation, dedicated to freedom and equality and to eradicating past tyrannies, should have shown so little concern for the freedom and equality of its women. Yet from the very beginning, women were again, as they had been in Europe, denied the right to vote, excluded from the town meetings and the state and Federal legislatures, ignored by the Constitution. Nor was this exclusion any less deliberate than had been the exclusion of Negroes. In a letter to her husband at the Constitutional Convention, Abigail Adams wrote:

> My dear John: By the way, in the new code of laws, I desire you would remember the ladies and be more generous and favorable to them than were your ancestors. Do not put such unlimited power in the hands of husbands. Remember, all men would be tyrants if they could. Your loving wife, Abigail.

This request was, however, a little too revolutionary for Mr. Adams. He replied: "Depend upon it, my dear wife. We men know better than to repeal our masculine systems."

Nearly 200 years later, the government of our nation is still a masculine system. Women won the right to vote only 51 years ago, after a century of struggle in its most political sense. To gain support for the Nineteenth Amendment, women mastered every political technique—lobbying, canvassing, doorbell-ringing, parading, demonstrating. With such experience, women should be well qualified for political participation. Yet in 1971, President Nixon filled only 13 out of 300 Administrative posts with women, and three of those 13 are White House secretaries. Out of 3,796 government jobs of GS-17 level (generally delineating the policy-making levels in government), only 58, or 1.6%, are filled by women. No women

17

have ever been appointed to the Supreme Court, despite a good number of highly competent female Federal judges. And Congress boasts only 12 women, one of whom was originally a replacement for her husband. On the state and local level, there are currently no women governors and only a handful of women mayors. In short, women have gained very little power since Adams' rebuke, or even since the Nineteenth Amendment.

Women are conspicuously absent from all branches of government, but their absence from Congress is most offensive. Women, who constitute 51.3% of the population and 53% of the electorate, are only 2.5% of the House of Representatives and 1% of the Senate. Congress—the representative of the people—is surely one of the most unrepresentative bodies in the world.

Both Congress and women have suffered from the lack of true representation. A review of the treatment of issues now before Congress highlights that male legislators are trapped by their sex when presented with women's issues.

In the Senate, for instance, one of the first issues of the 1971 session was whether three female pages, appointed by Senators Harris, Javits, and Percy, should be received into the male sanctuary. In special hearings on this matter, opponents of "integration" cited the high incidence of purse-snatchings near the Capitol, the strenuous activity involved in the job, and the housing problem as reasons for excluding girls. Senator Percy, whose appointee had received the President's Award for Physical Fitness, assured a skeptical committee that girls are easily capable of handling the exercise and the small amount of documents that must be carried, and that the government could easily provide any necessary housing or escorts. None of the Senators considered that the girls and their parents had all weighed the dangers and stresses and had decided that they could handle them. The Senators, who finally approved the girl pages, seemed unable to transcend their paternalism.

Of much broader concern are the child care bills now under consideration in both houses of Congress. Many of the child care bills authorize funds exclusively for the poor, and Congress in general tends to view child care as a poor woman's problem. Only two bills in the House, the Abzug-Chisholm bill and the Brademas bill, attempted to expand availability of child care facilities to the working and middle classes. Both of these bills reserved a certain proportion of funds and space for the poor (although "poor" was differently defined in the two bills), freeing remaining space and funds for higher-income groups. Mr. Brademas included this provision to assure that child care facilities were not merely custodial, but provided educational and developmental opportunities. By integrating income levels, the poor (often Black) children would be stimulated and taught by the "culturally advantaged" middle-income children; middle-income children would gain perspective on racism and other social problems.

What Mr. Brademas and everyone else in the House failed to perceive was that child care is not only a poverty issue, it is also a woman's issue. In nearly all American families, child care is exclusively a woman's responsibility. So long as child care facilities are available only to the rich,[1] only rich women can seek employment, go to school, or otherwise develop their talents. It is obvious that child care must be available to poor women, so that they can seek employment and provide for their families. Most working poor, lower-middle and middle-class women need and want quality and inexpensive day care so that they too may have a life outside the home.

The Abzug-Chisholm bill attempted to assure facilities for the non-poor, on a paying basis according to income, by gradually decreasing the proportion of funds reserved for the poor—from 65% to 55% over three years. This issue, however, will be lost in the male-dominated committee, and women will gain only incidentally from a series of poverty bills which happen to concern poor women. In the Senate, the woman's issue has been neither researched nor raised, so no provision for non-poor women has been made. The working poor woman will be penalized for having worked despite the unavailability of quality daycare, and the middle-class woman will continue to be confined to the home.

The most visible and vocal issue in Congress is, of course, the Equal Rights Amendment. Debate and tactics on this issue are among the most histrionic in Congress. In 1970, after 48 years in Committee, the Equal Rights Amendment was sent to the floor of the House on a petition of discharge. The Amendment passed the House by a vote of 350–15. But the Senate attached a series of crippling riders, and women withdrew their support for the Amendment. In 1971, the House Judiciary Committee reported out the Equal Rights Amendment with a rider exempting women from the draft and exempting all state laws "which reasonably promote the health and safety of the people," in effect, exempting all laws which currently discriminate against women. In the Senate, the chairman of the Judiciary Committee filibusters the amendment to block consideration by the full Senate.

Once again, the male legislators are unable to transcend their

---

[1] Estimates in Congress on the cost of quality day-care ranged from $1300 to $2800 per child per year.

19

male self-image to represent their women constituents. Many legislators (probably not a majority, but many of the most powerful
committee chairmen) do not want to subject women to military
conscription, nor do they want to release women from the oppressive, state "protective laws." Why women must be exempted from
the draft is unclear, but the justification seems to fall somewhere
between chivalry and a belief that women could not be trusted in
combat. Perhaps the real objection is a fear that women would not
accept war psychology and would inject a note of pacifism into the
military machine.

The vocal concern for state protective laws is also puzzling. It is
by no means ordained that protective laws which protect women
more than men would be stricken by the Equal Rights Amendment;
it is equally likely that the courts would instead extend the laws to
protect both sexes. This would seem more within the intent of the
legislature, if the courts could avoid the appearance of legislation
rather than interpretation. Assuming, however, that protective laws
would fall, women would for the first time have access to tough but
well-paid jobs.

Protective laws are now the single greatest obstacle to a totally
integrated work force. Employers use protective laws to exclude
women from jobs which they are perfectly capable of performing,
and which offer greater training, pay, and mobility. Several legal
challenges to these laws have been litigated under Title VII of the
1964 Civil Rights Act where the employer has used protective laws,
regardless of actual job requirements, to confine women to low-pay-
ing jobs and to separate seniority systems.

Of course, it is true that some women cannot regularly lift 30
pounds, or 40 pounds, or whatever the maximum weight happens to
be. It is also true that some women can easily lift that amount,
while some men cannot. Most women, in fact, occasionally lift
heavier items in housekeeping. Evidence indicates that in any event,
few employers require heavy items to be lifted; they use a crane,
or a pulley, or a dolly, or some other mechanical means.

Likewise, hour limitations should not be any lower for women
than for men; what is too long for women is too long for everyone.
So long as women are required by law to work shorter hours, employers will be reluctant to hire them. Conversely, those who wish
to work long hours for lucrative overtime pay are prevented from
doing so by "protective" laws.

Protective laws which protect women more than men are based
upon the stereotype of frailty. This is unjustified and restrictive. If
protective laws are necessary, a legislature should be able to establish a basic, *human* protection which allows individuals of both

sexes to demonstrate their capacity to exceed the limit. Such human limits would also be a proper subject for union negotiations by unions equally solicitous of its women's interests as its men's. Congress must be able to transcend its stereotyped chivalry to understand the issues, and to afford women the same opportunities that are afforded to men—on the same basis of individual capabilities.

Since Congress has been unable to transcend its sexual bias, the sexual bias of Congress must change. Members of Congress are finally becoming sensitive to the political power of women. Women are running their offices, typing their speeches, filing, answering phones, answering letters. The government could not run for a single day without them. Women are also 53% of the electorate, and they vote more conscientiously and frequently than do men. Women have a right—and a duty—to state their needs fully and boldly and to assure that those needs are met. Experience shows that those needs will be met only when women represent themselves in Congress.

Thus, the National Women's Political Caucus was formed to attain full representation of women in government. Three hundred women from 26 states and the District of Columbia met in Washington, D.C. in early July 1971 to discuss how to thrust women into politics. The women who attended were of all ages, colors, classes, and political persuasions, although Democrats seemed predominant. The group was diverse, articulate, and aggressive—by definition, it seemed, prone to factionalism. Yet there was practically no disagreement on the nature and breadth of women's issues, and disagreements as to tactics were compromised—at least temporarily—in the interest of unity. Perhaps the single most remarkable aspect of the Caucus was its determination to appeal to all women.

After 50 years of suffrage, the time has come for women to use their vote to attain power over themselves. The Caucus resolved to double or triple the number of women in Congress in 1972 (women would then be 8% of Congress, or 1/6 represented). By 1976, the Caucus hopes to force the political structure to mirror reality—with 50% or more positions of power filled by women, and perhaps a woman in the White House. As a matter of right, women must be fully represented in all branches of government.

To achieve such monumental gains, the Caucus must build a practical, realistic, political movement that is broad-based and united. Mass support can be attained only by addressing the interests of poor women, third-world women, and middle-class women. Women will have to be aggressive—even pushy—to fight the entrenched male bureaucracies; after all, candidates are not nominated simply because they are most highly qualified. Women, however, have been doing the "support" work—the real work—of politics for years. They know how to organize political movements; now is the time to organize their own.

On these sentiments, the Caucus established a national structure and formulated policies, priorities, and guidelines for the organization of local machines. The first policy decision was the agreement that the Caucus would not, at this point, become a woman's party, but would operate within established party structures. If women cannot make headway within party structures, the Caucus will run its own slate of candidates or work outside the political parties.

Congress is now dominated by male, white, middle-aged to old, upper middle-class "representatives." This is not the kind of Congress that the Women's Political Caucus wants to perpetuate. Rather than replacing a white male elite with a white female elite, the Caucus intends to elect a diversity of women: Black, white, Indian, Puerto Rican, Chicano, Asian; welfare mothers; union women, factory workers, farm workers, secretaries, teachers, artists, doctors, scientists, housewives, lawyers, businesswomen; young, old, middle-aged; poor, working poor, middle-class. Such a Congress would be more truly representative, better prepared to deal with the complex problems which beset our society, and unlikely to tolerate laws and procedures which now discriminate against women, the poor, the young, and any underrepresented minority.

Perhaps more important, such a Congress could make the shift in priorities that is necessary if social change and justice are to become realities. The conference revealed that regardless of party affiliation, women are committed to changing the direction of society and of the family. Guidelines on important election issues, endorsed by the whole conference, reflected the consensus for change. Perhaps sustained absence from the political structure has given women the outsider's objectivity to see where and how society has gone astray.

Some of the women's issues endorsed by the Caucus include:

1. Immediate passage of the Equal Rights Amendment;
2. Repeal of all laws affecting a woman's right to decide her own reproductive and sexual life;
3. Amendment of the 1964 Civil Rights Act to eliminate discrimination against women in public education, public accommodations, public facilities, and all Federally assisted programs;
4. Enforcement of existing anti-discrimination laws such as Title VII, the Equal Pay Act, and Executive Orders, and includes strengthening EEOC;
5. Elimination of the tax inequities affecting women and children;
6. Extension of the Equal Pay Act of 1963 to cover workers now ignored—professional, executive, and administrative, and extension of minimum wage to cover all workers, including domestics;
7. Increase and extension of unemployment insurance;
8. End to all kinds of discrimination in educational institutions;

The Struggle for Representation

9. Fair treatment of working women, regardless of marital status and including child care deductions, maternity benefits, voluntary parental leave (for men and women), and elimination of discriminatory social security laws.

Priorities which apply to society as a whole include:

1. Comprehensive and preventive health care for all Americans;
2. Legislation, enforcement, and education to preserve the environment;
3. Fair treatment in housing—including elimination of discrimination against women, especially welfare mothers;
4. Adequate income for all Americans;
5. End to hunger and malnutrition;
6. Community controlled programs for free child care, incorporating education, health, and child development; free programs for the aged;
7. Adaptation of institutions to the changing work patterns accompanying the humanization of both sex roles.

Sufficient funds for such broad social programs can come only from the government. The government, however, is presently squandering resources on foreign wars and munitions. The Caucus recognized that it could not realistically engage in a struggle against sex discrimination and against minority discrimination without also engaging in a national peace movement to free available resources. Therefore, foremost on the list of priorities to be changed is the demand for immediate withdrawal from the war in Vietnam, and cessation of the arms race and violence as a "masculine" way of resolving conflict.

The consensus on priorities and goals is encouraging but the difficult question of tactics remains. Some women still must be educated—to be sensitized; but those women who are already aware want representation now. The Caucus decided that women could be educated at the same time that other women are elected by raising women's issues at every election and by publicizing candidates' records on the issues. Meanwhile, new women will be registered and encouraged to vote for women candidates endorsed by the National Women's Political Caucus, crossing party lines when necessary. Party structures will be confronted and reformed to assure women an equal voice in decision-making and the selection of candidates. National support will be rallied for women candidates willing to fight for women and all underrepresented groups. Women if necessary will form coalitions with groups with similar objectives. Most important, women must be trained to organize at state and local levels to accomplish their objectives.

To assure that organization begins immediately, the National Women's Political Caucus elected 21 women to act as a continuing Policy Council, with authority to act in the name of the Caucus, establish and nominate necessary committees, and to increase its number to 25 by appointing 4 additional women. The suggestion of a Constitution and bylaws were specifically rejected to assure maximum flexibility. The Policy Council represents a diversity of geographic areas, political affiliations, ethnic, economic, and age groupings; but it plans to increase its diversity by appointing young women and women of Spanish-speaking origin to the remaining four slots. The Council meets at least monthly, and has established an office in Washington, D.C.

State caucuses will be organized in at least 26 states and the District of Columbia, and eventually in all states and territories. These state and local caucuses will be the real centers of issue formulation and political action, with access to financial aid, expertise, and speakers from the National Caucus. Each state, territory, and the District of Columbia will elect one woman to sit in a National Assembly, which together with the National Policy Council will be the policy-making body.

The National Caucus has already taken on the task of monitoring the selection of delegates to the 1972 presidential nominating conventions. In 1968, only 13% of the Democratic delegates and 17% of the Republican delegates were women; of 108 state delegations at both conventions, only one was chaired by a woman (Edith Green of Oregon). The Democratic Party has already agreed to challenge delegations in which women of all ages, races, and socio-economic levels are not reasonably represented. The Caucus has made a similar demand of the Republican National Committee to enforce its own guidelines promulgated at its July meeting.

In 1972, women will run as convention delegates and for local, state, and national offices. The Caucus will campaign for women—and men—candidates who are strong on women's issues. Republicans and Democrats agree, however, that the Caucus must do more than limit itself to the goal of more women in office, regardless of their stand on issues. Racist candidates will not be supported even if they are feminist. With the power of vote and organized efforts, women can play a significant role in the National Party Conventions, in the formulation of platforms, and in the choice of candidates.

Women already have the capacity to build the kind of humanistic society in which men and women can fully express their creativity and talents. Courage is contagious. As more women organize and speak out, they will win the political power to which their sheer numbers, their rights as citizens, their ability, and their experience entitle them. For this movement has compromised its differences to appeal to all women who must work together if women are to gain the power they deserve. The real silent majority is about to vocalize.

1. Articles and Pamphlets

BROPHY, BRIGID. "Women" in *Don't Never Forget; Collected Views and Reviews.* New York, Holt, Rinehart and Winston, 1966, pp. 38–44. (Originally published in the *Saturday Evening Post,* November 1963.) Writing in her usual astringent style, Brigid Brophy takes on modern society's treatment of women.

BUCK, PEARL S. "The Education of Women" in *To My Daughters, With Love.* New York, John Day, 1967, pp. 157–175. Pearl Buck says, "Woman is still living in the age of man's vengeance."

COMFORT, ALEX. "The Naked Lady" in *Darwin and the Naked Lady; Discursive Essays on Biology and Art.* New York, Braziller, 1962, pp. 100–118. On art and eroticism seen from an exclusively male viewpoint; women considered as art objects, sexual objects, passive receivers of erotic pleasure—never as viewers or doers. The artist is always considered as a man. A good example of unconscious sexual stereotyping.

DECROW, KAREN. "Women and Politics" in *Mademoiselle,* vol. 70, no. 4, February 1970, pp. 34–36. The story of what happened when a militant feminist ran for mayor of Syracuse, New York.

FREEMAN, JO. "The Building of the Gilded Cage," unpublished paper, 1969. A sharp assessment of the socialization and social control of women, and of the agents of that social control; legal, sociological viewpoint and references.

FRISOF, JAMIE KELEM. "Textbooks and Channeling," in *Women: A Journal of Liberation,* vol. 1, no. 1, Fall 1969, pp. 26–28. An analysis of five social studies textbooks and their presentation of women in contemporary life.

GAGNON, JOHN, and WILLIAM SIMON. "Is a Women's Revolution Really Possible?" in *McCall's,* October 1969, pp. 76 ff. If women were to be truly liberated our society would have to change so radically in work, family, and sex, we would hardly recognize it. Are men or women ready or capable of such change?

GALT, WILLIAM E. "The Male-Female Dichotomy in Human Behavior: A Phylobiological Evaluation," in *Psychiatry*, vol. 6, 1943, pp. 1–14. Galt was assistant to Trigant Burrow, a pioneer in group psychiatry. He sees "normal" sex life as a restriction of the organism's response. For a discussion of the ideas in this article see Betty Roszak's "The Human Continuum" in this anthology.

GINOTT, HAIM. "Sexual Role and Social Function" in *Between Parent and Child*. New York, Macmillan, 1965, chapter 10. This influential manual of child psychology preaches the traditional sexual virtues: boys must be raised to be he-men and breadwinners; girls to be shy maidens and homebodies. A continuing best seller, the book is a striking example of how popular psychology can be used to legitimize the oppression of women.

LIMPUS, LAUREL. "Liberation of Women: Sexual Repression and the Family," a reprint from *This Magazine Is About Schools*. Boston, New England Free Press, Spring 1969. An attack on woman's role as defined by the family.

"Little Mommy, You Have a Long Way to Go," *Association of American University Women Journal*, vol. 63, no. 2, January 1970, pp. 57–61. A panel discussion of women's liberation.

MCCARTHY, MARY. "The Tyranny of the Orgasm," in *On the Contrary*. New York, Farrar, Straus and Cudahy, 1951, pp. 167–173. Review of Lundberg and Farnham's *Modern Woman, the Lost Sex*. Good in its opposition to the "anatomy is destiny" school of thought.

MASLOW, ABRAHAM H. "Self-Esteem (Dominance-Feeling) and Sexuality in Women," in *Journal of Social Psychology*, vol. XVI, 1942; reprinted in Ruitenbeek, Hendrik M., ed., *Psychoanalysis and Female Sexuality*. New Haven, Conn., College and University Press, 1966, pp. 161–197. Women's sexual attitudes are more the "functions of personality and social and cultural relationships than of sheer biological endowment." Maslow finds that women with a high sense of self-esteem are sexually aggressive and more responsive than those with low self-esteem.

MASLOW, ABRAHAM, H. RAND, and S. NEWMAN. "Some Parallels Between Sexual and Dominant Behavior of Infra-Human Primates and the Fantasies of Patients in Psychotherapy," from *Journal of Nervous and Mental Disease,* vol. 131, 1960, pp. 202–212. Dr. Maslow and his associates conclude that the dominance/submission sex relationship is a sign of immature development and leads to a diminution of human sexuality.

MORGAN, ROBIN. "Women's Liberation," in *WIN Magazine,* Feb. 15, 1969, pp. 10–12. An excellent review of the movement.

O'NEILL, WILLIAM L. "Feminism as a Radical Ideology," in *Dissent; Explorations in the History of American Radicalism,* ed. by Alfred F. Young. De Kalb, Ill., Northern Illinois University Press, 1968, pp. 273–300. Good historical study of why the first wave of feminist activity failed.

PHELAN, LANA CLARKE. "Abortion Laws: The Cruel Fraud," speech delivered at the California Conference on Abortion, Santa Barbara, Calif., February 10, 1968. Reprinted by the Society for Humane Abortion.

PIERCY, MARGE. "The Grand Coolie Dam" in *Leviathan,* vol. 1, no. 6, Oct./Nov. 1969, pp. 16–22. Things are getting worse, not better, for women in the movement. The double standard reigns in radical male behavior.

PRIESTLEY, J. B. "Women Don't Run the Country," in *Essays of Five Decades.* Boston, Little, Brown, 1968, pp. 239–243. (Originally published in *Saturday Evening Post,* December 12, 1964.) Contrary to prevailing views, there is no "matriarchy" in the U.S., according to Priestley. Rather *Logos,* or masculinity, dominates, and we need the healing power of *Eros,* or femininity.

REEVES, NANCY. *Stereotypes of Woman's Place,* pamphlet. Los Angeles, University of California, 1969. A witty, stylish assessment of women in our society. Used as a text in Reeves's course at U.C.L.A.

RICHIE, JEANNE. "Church, Caste and Women" in *Christian Century,* vol. LXXXVII, no. 3, January 21, 1970, pp. 73–77. Clergymen are unconcerned while women demand more responsibility, less "volunteerism" in the church, as well as recruitment to the ministry.

RIEFF, PHILIP. "Sexuality and Domination," parts IV and V in *Freud: The Mind of the Moralist.* New York, Anchor Books, 1961, pp. 191–204. Shrewd analysis of the significance of Freud's misogyny. Rieff shows how Freud's hostility to women underlies his psychoanalytic theory.

SHAW, GEORGE BERNARD. "Woman-Man in Petticoats," in *Platform and Pulpit,* ed. by Dan H. Laurence. New York, Hill and Wang,

1961, pp. 172–178. In this speech delivered in 1927 Shaw argues away all the stereotyped differences between male and female.

SIMON, WILLIAM, and JOHN GAGNON. "Psychosexual Development," in *Trans-action*, vol. 6, March 1969, pp. 9–17. "We see sexual behavior . . . as scripted behavior, not the masked expression of a primordial drive."

THOMAS, KEITH. "The Double Standard," in *Journal of the History of Ideas*, April, 1959, pp. 195–216. Relates the mystique of female chastity to property rights.

UNWIN, HARRIET. "In a Man's World; the Best of Both Worlds," in *Anarchy* (London), vol. 5, no. 56, October 1965, pp. 302–310. Discussion of Betty Friedan's book and its implications for British women.

WILLIS, ELLEN. "Whatever Happened to Women?—Nothing, That's the Trouble," in *Mademoiselle*, vol. 69, no. 5, September 1969, pp. 150 ff. Pop-critic for *The New Yorker* and member of N.Y. Redstockings glares at the master-slave relationship.

ZILBOORG, GREGORY. "Male and Female," in *Psychiatry*, VII, 1944, pp. 257–296. Fascinating review of "phallocentric" psychoanalysis; discusses the work of Lester F. Ward, a late nineteenth-century sociologist who attacked male supremacy.

2. Books

BIRD, CAROLINE. *Born Female: The High Cost of Keeping Women Down.* New York, David McKay, 1968. Especially good on the economic facts of life for women.

BRIFFAULT, ROBERT. *The Mothers: The Matriarchal Theory of Social Origins*, abridged ed. by Gordon Rattray Taylor. New York, Universal Library, Grosset and Dunlap, 1963. First published in several volumes in 1927. A study of the matriarchal nature of primitive society. Briffault sees monogamy as a late development of the patriarchy.

CARSON, JOSEPHINE. *Silent Voices: The Southern Negro Woman Today.* New York, Delacorte Press, 1969. Deals movingly with the overwhelming poverty, drudgery, and struggle of the Southern Negro woman.

FERGUSON, CHARLES W. *The Male Attitude.* Boston, Little, Brown, 1966. Demonstrates how masculine thinking has dominated the course of American history; examines development of the gun, slavery, and the machine as male institutions. A much neglected work.

FIGES, EVA. *Patriarchal Attitudes: Women in Society.* London, Faber and Faber, 1970. An English novelist examines historical attitudes toward women; especially good for the selection of quotations from Rousseau, Freud, and Otto Weininger.

FLEXNER, ELEANOR. *Century of Struggle.* Belknap Press of Harvard University, 1959. History of American feminism.

FRIEDAN, BETTY. *The Feminine Mystique.* New York, Norton, 1963. The book that started it all.

JEANNIERE, ABEL. *The Anthropology of Sex.* Foreword by Dan Sullivan. New York, Harper, 1967. French Catholic anthropologist looks at the stereotypes of male and female; Sullivan's excellent foreword discusses De Beauvoir, love, sexuality, and the Christian tradition.

KANOWITZ, LEO. *Women and the Law: The Unfinished Revolution.* Albuquerque, University of New Mexico Press, 1969. Carefully documented scrutiny of legal discrimination on the basis of sex in the U.S.

KRADITOR, AILEEN S. *Ideas of the Woman Suffrage Movement, 1890–1920.* New York, Columbia University Press, 1965. A study of both profeminist and antifeminist thought in America.

———. *Up From the Pedestal: Selected Writings in the History of American Feminism.* Chicago, Quadrangle Books, 1968.

LAWRENCE, D. H. *Assorted Articles.* New York, Knopf, 1930. A collection of brief essays, several of which deal petulantly with the "cocksure" women of the day. Classic statements of defensive masculinity by the author of *Lady Chatterley's Lover.*

LEFORT, GERTRUDE VON. *The Eternal Woman: The Woman in Time, Timeless Woman.* Milwaukee, Bruce, 1954. Woman as bearer of salvation; Catholic viewpoint on the veil, mystery, and chastity.

LIFTON, ROBERT JAY, ed. *The Woman in America* (The Daedalus Library). Boston, Houghton, Mifflin, 1964. Contains a number of good articles, including Alice Rossi's "Equality Between the Sexes: An Immodest Proposal."

LUNDBERG, FERDINAND, and MARYNIA F. FARNHAM. *Modern Woman: The Lost Sex.* New York, Harper, 1947. Women seen as passive sufferers. This is the book refuted by Mary McCarthy in her article "The Tyranny of the Orgasm."

MARDER, HERBERT. *Feminism and Art; A Study of Virginia Woolf.* Chicago, University of Chicago Press, 1968. See especially his chapter, "Feminism and Art" for a perceptive study of V. Woolf's feminist ideas.

MASTERS, R. E. L., and EDUARD LEA. *The Anti-Sex: The Belief in the Natural Inferiority of Women: Studies in Male Frustration and Sexual Conflict.* New York, Julian Press, 1964. Hate-filled selections by misogynists through the ages, including Aristophanes, Juvenal, Schopenhauer, Jonathan Swift, and Otto Weininger among others.

MEMMI, ALBERT. *Dominated Man: Notes Toward a Portrait.* New York, Orion Press, 1968. Chapter on women deals mainly with Simone de Beauvoir. Illuminating on the psychology of oppressed and oppressor with a definition of racism that would apply just as well to sexism.

MERRIAM, EVE. *After Nora Slammed the Door: American Women in the 1960's: The Unfinished Revolution.* Cleveland, World Publishing Co., 1964. Cleverly written indictment of women's role.

O'NEILL, WILLIAM L. *Everyone Was Brave: The Rise and Fall of Feminism.* Chicago, Quadrangle Books, 1969. Scholarly account of early American feminism and its demise.

PARTURIER, FRANÇOISE. *Open Letter to Men.* New York, Heinemann, 1968. Reply to previously published *Open Letter to a Woman of Today*, by André Soubiran (Heinemann); French feminist viewpoint, dedicated to Simone de Beauvoir; light, whimsical, but filled with a sense of outrage.

PHELAN, LANA CLARKE, and PATRICIA MAGINNIS. *The Abortion Handbook for Responsible Women.* North Hollywood, Calif., Contact Books, 1969. Down-to-earth discussion of all phases of abortion, including what to do and what not to do. Hypocrisy of the medical profession exposed.

SCHMALHAUSEN, SAMUEL D., and V. F. CALVERTON. *Woman's Coming of Age: A Symposium.* New York, Liveright, 1931. Essays by Charlotte Perkins Gilman, Havelock Ellis, Dora Russell, Rebecca West, and others.

STERN, KARL. *The Flight from Woman.* New York, Farrar, Straus and Giroux, 1965. Idea of woman as muse and closer to nature than men. Stern is a believer in sexual polarities: "masculine rationalism" versus "feminine intuitiveness."

STOLLER, ROBERT J. *Sex and Gender: On the Development of Masculinity and Femininity.* New York, Science House, 1968. Refutes "innate differences" theory of masculine-feminine behavior: ". . . insofar as the development of gender identity is concerned in almost all humans, by far the most powerful effect comes from postnatal psychodynamic factors. . . ."

WATTS, ALAN. *Nature, Man and Woman.* New York, Pantheon, 1958. Sex as cosmic union; opposed to grasping, power-play aspects of Western attitude toward nature and sex.

WEININGER, OTTO. *Sex and Character.* London, Heinemann, 1906. Rabidly antifeminist tirade.

WOOLF, VIRGINIA. *A Room of One's Own.* New York, Harcourt, Brace, 1929; and *Three Guineas,* London, Hogarth Press, 1938. Imaginative treatments of the intellectual and economic exploitation of women.

WRIGHT, SIR ALMROTH. *The Unexpurgated Case Against Woman's Suffrage.* New York, Paul B. Hoeber, 1913. Well-known antifeminist book of the prevote era.

3. Fiction and Drama

This is obviously only a small, personal selection from the vast number of works of literature which deal with woman's struggle for sanity and social equality.

DRABBLE, MARGARET. *The Millstone.* New York, Morrow, 1965. Adventures of a young unmarried woman who decides to have her baby on her own in London. Harrowing and beautifully written.

GILMAN, CHARLOTTE PERKINS. "The Yellow Wall-Paper" in *Ghostly Tales to Be Told,* ed. by Basil Davenport. New York, Dodd, Mead, 1950. Anthologized widely as a horror story, it is in fact the real experience of Mrs. Gilman. The woman in the wallpaper trying to get out is . . . herself, trying to become real. She states in her autobiography, *The Living of Charlotte Perkins Gilman,* that she wrote the story in 1890 after a nervous breakdown, following which she became subject to fits of depression all of her life.

GELLHORN, MARTHA. *Two by Two.* New York, Simon and Schuster, 1958. Bitter-sweet collection of short stories on modern marriage and love.

GODARD, JEAN-LUC. *La Femme Mariée.* Film about the life of a married woman who is deeply alienated; she has the same empty relationship with both her lover and her husband. When she finds she is pregnant and asks the doctor for an abortion, he refuses to advise her. She is the epitome of woman as exploited by the advertising image.

GRANVILLE-BARKER, HARLEY. *The Madras House,* in *Edwardian Plays,* ed. by Gerald Weales. Mermaid Dramabook, New York,

Hill and Wang, 1962. Drawing-room melodrama which mirrors Edwardian preoccupation with women's place.

KAUFMAN, SUE. *Diary of a Mad Housewife.* New York. Random House, 1967. Bitter, but hilarious account of an urban wife's marital tribulations.

LAWRENCE, D. H. *The Daughter-In-Law,* in *Complete Plays* (Phoenix ed.). London, Heinemann, 1965. Play about a brutish coal-miner, his wife, who has cultural aspirations, and his mother, who seeks to dominate them both. The scenes of marital conflict are as bitter and powerful as any of Strindberg's.

LESSING, DORIS. *The Golden Notebook.* New York, Simon and Schuster, 1962. Fictional life of a woman struggling to be free and herself in contemporary London.

PAVITT, DAWN, and TERRY WALE. *The Bond.* A B.B.C. Television Play. A young woman gradually becomes aware of her marriage as bondage. Excellent for use as an introduction to all problems of women's liberation. Should be screened on as many educational TV outlets as possible.

PLATH, SYLVIA. *The Bell Jar.* London, Faber and Faber, 1966. Novel about a girl who doesn't, can't, and won't fit in, and her horrifying experiences of psychosis in a mental hospital.

SHAW, GEORGE BERNARD. *Getting Married,* in *Edwardian Plays,* ed. by Gerald Weales. Mermaid Dramabook, New York, Hill and Wang, 1962.

STRINDBERG, AUGUST. *Married: Stories of Married Life,* trans. by Ellie Schleussner. London, Frank Palmer, 1913.

WELLS, H. G. *Ann Veronica: A Modern Love Story.* New York, Harper, 1909. Ann Veronica, a spirited, intelligent girl, runs away from her repressive father to London, joins the suffragettes, gets arrested, and falls in love on her own terms. The epilogue—disappointingly—finds her a respectable married woman.

72 73   12 11 10 9 8 7 6 5 4

ORGANIZING FOR FREEDOM

Penina Migdal Glazer

THE SUFFRAGE MOVEMENT was probably the largest, most well-organized and effective feminist movement in the history of the struggle for women's rights. These feminists have been eulogized for their great accomplishments and criticized for their too narrow vision. Yet, who were the suffragists? What were their goals? They included left-wing radicals like Emma Goldman who spent years in jail and exile, middle-class respectables, and upper-class matrons like Alva Vanderbilt Belmont who spent millions of dollars to be accepted into New York's "400."

All of the women agreed on one premise—women's rights should be expanded. Beyond this they often followed separate paths. The moderates wanted equal rights; they demanded that they be integrated into a male-dominated society from which they were overtly excluded. Their more radical colleagues rejected this goal. For them the fight for women's rights was part of a larger quest for social change. What good would the ballot be for people too poor and too exploited to use it?

The major works on the history of women focus on the former stance. But this emphasis alone does a disservice to the complexity and richness of a social movement. It is much more useful to analyze several feminist movements, united in certain goals and actions yet distinct in their ultimate goals and strategies. We need to know not only about the Susan B. Anthonys and the Carrie Chapman Catts, but also about the ideas and programs of the women socialists, anarchists, and progressive urban reformers. These deeply committed activists sought to change basic social and political institutions through involvement in unionization, internationalist and peace movements and through efforts to change State, family, and church.

There are a number of good books on the more conservative wing of the suffrage movement. Aileen Kraditor, in her study *Ideas of the Woman Suffrage Movement, 1890–1920*, has pointed out that the major organizations were very much characterized by their middle-class composition and middle-of-the-road allegiance. Leaders of the National American Women's Suffrage Association (NAWSA) no longer spoke in the idealistic rhetoric of an earlier generation of abolitionists for whom the ballot had been a lofty and distant ideal. The new generation was determined to be politically effective and largely shunned arguments of justice, universal suffrage, and unqualified democracy. By the turn of the century, women had gained a number of civil rights including the right to own property and access to higher education. Considering themselves intelligent Americans who were eminently qualified to vote, they allied themselves, often for the sake of expedience, with anti-Negro, anti-foreign, and sometimes anti-labor groups. Miss Kraditor develops this theme in great detail, noting exceptions, regional differences, and inconsistencies within this branch of the movement. She has established quite clearly the limited social and institutional changes sought by the NAWSA and its great leaders such as Susan B. Anthony, Carrie Chapman Catt, or Anna Howard Shaw.[1]

My major focus in this essay is with those more radical women who recognized the grave limitations of the position that the vote alone would fundamentally alter women's role in society and government, and who sought to integrate the quest for the ballot into a more broadly conceived program for change. One alternate model to the suffragists' demand for their civil rights was initiated in the 1880's when a number of women related their own conditions to a more general critique of American society. The list of names of these dedicated women is very long and includes upper-class reformers (Margaret Dreier Robbins), middle-class leaders (Jane Addams, Lillian Wald, Mary McDowell), and working class women (Agnes Nestor). Among this group there was a constantly shifting emphasis between the need for women to work for feminist causes and for women to struggle to make society more democratic, more just, and more humane. For them, social change for women was part of a larger effort against exploitation to which they devoted their lives. This was an age when large numbers of extraordinary women became involved with the society, the world, and its deep-seated, multi-faceted social problems. Their struggle for institutional reform is an important chapter in American history.

The Settlement House Movement

The 1880's produced the first generations of female college graduates from Cornell University, Smith College, Bryn Mawr, Oberlin, Rockford Seminary, and a number of other schools which had opened their doors for preparatory and college level work for members of the "fair and uneducated" sex. Now the first graduates found themselves with a reasonably good education and nothing to do. They were concerned that they had become educated, well-travelled dolls who would have no impact or importance.

---

[1] A. Kraditor, *Ideas of the Woman Suffrage Movement, 1890–1920,* New York: Columbia University Press, 1965.

Organizing for Freedom

Their determination to prevent this resulted in their involvement in a number of crucial projects. Their role in the founding of the urban settlement houses was perhaps most far-reaching. Conscious of their elitist position and committed to avoiding *noblesse oblige* charity works, they moved into the slums of New York, Chicago, and Boston to live among the people as neighbors, friends, and community organizers. The memoirs of Jane Addams, Mary Simkovitch, and Lillian Wald vividly record the spirit and energy of these women. The records of the College Settlement Association document the substantial number of alumnae who worked and resided, for varying periods of time, in the Settlement houses. Through these institutions they became socially committed, political activists. They worked for institutional innovations (e.g. public health nursing), political reform, redistribution of resources (unionizing workers, organizing immigrants), and women's rights.

Mary McDowell, a settlement worker who was an important figure in the women's labor and political movement, incorporated many of the outstanding characteristics of the feminine leaders of her generation. Born to a relatively affluent family just before the Civil War, Miss McDowell was brought up on the glory of Lincoln and the cause of the North for which her father had fought. Although she was not a college graduate as so many of her settlement worker colleagues were, she did prepare for teaching in the newly founded, and still experimental, kindergartens. Her young adulthood was spent in Chicago where she came under the influence of temperance leader Frances Willard and was exposed to a number of the reform movements which characterized the late nineteenth and early twentieth century.

As a resident in Hull House, with close acquaintances in the Northwestern University faculty and in the University of Chicago's fledgling sociology department, she further established her connections with the liberal activists of that period. Miss McDowell went beyond a fashionable involvement in a few middle-class projects when she moved to Packingtown, back of Chicago's stockyards, to head the University of Chicago Settlement House. Immediately concerned with the abysmal living conditions of immigrant employees in the large meat packing corporations, she became a leader in the organization of workers and a supporter during their strikes.

From that point on her long career was marked by her commitment to basic reforms in the social and political system. This was a difficult job amongst men and almost unheard-of for women. Active in the legislative battle for the eight-hour day, dedicated to including white and black women in the labor movement, committed to the battle for women's suffrage and participation in politics, she

31

increasingly expanded her definitions of pressing problems and her reform goals.

The tying together of the problems of women with the struggles of the working class was critical for Mary McDowell and other settlement workers' entire conception of feminism. It removed these women from the narrow provincialism which often led more moderate feminists to equate the status of middle-class women with all women.[2] The conscious attempt to unify these issues represented a radical departure from the "vote-above-all" women and also from the most militant feminists who sought equality for women to the exclusion of any class interests.

Settlement workers and organizers were often accused by conservatives of engaging in dangerous socialist and anarchist ideas, defense of violence and illegal disruption of the social order. Radicals, on the other hand, were appalled by the settlement workers' abysmal lack of recognition of the importance of class consciousness, and feared that they were middle- and upper-class spies who would co-opt or sell out working women and men. In fact, their political theory was a dynamic combination of conservatism and radicalism which was peculiarly effective in this period of urbanization, industrialization, and the legitimation of unionization.

While there was considerable range of political orientations within Settlement associations, the prevailing views of leading feminist organizers such as Mary McDowell, Florence Kelly, or Jane Addams, was one of expanding class cooperation and rejecting exclusive concern with middle-class women's quest for equality in favor of identification with labor's interests. To Jane Addams, the founder of Hull House, concern with the labor movement symbolized the "recognition of the fact that it is a general social movement concerning all members of society and not merely a class struggle."[3] Even those Settlement workers who called themselves "socialists" were fundamentally committed to class cooperation as a major means of improving the human condition. Particular emphasis was often given to the special problem of female labor. Hull House, for example, was the place where women shirtmakers and cloakmakers were organized. At this same notable Settlement one of the earliest female organizers, Mary Kenny O'Sullivan of the bookbinders' union, was convinced that her suspicions of the

---

[2] See Gerda Lerner's discussion of this in "Women's Rights and American Feminism," *American Scholar*, XL (Spring, 1971), 235–248.

[3] Jane Addams, *Twenty Years at Hull House*, New York: New American Library, 1961 edition, p. 158.

Organizing for Freedom

middle-class ladies were unfounded; that "outsiders" could be useful to working women. Thereafter, working class and middle-class organizers in the Settlement worked closely in a variety of efforts, and in 1903 organized a federation of unions, the Women's Trade Union League.

This was in contrast to strong anti-labor attitudes which the public at large held in response to radical organizing efforts and which was reflected in the positions of moderate and conservative suffragists. In 1893 the NAWSA passed a resolution that woman suffrage would solve the *problem* created by having illiterates (foreigners) vote. After the turn of the century the organization became officially more sympathetic to the needs of working class women and justified the ballot as necessary to improve their conditions. Nevertheless, for most, the concern was mostly a formality. The ballot was the real goal and the problems of labor were secondary, if important at all. In 1906, for example, an important labor leader accused the suffragists of "rescuing" and doing things "for" and not with working class women. Despite their desperate need of the vote for political and economic power they were still almost totally unrepresented at suffrage conventions.[4]

Although there was some division in the settlement houses when major strikes resulted in violence, the main thrust of the settlement reformers was strong sympathy for workers and active involvement in the major labor issues and struggles. Mary McDowell, for example, was called upon to arbitrate between the workers and the meat companies of Chicago. Others aided during strikes by picketing, providing funds, and educating the hostile middle class.

> That a Settlement is drawn into the labor issues of its city can seem remote to its purpose only to those who fail to realize that so far as the present industrial system thwarts our ethical demands, not only for social righteousness but for social order, a Settlement is committed to an effort to understand and, as far as possible, to alleviate it. That in this effort it should be drawn into fellowship with the local efforts of trade unions is most obvious.[5]

Jane Addams went beyond a call for good will and support. She maintained that the involvement by Chicago Settlements in strikes, particularly of unskilled workers, led her and her colleagues to demand unprecedented State regulation which would benefit workers.

[4] Kraditor, pp. 148–151.
[5] Addams, p. 166.

33

that as the very existence of the State depends upon the character of its citizens, therefore if certain industrial conditions are forcing the workers below the standard of decency, it becomes possible to deduce the right of State regulation.[6]

The demand for cooperation among social classes for bettering working conditions reflected an organic view of society. "The highest standards of living for the American worker," wrote Mary McDowell,

> will be attained only after he becomes a partner and a real cooperator with his employer . . . The question whether this fuller life has in it the elements of a higher and finer spiritual life for the children of the worker will have to be answered by society as a whole, for no side of life is independent of the others.[7]

This theory of total responsibility for all people quite naturally led reformers to engage in multi-faceted causes. Mary McDowell was as involved with the attempt to modernize garbage collection and dumping which would inhibit disease in slums near the dumps as with the effort to secure the eight-hour day or the vote for women. As she saw it, each reform brought people closer to the democratic ideal. Means and ends were not to be confused. The ballot was a primary tool for social regeneration but not the end product. Similarly, resolution of bread and butter issues was necessary but not sufficient.

> Industry in the future may have to add to the wage-earners income something beyond just the necessities of the human animal for food, shelter, clothes; to these may have to be added recreation, more education, provision for the future.[8]

The Formation of the Women's Trade Union League

At the same time as they were maintaining the need for strong integration of classes, these women recognized a need for separatist organization of female workers. By the end of the nineteenth century, the problem of women workers was extremely serious. The rapidly expanding industrial system drew large numbers of women to work in the factories. By 1900 there were an estimated

---

[6] *Ibid.*, p. 168.

[7] *Mary McDowell and Municipal Housekeeping*, compiled by Caroline Hill, Chicago, p. 66. (Undated, published privately.)

[8] *Ibid.*, p. 66.

6,000,000 working girls and women. Exploited by the employers, this unskilled working force was also discriminated against by male unionists who defined them as cheap labor threatening their jobs and wages. To combat this dissension Mary McDowell, along with a number of other women, borrowed the notion of separate organization for women from England, and helped to found the Women's Trade Union League.

Although there had been a number of spontaneous united efforts by women workers earlier in the nineteenth century, they had been unable to sustain a permanent organization beyond an immediate crisis. In the 1890's a small group of Irish working girls followed a spontaneous abortive strike with the organization of the "Maud Gonne" Club (named after the famous Irish patriot). Mary Mc-Dowell and labor organizer Michael Donnelly, with whom she worked closely in the Chicago stockyards, eventually helped these girls transform the club into a local of the Amalgamated Meat Cutters and Butcher Workmen of North America. This marked the beginning of a major and difficult organizing effort.

Most women entered the labor market as very young, unskilled low-paid workers, traditionally the most difficult type of workers to organize. Many female workers believed their employers' admonitions that women unionists were unfeminine. Youthfulness, lack of education, and the nature of feminine training all militated against women asserting themselves. Large numbers of these young women were too inarticulate to vent their grievances and state their ideas at meetings. Without speaking or participating it was difficult to engender high degrees of commitment.[9]

Yet some excellent leadership did emerge. Women like Agnes Nestor and Mary Kenny O'Sullivan became figures of national importance. Slowly, a few unions developed strong organizations. The glovemakers and bookbinders were among the first to organize women successfully. In 1903 these separate unions federated into the National Women's Trade Union League as a separate group within the rising American Federation of Labor. The A.F. of L. officially welcomed and recognized this special female effort, but in practice often neglected or discriminated against women workers. It took a long time for the A.F. of L. to recognize that equal pay for equal work benefitted men as well as women workers.

In its earliest years the National Women's Trade Union League undertook organization primarily in Chicago, New York, and Boston.

---

[9] Gladys Boone, *The Women's Trade Union League*, New York: Columbia University Press, 1942, p. 60.

In these areas it attempted to aid and serve strikers and workers through the formation of working girls' clubs and through the investigation of bad working conditions for women and children. During major strikes such as that of 40,000 garment workers in 1909-1910 the League handled all clerical work, rented halls, provided speakers, arranged bail for arrested strikers, and attended court cases.[10] National conferences were called in an attempt to foster strength and unity. A regular column on the Women's Trade Union League was featured in the organ of the A.F. of L., the *Union Advocate;* in 1911 the League began publishing its own journal, *Life and Labor,* which was edited by the well-known labor leader and journalist, Alice Henry. The journal dedicated itself to all the problems which faced working women and was an educational organ on feminine as well as working class issues.

The message was quite simple. The organization of women into trade unions was primary. Beyond that the League fostered interest in conditions of women all over the world. Suffrage progress in a variety of countries was noted monthly. An active campaign to buy union-label goods was featured and model lessons for immigrants to use in learning English prepared by the Education Committee of the N.Y. League were included regularly.

Lesson III. Home Work

I am a piece worker.
The forelady gives me some work.
I finish the work.
I ask for more work.
There is no more work.
I have earned only forty cents.
I put on my hat and my coat.
I go out through the office.
I see some women there.
The forelady gives them bundles of work.
They are home workers.
The boss has work for them.
He had no work for us.
Home workers save the boss money.
He does not pay rent for them.
He does not pay for their gas.
He does not pay for their needles and thread.
They do not ask for higher prices.
They can work all night.
They make our season short.
They keep our prices down.
They spoil the trade.[11]

[10] *Memoirs of Alice Henry,* Melbourne, 1944, p. 52.
[11] Violet Pike, "New World Lessons for Old World People," *Life and Labor,* II (February 1912), 48–49.

Organizing for Freedom

The feminist theme in *Life and Labor* was very strong. Articles about fighters for women's education such as Emma Willard and Mary Lyon, and feminist abolitionists of earlier generations were featured as were creative poems, essays, stories, and humorous anecdotes advocating women's rights. Radical feminists like Charlotte Perkins Gilman were defended in biographical essays. Strikes, labor investigations and political events relevant to labor were reported. Socialists, Progressives, liberal Republicans, and Democrats were represented among the contributors.

The leaders of the League were absolutely committed to raising the total standards of women through organization "particularly standards of independence in thinking and of self-dependence in action." In mixed unions, they maintained, women rarely influenced policies. Male union leaders often neglected women members and regarded the organization of women as futile. For these reasons League spokesmen continued to reiterate their commitment to organization for women. "Not for their own sakes only, but for the sake of the labor movement and for the sake of the community."[12]

Early organization depended on the money, efforts, and talents of middle-class women. Originally much feared as spies for the employers, a number of well-to-do organizers became indispensable to the growth and success of the W.T.U.L. Margaret Dreier Robbins, who moved to Chicago when her husband became head resident of a settlement house, was in the 1890s rejected for membership in an early women's union (Dorcas Federal Trade Union). Her understanding of the resistance to middle-class membership and her unfailing devotion of time and wealth to feminine unionism led her in 1907 to become the national president of the W.T.U.L. and one of its major leaders for several decades.

To these Allies, as the non-working members were known, the Trade Union movement meant more than shorter hours and higher wages. It represented an important extension of democracy.

> Self-government in the day's work—a government of the people, by the people, for the people is to be established in the workshops of the world.[13]

The organization took on moral fervor. Emily Greene Balch, president of the Boston League, captured the breadth of their commitment in her recollections.

> (We understand) trade unionism not as a struggle for material advantages for a limited class of people but in the same sense in which I

---

[12] *Memoirs of Alice Henry*, pp. 50–51.
[13] M. Robbins, "Self-Government in the Workshop," NWTUL pamphlet, undated, unpaginated, Sophia Smith Collection, Smith College.

understood my teaching at Wellesley College, as a part of a wide-spread and many-sided effort for juster and more humane social relations everywhere. There was a great deal of idealism in the trade union movement of the time as we saw it, and it has been one of the sad experiences of my life that it has done so relatively little for the weakest and most unskilled laborers.[14]

Through trade union schools for democracy and citizenship the affluent Allies hoped to awaken responsibility and initiative in young working girls. The unions, they believed, would resist the choking of intellectual and moral powers of workers. Restriction of economic opportunity like the abrogation of political rights for women was costly to the entire society.

> In every workshop of thirty girls there are undreamed of initiative and capacity for social leadership and control—an unknown wealth of intellectual and moral resources.[15]

It would be good for the individuals and good for the human race, they argued, to release these energies.

The League ultimately developed into a very broad-based organization. Its greatest success was the legitimation of unionism as a feminine and proper form of activity. Through active pressure on the middle-class Women's Clubs, questions of industrial conditions and problems of the working class were brought to the attention of the more affluent. Continually speaking, lecturing, writing, women like Mrs. Robbins, Mary McDowell, Alice Henry, and Agnes Nestor made local problems national issues. Through the prominence of the more well-known Settlement workers (Jane Addams, Florence Kelly, Emily Greene Balch) the results of factory investigations were brought before Congress and Presidents Theodore Roosevelt and Woodrow Wilson to urge legislation and regulation.

The implications for the development of political theory were far-reaching. There was unanimous belief that the vote, as the ultimate measure of political exclusion, rightfully belonged to women. It was the only means through which women could influence the major issues which were central to their lives and the lives of their families—education, health, sanitation, working conditions. But political action was larger than suffrage. Effective action demanded unity through organization, education and social activity and this was the program of the Trade Union League. As a concerted effort was made to respect political activists and suffrage workers alike,

---

[14] Quoted in M. Randall, *Improper Bostonian*, New York: Twayne Publishers, 1964, pp. 83–84.
[15] Robbins, "Self-Government."

as shown in Charlotte Perkins Gilman's poem which appeared in
Life and Labor in 1912.

The Socialist and the Suffragist

Said the Socialist to the Suffragist:
"My cause is greater than yours!
You only work for a Special Class,
We for the gain of the General Mass,
Which every good ensures!"

Said the Suffragist to the Socialist:
"You underrate my Cause!
While women remain a Subject Class,
You never can move the General Mass,
With your Economic Laws!"

Said the Socialist to the Suffragist:
"You misinterpret facts!
There is no room for doubt or schism
In Economic Determinism—
It governs all our acts!"

Said the Suffragist to the Socialist:
"You men will always find
That this old world will never move
More swiftly in its ancient groove
While women stay behind!"

"A lifted world lifts women up,"
The Socialist explained.
"You cannot lift the world at all
While half of it is kept so small,"
The Suffragist maintained.

The world awoke and tartly spoke:
"Your work is all the same;
Work together or work apart,
Work, each of you, with all your heart—
Just get into the game."[16]
Charlotte Perkins Gilman

For most of the women dedicated to reforming labor conditions,
politics was necessarily a humanitarian and inclusive enterprise. The
aim of female participation was betterment of self and loved ones
in an increasingly complex society. As women moved into positions of social responsibility, all of humanity would benefit. Similarly
as workers were given rights, dignity, and humane conditions, all
members of the society would live in greater spiritual harmony.

---

[16] Published in *Life and Labor*, II (February 1912), 61.

The Massachusetts Review

It is part of the logic of this philosophy that exclusive absorption in a narrowly defined suffrage movement would be antithetical to their goals. As time went on they increasingly broadened their range of activities, spending some of their most important years on internationalist and peace movements. Emily Greene Balch lost her job as professor of economics at Wellesley College during World War I, but both she and Jane Addams were later honored with Nobel Peace Prizes for their untiring efforts with the Women's International League for Peace and Freedom.[17]

Conclusion

The position ultimately developed by the settlement house, trade-union group was a multi-faceted and complicated one and incorporated many of the tensions which were and still are inherent in the feminist movement. Harold Cruse, in his monumental book on Negro intellectuals, has characterized black history as caught between two strains—separatism and integration—and never able to accept one to the exclusion of the other.[18] This description can well be applied to the feminist movement—the desire to be treated equally and yet maintain a separate identity (culturally, politically, socially) has been evident in many cases. The tension between the fight for equal rights and the special needs of women can readily be seen amongst the urban, labor reformers of the late 19th and early 20th century.

Their commitment to an organic view of society—the ultimate dependence of rich as well as poor on the well-being of all groups —underlay their militant, reform campaigns for equal rights. These rights meant economic independence, adequate health facilities ranging from garbage collection to medical benefits, suffrage, education, and innumerable other reforms which they deemed essential.

At the same time they perceived women as a special group. They lobbied and worked diligently for legislation to protect women from abominable working conditions (regulation of hours of work per week) and quickly saw the need for separate political and economic organizations for women (Women's Peace Party, Women's International League for Peace and Freedom, politicization of Women's Clubs as well as the Trade Union League were all organizations in which these reformers involved themselves). Mary McDowell

---

[17] These are the only two American women ever awarded the Nobel Peace Prize.

[18] H. Cruse, *The Crisis of the Negro Intellectual*, New York: William Morrow and Co., 1967.

40

chastized those who ignored the special qualities of women while deploring lack of economic equality. "We are not cheered," she wrote, "when outsiders talk about equality of men and women in the economic field, for we know that at present there is no such equality . . . when men bear the children, care for the home making, and work for wages, all at the same time, then we can join the extreme feminists" in their total commitment to equal rights.[19]

The separate and special character with which they treated women often resulted in opposition to those militant feminists who dedicated themselves exclusively to equal rights and integration into male society. The Women's Trade Union League opposed and lobbied against equal rights legislation proposed by the militant feminists in the National Women's Party in 1922. The League advocated a policy of seeking separate legislation to deal with specific issues of inequality. They maintained that the effort to gain labor legislation for women entitling them to minimum wages, maximum hours, necessary provision of seats in factories and stores had brought considerable improvement for working women which would be invalidated by an equal rights amendment.

> We wish to expend our efforts upon our constructive program for the improvement and extension of industrial standards for women, and not be forced to exhaust our resources in defense of what we have won.[20]

Committed to a broad view of women's needs, the leaders of the National Women's Trade Union League condemned the affluent women who would benefit by an equal rights amendment at the expense of protective legislation for working class women.

> There are national and state organizations of salaried and professional women who are not working in the interest of their less privileged sisters, but have the point of view of the manufacturers' associations . . . The extreme feminists, because they do not know the human side of economics, and love the academic sound of "equality of opportunity," are not lending a hand to the young sisters in the grip of the industrial machine. It is a hard, uphill fight.[21]

In effect these leaders refused to allow class interest to play off one group of women against another. If total integration and equal rights had to wait, that was clearly subordinate to identification with the less powerful—the underdogs of the system.

---

[19] M. McDowell, p. 53.
[20] "Protective Legislation in Danger," WTUL Report (November 1922), Sophia Smith Collection, Smith College.
[21] McDowell, p. 54.

Some of their arguments for the special position of women led them to rather specious positions on certain political issues confronting feminists. Jane Addams, for example, chose to lobby for women's suffrage because it was an indispensable tool in an increasingly complex society in order to fulfill responsibility for home and children—to obtain hygienic conditions, proper food, clothing and education.

> if woman would keep on with her old business of caring for her house and rearing her children she will have to have some conscience in regard to public affairs, lying quite outside her immediate household. The individual conscience and devotion are no longer effective.[22]

Jane Addams, who deliberately resisted the life of upper-middle class society and rejected family and children in favor of active social and political involvement, was defending the vote on the most conservative grounds—that it was necessary to be good wives and mothers. Traces of a broader argument did play a minor role in her suffrage writings. Rejecting the notion that women should operate through influence on men in her family she wrote:

> I believe . . that nothing is gained when independence of judgment is assailed by "influence," sentimental or otherwise, and that we test advancing civilization somewhat by our power to respect differences and by our tolerance of another's honest conviction.[23]

Here and in other writings, Miss Addams begins to approach the more radical argument that women's ideas are valuable and must be allowed to enter into the marketplace of ideas—not to enhance her role as wife and mother, but because all human beings have a right and obligation to contribute to the social and political process. Nevertheless, the dominant tone in her suffrage writings is the need for women to perform traditional functions in a complex system.

There was an inevitable tension between their integrationist (vis-à-vis class issues) and separatist commitments (on the feminist issue). The result can be observed in the need to justify and explain the position of women in the society. This emphasis served certain ends but was only partially beneficial to the advancement and redefinition of women's place—social, economic, and political.

Nevertheless, the lessons of these settlement and labor leaders are monumental. In a period when we are once again plagued by

---

[22] "Why Women Should Vote," *Ladies Home Journal* (January 1910), reprinted in C. Lasch (ed.), *The Social Thought of Jane Addams,* New York: Bobbs-Merrill, 1965, p. 145.
[23] *Ibid.,* p. 150.

the tensions between integration and separatism, between organizing for short-range goals and maintaining long-range visions, the examples of our predecessors are most valuable. This was a generation of women of privileged background, who were determined not to become educated frills. They invested their intelligence and moral energy into effecting a better world. They kept a vision of peace, justice and equality while working for specific goals—unions, voting rights, municipal reform. Their ability to tie their commitment to women's rights to other kinds of reform made them amongst the most profound feminists of their time. They recognized that the right to vote accomplishes little by itself—especially for women working in ill-equipped factories sixteen hours a day. They recognized the need for constant political pressure and action—for organization and activity both nationally and internationally.

The number of women with notable careers in labor, politics, settlement work, education, public nursing, and the peace movement was impressive. The next generations, suffering from postwar reaction and subsequently from the great depression, were not able to sustain this energy level. As this generation of settlement leaders died, the nature of the settlement houses changed. Their careers were clearly tied to a larger reform mood which prevailed in the country and part of their success was due to larger social, economic, and political forces. Their example and accomplishments are noteworthy. Although they moved fairly easily into the world of practical politics, these reform leaders refused to sell out their vision of a better world for short-term gains of the vote or settlement funding or easy approbation. By maintaining this tension of long-range vision and short-term goals, these women were able to carry out more than forty years of active reform and to identify problems which feminists today must not neglect.

BIBLIOGRAPHICAL NOTE

For further study of this problem the reader is advised to consult the useful and enjoyable autobiographies and biographies of settlement and reform leaders. Some of the best are: Jane Addams, *Twenty Years at Hull House, The Memoirs of Alice Henry;* Lillian Wald, *Windows on Henry Street,* Mary McDowell and *Municipal Housekeeping* (compiled by Caroline Hill); Mary Simkovitch, *Neighborhood* and Agnes Nestor, *Woman's Labor Leader.* Some of the more important biographies are H. Wilson, *Mary McDowell, Neighbor,* Chicago: University of Chicago Press, 1928; Mercedes Randall's biography of Emily Greene Balch, *Improper Bostonian,* New York: Twayne Publishers, 1964; James Linn, *Jane Addams,* New York: D. Appleton-Century, 1935. Christopher Lasch has edited *The Social Thought of Jane Addams,* New York: Bobbs-Merrill, 1965 and has an important essay on Miss Addams in his book, *The New Radicalism in America,* New York: Random House, 1965. Arthur

The Massachusetts Review

Mann, *Yankee Reformers in the Urban Age*, New York: Harper & Row, 1954 has a good chapter on Vida Scudder. Two pertinent studies of the women's rights movement are E. Flexner, *Century of Struggle*, Cambridge: Harvard University Press, 1959, and A. Kraditor, *Ideas of the Woman Suffrage Movement, 1890–1920*, New York: Columbia University Press, 1965. Gladys Boone has an old but useful monograph of *The Women's Trade Union League*, New York: Columbia University Press, 1942. The most comprehensive study of the settlement movement is Allen F. Davis, *Spearheads for Reform*, New York: Oxford University Press, 1967. Some of the better libraries, like the Sophia Smith Collection at Smith College have the Women's Trade Union League journal, *Life and Labor* and a number of the League's pamphlets and records. A good example of the tone and substance in these documents is the following, from *Life and Labor*, II, 4, April, 1912:

"TIME IS PASSING:

I have so much I want to say. What bothers me most is time is passing. Time is passing and everything is missed. I am not living, I am just working. But life means so much, it holds so much, and I have no time for any of it; I just work. Am I not right?

In the busy time I work so hard; try to make the machine run faster and faster because then I can earn some money and I need it, and then night comes, and I am tired out and I go home and I am too weary for anything but supper and bed. Sometimes union meetings, yes, because I must go. But I have no mind and nothing left in me. The busy time means to earn enough money not only for today but to cover the slack time, and then when the slack time comes I am not so tired, I have more time, but I have no money, and time is passing and everything is missed.

Romance needs time. We can think about it, yes, but to live it needs time. Music I love, to hear it makes me happy, but it is passing. The operas and the theatres and the dramas, they are here but to me they are just passing. To study, to go to high school, to the university, I have no time and I have no money.

Then the world is so beautiful. I see the pictures of the trees and the great rivers and the mountains, and away back in Russia I was told about Niagara Falls. Now why if I work all day and do good work, why is there never a chance for me to see all these wonders?

I have been thinking. First we must get a living wage and then we must get a shorter work-day, and many, many more girls must do some thinking. It isn't that they do not want to think, but they are too tired to think and that is the best thing in the union, it makes us think. I know the difference it makes to girls and that is the reason I believe in the Union. It makes us stronger and it makes us happier and it makes us more interested in life and to be more interested is oh, a thousand times better than to be so dead that one never sees anything but work all day and not enough money to live on. That is terrible, that is like death.

And so now the Women's Trade Union League has helped me so much, and the Union has helped me so much, and I want to help others, and so we must have 'Life and Labor' written in Yiddish too so that all the Jewish girls can understand. And then I think we ought to have it in Polish and Bohemian and Lithunian [sic] and Italian. Can you do this? How can I help you to do it?

'Life and Labor' is great!   —ANNA RUDNITZKY"

SEX-ROLES AND SEXUAL ATTITUDES IN SWEDEN: THE NEW PHASE

Sondra R. Herman

"When you say equality, people see there isn't any, and so you have a sharpening of demands and expectations."

PRIME MINISTER OLAF PALME, June, 1970.

IN OUR TELEVISED world-village, revolts still have a national colora- tion. French students fared better with workers in Paris in May, 1968 than American students did in New York in May, 1970. Alexander Dubcek and former Chancellor Roger Heyns of the University of California may some day exchange memoirs, but Berkeley is not yet Prague. The sisterhood of feminists also en- counters very different national establishments and cultures. In the United States the fierce and competitive spirit of Woman's Libera- tion reminds us that this was once a society imbued with Social Darwinism. The suffragettes appear too genteel for their successors. Today's women have the example of the Black revolution.

In the Soviet Union it is difficult to speak about revolution, except the old one. Woman's obligation to work outside the home is a fundamental tenet of Communist life. Russian women are better represented in the professions than the women of other nations. Equality has its problems however. Employed married women, it has been estimated, spend an average of five hours a day on house- work and child-care. A writer in *Voprosy ekonomiki* noted a marked trend among such women to abort second and especially third pregnancies. Although child-care centers are plentiful, women still tend to stay home from work for over a year after the birth of a child, rather than for the three months they are usually granted. Such responses to their double role (especially the abortions) have been called very "undesireable to society." While part-time jobs are discussed, few appear. The Soviets have not considered reciprocal adjustment of parental duties. Mother still has two jobs.[1]

In contrast to Soviet conservatism and American combativeness, the Scandinavian approach to sex-role equality seems both quiet and

---

[1] A. K., "A Demographic Problem: Female Employment and the Birth-rate," *Voprosy ekonomiki,* trans. by Arlo Schultz in *The Soviet Review,* XI, no. 1 (Spring, 1970), pp. 76–81; see also Edmund Nash, "The Status of Women in the USSR," *Monthly Labor Review* (June, 1970), p. 43.

daring. Women constitute approximately the same percentage of the Swedish as of the American labor force (almost forty percent), but hardly any are employed as household helpers for other women, and their representation in the professions has been steadily rising during the last twenty years. The Swedish government has experimented with a number of changes designed to stimulate woman's gainful employment. The system of taxation was changed recently, making it pay for the married woman to work. The government has experimented with part-time jobs for both parents of very young children. Financial support for locally organized child-care centers is rising. The schools are purposefully educating boys and girls for more androgynous sex-roles. Considering freely a variety of programs, the Swedes even allow such phrases as "house husband" to enter their vocabulary. Still the discussion remains dispassionate and the tone rather bureaucratic. A major effort to revolutionize the most deeply entrenched attitudes toward sexual roles has brought no open conflict, although there are clearly perceptible differences of opinion. Even where political influence is at stake, as in the Parliament where thirty-four seats were lost in the shift to a unicameral system in 1971, and where the woman's organizations are struggling to maintain the seats now held by women, reasonable compromise prevails.

Reentering the United States from Stockholm to the tune of silly sex-war cartoons, women crashing into men's bars and popular periodicals predicting an increase in violence on a new front, one experiences a shock. Everyone seems to be shouting to be heard. The white males are readying for a new siege. The feminists' dramaturgy with witches recalls some of the worst moments of a mythic barbarian age. In Scandinavia, but particularly in Sweden, the setting is one of good manners, formality, and a serious commitment to social role equality as well as to sexual liberation.

Ironically, the Swedish tradition of patriarchal and active government has been the largest factor in women's drive for equality. The Swedes receive, if they do not always accept, official or semi-official guidance in virtually every aspect of the sex question. The National Association for Sex Education, known as the RFSU (Riksforbundet for Sexual Upplysning), has shared in governmental responsibility for encouraging family planning and family counseling. It is a voluntary organization, however, whose chief effort goes for propaganda toward a freer and more responsible sexuality. Ready for the subway kiosks and factory walls is the latest RFSU poster which reads, "You don't *have* to go to bed together." As one columnist has remarked, the Swedes, who frequently lack a "half-way station of demonstrated warmth," can now relax. The sex educators have informed them that, after all, intercourse is not an obligation! They can just be friends. In a culture where privacy, especially the privacy of the deeper emotions, is cherished, such an attempt to mold private attitudes is, nevertheless, common. How much easier it becomes, then, to discuss more traditionally public issues such as married women's tendency to neglect their own education, or the extent to which fathers might participate in child-care centers. Here the radio campaigns, the Royal Commissions, the position-papers proliferate, and one rarely hears complaints about the public sector.

The whole cool and determined but well-mannered attempt to debate what in some cultures is undebatable, reminds visitors of the skilled traditions of Scandinavian diplomacy. The Scandinavians share an unspoken consensus that the war between the sexes, while fine on the stage and in novels, is really as pointless and wasteful as war between nations. Having understood the potentialities for destruction, they rather pointedly give prizes for peace. Swedish feminists are now studying the demands and difficulties of the *man's* role in the society and in the economy, rather than attacking masculine chauvinists under a banner labeled "Women's Rights."

The Fredrika Bremer Association (founded in 1884 and including both men and women among its 11,000 members) calls today for planned economic changes to allow women to relieve men's burdens. Taking a cue from the 1956 study by Viola Klein and Alva Myrdal, *Women's Two Roles,* the Swedish feminists insist that any society that shortens men's lives with ulcers and heart attacks, while preventing women by the millions from performing any useful labor is clearly in need of substantial change.[2]

In general, the Social Democrats support this proposition. Whether they go as far as the Bremer Society in insisting that women be part of a unified labor supply is another question. At the moment Sweden's industrial economy is overheated. Having a population of eight million and a persistently low birth-rate, the country is experiencing a severe labor shortage. Thousands of workers have come up from Southern Europe, especially from Yugoslavia, but they are not enough. The social planners somehow must integrate the women, the largest available underemployed group, into the economy. For the moment, then, the Government and the voluntary and non-partisan Bremer Society have parallel goals.

---

[2] *Women's Two Roles: Home and Work* (London, Routledge & Kegan Paul, Ltd., 1956; 2nd ed. 1968), p. 186; *Hertha* (Stockholm, Fredrika Bremer Association, no. 3, 1970).

II

WHETHER THIS transformation will actually take place, whether
the second feminist struggle will be as successful as the first is
difficult to predict. The first struggle for women's rights in Scandinavia lasted for almost one hundred years, from the middle of the
nineteenth century to the beginning of World War II. No one
looked upon old Sweden as Americans once looked at America as
a "woman's country." On the contrary, Swedish laws and customs
were strictly patriarchal; women were undoubtedly subservient,
well into the first decade of the twentieth century. Then, the transition to a highly industrialized economy, to an urban society, and to
social and political democracy came swiftly and the position of
Scandinavian women advanced sharply with that of other groups
who had been powerless under the patriarchy. Sometimes American
feminists today, taking a cue from the Norwegian-American econo-
mist Thorstein Veblen, wonder if they have "suffered the penalty
of taking the lead."

In the latter half of the nineteenth century, Sweden experienced
severe problems of population displacement. As industrialization
was just starting, thousands of people emigrated to the United
States to escape rural poverty. At the same time, many farm families
came to the only major city—Stockholm. For reasons not entirely
clear, there were many more women then men. Their families could
not support them, but they were legally barred from paid employment. Prostitution was rife and poverty widespread. In this situation the Swedish woman's rights organizations, although chiefly composed of more protected middle-class women, necessarily focused
upon the most basic human right of all—the right not to starve.
Rather than campaign for the vote as the key to all else, the
feminists fought for woman's paid employment, for the right to
earn as well as to own property. They campaigned for a new form
of marriage that would give the wife some property and some
authority over her children. Always before Fredrika Bremer and
her successors were reminders of those pitiable women who adver-
tised for any work or any home where they would be "treated with
kindness." The development cooperatives owned and managed by
women were part of the feminist campaign. These movements, then,
could not be called in the strictest sense suffragette.[3]

Starting in the 1880's another struggle, largely literary, was conducted with many fiery quarrels and dramatic encounters—a cam-

---

[3] Hanna Astrup Larsen, "Sweden's Unique Organization of Women,"
American Scandinavian Review, I, no. 3 (May, 1913), pp. 14–17.

paign for free discussion of sexual issues and for open consideration of women's sexual nature as well as of her economic needs. When the "moralists and immoralists" in this struggle included the greatest figures in Scandinavian literature, Ibsen and Bjørnson, Brandes and Strindberg, the feminists could not ignore it. By and large they took sides with the moralist Bjørnson and against the deeply anti-feminist Strindberg.[4] However, the established Lutheran Church to which over 90 percent of the population belonged (and to which over 90 percent still belongs) upheld the traditional Christian virtue, chastity, and with it the proprietorship of men in the bourgeois marriage.

As the society grew more secular in its values, Scandinavians more openly challenged the double standard, and feminists challenged the man's proprietorship. The bold Ellen Key, who, like Havelock Ellis, celebrated woman's difference from men and woman's obligation to remain womanly, nevertheless observed that the Church destroyed love by locking up sexuality in the "white sepulchre of lawful wedlock." The morbid images associated with a rigid or twisted sexual morality seemed almost as common in Ellen Key's day as they are today in Ingmar Bergman films. Key asserted that the instinctive desire for motherhood was an essential part of woman's nature and therefore should be protected as her right—whether or not she married.[5] While Key's works were more popular in Germany and among some American intellectuals than they were at home, her emphasis upon free motherhood and close ties between family and community found response in some of the social policies of the twentieth century.

Very probably, however, these open discussions of sexuality and sexual rights accorded with the actual beliefs of an earlier silent majority. While the Church proclaimed premarital chastity, the rural population (although obediently church-going) knew of another, livelier counter-tradition. It was quite common throughout the Scandinavian countryside for a man and woman to live together without benefit of clergy. In fact, premarital sexual relations were considered an important element in a couple's suitability. Sometimes, of course, the relationship was short-lived and casual; but frequently it was a serious time of testing. Often the couple decided to marry only when they learned the woman was pregnant. Thus for many people marriage was neither contract nor sacrament. It was a commitment taken after a trial marriage—a commitment to raise children together. Today this ancient custom has reemerged

---

[4] Elias Bredsdorff, "Moralists versus Immoralists: The Great Battle in Scandinavian Literature in the 1880's," *Scandinavica*, II (June, 1969), 91–111.

[5] Ellen Key, *Love and Marriage* (New York, G. Putnam's Sons, 1911).

in an urban, secular society. Premarital sexual relations among couples in love are not only accepted, but expected. True, the Church upholds premarital chastity and the Swedes, like their ancestors, still belong to the Church. But they follow rural custom.

In other ways, too, Scandinavian ruralism has prevented prudery from taking hold. Casual about nudity in the bath or at the beach, accepting sexuality much as they accept and appreciate physical culture, the Scandinavians like to remind visitors that "nature is our real religion." With a deep, almost mystical reverence for the woods, the high grass fields, and the shrouded lakes, the Swedes create an atmosphere about their lives that makes sexual double standards and old-fashioned morality quite ridiculous. Still, they continue to value privacy, a secrecy about feelings, and—in their frequent escapes to the countryside—solitude.

Significantly, in the early twentieth century both traditionalists and feminists rejected individualistic values for the primacy of the community. Not only did Ellen Key argue that the strength of the nation depended upon women devoting themselves to their children and the state protecting them in this devotion, but others combined social feminism with equal rights quite comfortably. Selma Lagerlöf, whose *Gösta Berling's Saga* remains the great romantic epic of Sweden, considered the vote essential to women but looked to the transformation of the state by the home. While many American suffragettes converted a similar theme into an overstatement of the case for the vote, the Scandinavian debate continued to embrace all the complexities—the relations between men and women, parents and children, and family and state. Eventually the transformation of the state became the overriding purpose of feminism.

While the Scandinavian feminists lacked certain American advantages such as early higher education for women, and state by state political experimentation, they benefited by their widespread readiness to accept governmental participation in social life. Starting in the late nineteenth century, coming to a peak in the period 1915 to 1921, the rush of feminist legislation overwhelmed the old forms. In the 30's, feminism and family welfare legislation merged.

III

IN 1915 ONLY unmarried women over twenty-one had property rights at all comparable to those of men. Married women were legally, as well as economically, dependent upon their husbands. In that year, however, Parliament changed the legal definition of marriage to that of a contract. The new divorce law allowed the dissolution of a broken marriage after a year's separation with each former partner dividing the property equally. This property division derived from the explicit assumptions that both partners brought

50

property to the marriage and that the woman's activity in managing the household and raising children constituted a financial contribution equal to that of her husband's wage earning. Four years later, when women as well as all men over twenty-one received the vote, several other changes took place in the marriage law. Children born out-of-wedlock were no longer "illegitimate." In the thirties they began to receive the same social aid as other children (or greater help where necessary). Ancient laws forbidding sexual relations outside of marriage were abrogated. Women soon received full legal guardianship over their children and became equally responsible under the law for the children's support. In the 1920's the higher public schools and universities allowed women to matriculate on the same terms as men. The Government Service admitted women, although few would enter this area of employment until World War II when it became the most common employment avenue for women.[6]

While the percentage of Swedish women in the labor force rose steadily from 2 percent in 1920 to approximately 40 percent in 1968 the critical period in Sweden as elsewhere was the 1930's depression. By launching a massive program of public works and family welfare, the governments of Scandinavia countered the usual temptation to drive women out of the labor-market on the grounds that there were too few jobs even for men. A proposed law to that effect met defeat in the Swedish Riksdag. But it was really the launching of the modern welfare state that made the difference. Equal pay laws covered first government and then private employment. The National Pensions Act provided equal pensions for men and women regardless of marital status.

When the plummeting national birth rate aroused consternation, the old laws prohibiting the distribution of contraceptive information were dropped. Family planning was encouraged. But in Sweden and in the other Scandinavian countries the term implied the encouragement of family stability and growth, not contraception in the face of overpopulation. Expectant mothers received preventive medical care, medicine, prenatal instruction, obstetrical and postnatal care, all free. School authorities provided free lunches to every child. State aid for housing for the poor was initiated; and this later became a governmental commitment to provide housing for all according to family size as well as income. Public assistance to needy families was shortly transformed into a flat cash allowance annually for each child (now 900 crowns). Public authorities aided

---

[6] Edith Anrep, *Some Features of Women's Status in Swedish Family Law* (Swedish Institute, 1962).

the mother of an out-of-wedlock child while attempting to win child support from the father. Later the child's inheritance claims on the father's family were deemed the same as those of children born in wedlock. Abortion laws were liberalized, although some medical and legal limitations remained. Finally, laws against adultery and against homosexual relations between consenting adults were abrogated.[7] Legally the old patriarchy was dead and in its place stood the modern welfare state committed officially to sexual equality and community responsibility for family welfare.

Social insurance became more inclusive and more sophisticated in the forties and fifties. The welfare-state, in itself, prevented the "retreat to the home" which American women experienced in the fifties. By the 1960's an appreciation for the complexities of the family-economy at different stages of life was fully evident in public policy. While heavy taxation levelled out extreme differences in living standards throughout the society, social insurance for mothers staying at home with young children, additional consumption allowances for each child, special provisions for families with three children or more, levelled out living standards throughout the individual's lifetime. The periods of greatest family expense were the periods most protected by insurance.

Recently, the government has made several subtle but vital contributions to the encouragement of both stable families and working mothers. As of January, 1971 it taxes each individual's income separately thereby keeping a married woman's income in a lower bracket than would be the case in a joint declaration. Prime Minister Palme has declared, "The principle behind the new proposal is that all people shall be regarded as economically independent individuals and that society shall adopt a neutral attitude as to the form of cohabitation which people chose." Secondly, it has granted "house husband's insurance," recognizing that it is not *always* mother who stays home. Third, it has initiated on a small scale, and encouraged trade unions and management organizations to plan for part-time work for fathers as well as for mothers of small children. In addition, it has surveyed the need for more child-care centers, made further investments in them, and has planned new housing with a view to reducing housework, and centralizing housecare activities where possible. Such public commitments encourage, if they do not guarantee, a positive and practical attitude toward the problems of

[7] Maj-Britt Sandlund, *The Status of Women in Sweden: Report to the United Nations 1968* (Swedish Institute, 1969), pp. 14–22, 71; Birgitta Linnér, "Social and Legal Aspects of the Family," Swedish International Development Authority, Seminar in Planned Parenthood and Sex Education in Sweden, April 6–24, 1970, p. 4.

working mothers. If anything can expose the roots of the sex-role tangle, this policy should.

IV

NEVERTHELESS, SWEDEN is far from a feminist utopia. Informal economic discrimination is widespread. Swedish women usually enter a different job-market from Swedish men. Although progress has been made, they are separate and unequal.

In the age-group of highest employment, ages 30 to 49, according to the International Labour Organization, 46.5 percent of the Swedish women worked for pay in 1969 compared with 42 percent in the United States and 31 percent in Canada.[8] In both the United States and Sweden severe wage disparities exist between men and women. 70 percent of the Swedish women gainfully employed earn less than $4500 a year while 80 percent of the Swedish men earn more than that.[9] Although examples of outright exploitation are rare, they do turn up. A woman member of the Riksdag recently investigated and exposed a large laundry in Northern Sweden in which women were working under conditions worthy of the worst of early industrialism. Horrified and shocked the Swedes, with their typical desire to expose their own faults, insist upon telling the story to foreigners. The laundry was forced to meet working standards. After years of legislation and less formal effort, Sweden still has two job-markets: the male job-market reaches from heavy factory labor to the most prestigious and well-paying executive positions. For the women, the jobs in heavy industry are opening up, but there is little room at the top. While an occasional woman becomes an executive and the number of the doctors and other professionals increases, the woman's job-market for the most part remains a low-paid one of clerks, beauticians, nurses, secretaries, shop assistants, and elementary school teachers.

Sweden has long had equal pay for equal work laws, but the Secretary of the Fredrika Bremer Association reported, "Jobs are sometimes reclassified so that men and women doing the same work appear to hold different positions. Then the men are paid more." The program of the Association meeting held in June 1970 still read: "We demand the same wage for the same job, equal rights to work in the home and outside it, and the right person in the

[8] International Labour Office, *1969 Year Book of Labour Statistics* (Geneva, 1969), pp. 23, 37.
[9] Anna-Greta Leijon, *Swedish Women—Swedish Men* (Swedish Institute, 1968), pp. 51–52.

53

right place regardless of whether that person be a man or a woman."[10]

In spite of governmental efforts to encourage women to take jobs, both the women themselves, and employers generally, tend to regard female participation in the economy as supplementary. This is a view that deeply troubles the leaders of the woman's rights organizations. They do not rest easy about the future. It is not at all certain that the percentage of women in industry and in the professions will continue to rise if there should be economic reversals. Editors, broadcasters, and columnists continue the sex-role debate as if in a hurry to push for one job-market while Sweden's economy is still overheated. If a recession occurs the women may well have the worst of it, for it is quite impossible to send thousands of immigrant male workers back to Southern Europe. Thus beneath the good manners anxiety lies. The women's drive is for "equality now."

Some of the greatest difficulties in achieving true equality in the job-market stem from the part-time and sometime nature of female employment. The consequences in Sweden are not really very different from those in the United States—lack of employer interest in training women; lack of woman's experience and qualifications for advancement; and above all, lack of female influence in the trade unions. If ever the goal of a unified labor market is to be reached, the women themselves will have to have a greater commitment to employment. They will have to find much greater support from the unions. These problems the women's societies recognize. "Women must not be regarded as marginal labour," the Fredrika Bremer program reads, "nor must they acquiesce in being treated as such." The demand is persistent and well-justified. The divided job-market has already had painful consequences. Both men and unmarried women tend to leave the cold, dark Northern areas where heavy extractive industries predominate. The women who remain in the North with their husbands have fewer opportunities to work there, but those who come South add to the woman-surplus in the cities. Being confined to a limited number of professions makes the situation worse. Moreover, unmarried mothers are the most needy participants in the job-market and their choices are few. They are also (comparatively speaking) the poor of Sweden and frequently are found in the lowest-paying jobs. Understandably, their children have priority in receiving places at child-care centers, but this does not improve the situation of other working mothers who need such services and frequently fail to find them.

---

[10] Interview with A. M. Fjellgren, Secretary of the Fredrika Bremer Association, June 10, 1970; Program of the Fredrika Bremer Association, 1970 resolutions.

Sex-Roles and Sexual Attitudes in Sweden

In Sweden as elsewhere child-care and housework problems are the greatest practical inhibitors of paid female employment. Household help is next to impossible to find since the Swedes are both too egalitarian to ask others to perform menial labor for them, and too proud to do it for others. Only the baby-nurse trainees, who need a period as mother's helpers, are available to supplement the housework of the mother herself, and there are never enough such helpers.

Most mothers, going out to work, would need to find child-care centers at least part of the time. A 1967 survey showed that there were 300,000 children under ten whose mothers worked more than fifteen hours a week. Half of the children (those between seven and ten) were in school; over half of the young children were home with mama. Only 40 percent of the six-year-olds were in nursery schools or day schools. But another 200,000 mothers said they would like to go to work if they could find a place in the day-care centers for their 350,000 young children.[11]

Many mothers and most often the younger fathers understand that children over the age of three need the social experiences of play groups and nursery schools whether or not mother goes to work. One finds however, occasional male resistance to the idea. "There is the long arm of the state reaching into the cradle," one man grumbled in a conversation about the kindergartens (quite forgetting some protective aspects of that long arm). "Many people feel children are indoctrinated in schools and seven is early enough," another reported. Possibly, resistance to heavier taxation lies behind such remarks. The kindergartens, all-day nurseries, and nursery schools are the creation and financial responsibility of local taxing districts—the communities. Some districts have many preschools. In Stockholm where over 50 percent of the married women work, there are free-time centers, day nurseries, private family nurseries, as well as nurseries attached to clinics and regular preschools. Outside the cities, these centers are rare. Again the greatest problems exist in the North where settlement is sparse and the prospect of a long bus ride for tiny tots is enough to keep the most ambitious mother home. There have been increasing financial contributions to the child-care centers from the central government, and increasing attention to the quality and variety of experiences the children have in them. In general the teachers seek to create the environment for spontaneous and imaginative play rather than to prepare the child for later formal learning.[12]

In spite of an increasing effort to provide child-care centers, their relative scarcity, outside of the major cities, remains one of the

---

[11] *Status of Women in Sweden*, p. 59.
[12] *Before School Starts* (Swedish Institute, 1970).

most serious problems for those thousands of mothers who want to go out to work.

In one respect, the future of the nursery seems bright. One rarely encounters in Scandinavia the pseudo-Freudian assumption common in America that the dependence of child upon mother is so exclusive that mother's going to work would constitute a trauma for the child. In fact, recent public discussion of sex roles in Scandinavia has emphasized the importance of *father* in the life of young children—especially in the life of young boys. Studies concerning the effects upon young children of mother's working outside the home have not been entirely conclusive. In one Stockholm study, the children of mothers, working full-time, under hard economic pressure, *did* present more behavioral problems in the early grades than the children of mothers who stayed at home. But children of mothers working part-time performed better than either group. Several important variables in the study, however, were neglected: the teacher's attitude toward these children; the family's education and social position; the father's presence or absence at home; the mother's attitude toward her work and her children. In addition, the most important elements are those too deep to measure at all, the quality of the parent-child relation and of the relations between the mother and father—the love in the family.[13]

"In Sweden," Birgitta Linnér, head of family counselling in Stockholm, remarked, "we never took to Freud. Of course, his ideas were influential among psychiatrists, but other ideas have had a stronger impact. Today, even our psychoanalysts consider Freudianism old-fashioned. It has little to do with our present debate over sex-roles. Since the thirties, the part played by the sociologists in advising the government has been much greater. Our main concern has been, for a long time, a secure family income and not firm social roles. I think most Swedish family counsellors would say that the discontented mother at home does more harm to her children than the mother who has interesting work outside the home. But we really want the woman, herself, to choose."[14]

v

WHILE MANY SWEDISH families still accept the traditional sex-roles of mother as homemaker and father as breadwinner, some interesting changes are taking place in the schools in the wake of the official position that this differentiation is somewhat harmful to society. A 1965 study (or rather series of studies) indicated that the girls still preferred the occupations of grade school teacher and

---

[13] *Women's Two Roles*, pp. 122–134.
[14] Interview with Mrs. Linnér, June 8, 1970.

medical workers while the boys thought of themselves as engineers and scientists and metal workers. The Swedish labor market supplying both expanding medical services and greatly expanding industrial services, could not afford this differentiation particularly if the medical workers were chiefly nurses, many of whom did not return to work after marrying. Traditional vocational counselling, early educational differentiation, and even primary school textbooks reinforced the dysfunctional choices. In 1966 experiments started in a few school districts. Today, by Swedish law, *all* primary school students must take handicraft training both in the traditional girls' crafts, cooking and sewing, and in the traditional boys' crafts, woodworking and metal work. No segregation by sex is allowed in the handicraft classes. "My son came home from school the other day," one mother told me "with the most delicious cake, which he had baked all by himself. He wanted to go right into the kitchen and make another." "What did you think of that?" I asked. "I think it's wonderful."

Vocational counsellors are now obliged to advise girls who choose the traditional women's occupations that they are choosing lower pay and probably fewer promotions throughout a lifetime. Girls who assume that marriage will be their major source of income are cautioned against such an assumption. Evidently, however, the vocational counsellors find it hard to break out of traditional status-role conceptions even when the law requires it, for the Fredrika Bremer Society has asked for a replacement of the present guidance system with a broader and more intensive program including study visits. Swedish feminists realize that unless young girls see married women successfully meeting professional demands, their promises of a future in the professions seem false. One productive woman physicist is worth a thousand words. And Sweden needs engineers and scientists. It becomes almost unpatriotic to steer a girl, talented in mathematics and the hard sciences, to another, more "feminine" occupation.

Beneath the policy level, however, the reality of feelings about sex-status roles and occupational differentiation is more difficult to probe. The tradition of Swedish privacy where deep emotions are involved obscures, just where one most wants light. Only a few glimmers come, and these are mostly from the statements of devoted feminists. You wonder whether the wish is father (or mother) to the thought. These glimmers, however, have such radical implications, that they are worth examining. About the same time the sex-role studies of occupational choices were published, a public discussion began over the question of the male's traditional role in the family and in the economy. Did men *want* to be the sole breadwinners? Did they accept the degree of isolation from their children that this role entailed? Swedish fathers, like American fathers, often find their shorter work hours lengthened again by semi-professional obligations and by commuting. Were they willing to play a double role at home and at work somewhat similar to woman's double role? Did they feel restricted, by the rigid demand that men never show feelings, always play the tough guy? The silent majority, finding the questions too dangerous, stayed silent. But on the radio, in newspapers, in magazines, those who replied gave surprising answers. Swedish men did *not* appreciate the clinging dependence of the traditional woman, and would approve of more women taking jobs. The tough guy role was singularly oppressive not only to women, but more especially to the men, who wished for a wider emotional range and thought the "locked in" attitude unhealthy. Above all, the father's isolation from his children was thought unsatisfactory.[15]

By 1970 the sex-role debate in Sweden moved on to new ground. Advocacy of more job opportunities for women and more government supported child-care centers became the *conservative* position. The man's assumption of a double role, virtually unthinkable in the United States, became the key position of the radical thinkers. As Dr. Kerstin Aner, member of Parliament, remarked, "We don't want to take anything away from men. On the contrary, we want to give them the privilege of meeting their children more often. We want to stop shutting the women *in* and the men *out*." Again the modern debate calls echoes out of Strindberg. The playwright viewed the real (as opposed to the legal) position of the father as powerless. Was he ever to be sure he *was* the father? What relation had he to his child? Motherhood seemed both more powerful and more dangerously irrational than fatherhood. Strindberg depicted beautifully in *The Father* how darkly and deeply beneath the rationality of modern man lay a longing for immortality through work and children; how vulnerable man would be, if he lost his children.

If women should achieve equal opportunity, not likeness, but equality with men, what will that mean for men? The Swedes raise the question because the possibility of more androgynous sex-roles seems very real in Scandinavia. And yet there is little evidence of a male backlash. Quite the contrary. Every year more young men work in child-care centers; more attend the baby-care classes; more share the housework with their working wives. In part the growing demand for efficiently planned housing, for higher quality child-care centers, for more adequate insurance coverage to care for the very young, very old, or ill at home reflects the break-

---

[15] Interview with Ying Toijer-Nilsson, editor of *Hertha*, June 10, 1970; also "Behöver mansrollen förändras?" *Hertha* (no. 3, 1970), pp. 2–14.

down of traditional roles. As more men accept, or even take into consideration, a double role, the demand for efficiency in housework and domestic duties increases.

With characteristic social imagination, the Swedish planners have seen how even the revolt of the young might be made to serve the needs of social democracy. As the young reject careerism, the trade-unions support part-time jobs for both parents of young children. As the rebels experiment with group marriages, the state orders a commission to study the code to make sure all marital forms are accommodated. Trial marriages and homosexual unions are already within the law. Not that the Swedish government has gone hippy. Far from it. Undoubtedly, many older and more traditionally-minded Swedes find the young as much of a trial as many Americans do. Instead of hitting them with flags, however, they study and accommodate. The decline of traditional masculine prerogative among the young has proved of real value to a government needing women in the labor force. Youth may want to drop out, but the planners find ways of pulling them in. No doubt devoted revolutionaries find Sweden deeply discouraging.

The youth rebellion reinforces, rather than challenges, the traditional Swedish displeasure at aggressiveness. Combative masculinity is very bad form in Sweden. When I asked various leaders of the Fredrika Bremer Society as well as Mrs. Linnér whether Swedish men did not feel threatened by the woman's drive for equality, they seemed barely able to understand the importance of the question to an American. Each one began, "No, no, Swedish men are not like that." How did they account for the ease with which the younger men adapt to the drive for equality?

"Of course, the process of education and discussion has gone on for a long time in Sweden," Mrs. Ying Toijer-Nilsson, editor of *Hertha*, replied. "Each time an issue is raised, the very nature of the discussion makes a variety of opinions respectable. I remember how the schoolboy teasing about the few men at home ended once the government seriously considered house-husband insurance." The entry of Swedish women into the labor market has been steadily increasing since the 1920's. The women in Sweden have not had the well-publicized reversals of American women, and therefore have eschewed radical postures and dramatic gestures designed to raise the consciousness. True, the Redstockings recently put on a mass demonstration in Copenhagen but the response in Sweden was both sympathetic and faintly condescending.[16] The cool, steady Swedish approach to status-equality might be a large factor in easing men's acceptance of the change.

---

[16] Interview with Ying Toijer-Nilsson, June 10, 1970.

Political factors also have an impact. The Fredrika Bremer Society is nonpartisan and small. Men as well as women join (although the male membership is tiny). But the society is committed to the same goals as the government itself, and the Social Democrats have been in power for over thirty years. Experience in organization has made the leaders wise. "We have never made this a question of women against men," reported Mrs. Fjellgren the organizational secretary. "And we haven't let ideology tie us up. Everyone who supports a more democratic social order can support our goals. But sometimes we run into a real conflict of interest. We would like to see more women in Parliament. And the man who fears he might lose his place to a woman is just the one most likely to say, 'Well, of course, the women should be represented on the committee on child-welfare.' He wants to keep us in *our* place and out of his! But most men do not see any conflict, because there isn't one." Nevertheless, she worried about the effects of the change-over to a unicameral legislature. Would women lose the political influence they had? It was not discrimination but female indifference that posed the greatest difficulties.[17]

Most of the people who considered the question of relative masculine defensiveness in Sweden and the United States replied differently. If a man has to prove that he is stronger, better, or smarter than women his own sense of masculinity must be lacking. Mrs. Birgitta Linnér was blunt about it. "Inner sexuality, if strong, needs no proof. Men who need the assurance afforded by very different sex-roles (and women who need strong differences in outward roles) are not very confident of their own sexuality. That type seems rarer in Sweden than in the United States." Mrs. Linnér was not certain of the explanation, but she rather hesitantly observed that the general sexual permissiveness and even perhaps sex education has something to do with the masculine confidence. "Sexual enjoyment itself is the deepest expression of masculinity and femininity. A man who needs to assert economic or political power over a woman reminds me of the man who needs to seduce a woman. He has to prove something. Here he would be considered very weak."

"You don't agree, then, with Prime Minister Palme, who is reported to have told reporters that Swedish and American sexual behavior is similar."

"Perhaps behavior is similar in some respects, but Swedish sexual attitudes are very different. Standards of masculinity and femininity are different."

The key difference, she thought, was the virtual absence of the

---

[17] Interview with A. M. Fjellgren, June 10, 1970.

double-standard, both in practice and in ideals. "We do not define the virgin as a good woman simply because she is a virgin. Nor does she become bad once she ceases to be a virgin. The woman as well as the man is fully entitled to whatever sex life she desires, so long as she harms no-one else. It is strictly her own business. If she doesn't want to have intercourse and the man does, well they wait for another time, I suppose. The bedroom is no testing-ground. Nothing has been proved one way or the other."[18]

In Scandinavia one finds a strong official emphasis upon the need for sexual knowledge uniting with an equally strong respect for the privacy and importance of intimate relationships. Old-fashioned chastity has not succumbed to modern looseness. Instead, a new ideal has emerged—mutuality.

The ideal of mutuality is apparent first, in the almost universal use of and approval of birth-control devices. Significantly, even the Lutheran Church approved the sale of condoms through vending machines in spite of its official opposition to premarital relations. Today the debate over different sexual morals goes on within the Church, while in the secular society pluralists have won. The use of birth-control devices and pills may have increased the woman's initiative in sexual matters as it quieted her fears, but it has certainly equalized risks. What has resulted from this acceptance of premarital relations and easy access to contraception and information? Again Mrs. Linnér reports: "It has probably complicated intimate relations in that both men and women expect more of each other. It has given the man much less control over the woman than he had before. But if it has allowed relations to be more relaxed and playful, then it is all to the good. You know, the young really do not behave so very differently than their elders, I think. But they act more openly and with less guilt."

Sex education, which has been a compulsory part of the school curriculum since 1956, and an experimental part for a decade earlier, contributed to this effect. The practice of discussing sexual matters frankly and realistically, term after term, in mixed classes of boys and girls, has eased somewhat the usual crises of teenage pregnancies and venereal disease. The curriculum planners have realized the necessity of combining studies of physiology with studies of family relationships, of the psychology of love-relations, and of different cultural standards. Detailed, explicit contraceptive information as well as information about venereal disease and the problems of sexual deviation are given to all groups over the age of fourteen. The sexual norm is supposed to be not hedonism, but mutual responsibility. Recently the old school textbooks which had

---

[18] Interview with Mrs. Linnér, June 8, 1970.

recommended premarital chastity were dropped as unrealistic. However, problems of transition abound.

It is easier, after all, to teach the "plumbing" than to inculcate sexual responsibility among adolescents. Educators are concerned that, in spite of the ready availability of contraceptives, the rate of teenage pregnancy and of venereal disease has not declined. The weak point in the whole program remains the embarrassed and reticent teacher. Frequently, a perfectly planned and carefully researched curriculum is never put into practice. Teachers delay the subject until the end of the term when "there is no time." Others simply cannot bring themselves to use accurate sexual terms. The youngsters still learn, therefore, that "something is wrong."[19]

Increasingly the teachers' summer workshops in sex education are used both to discuss new research findings and to aid the teachers who still feel uncomfortable with the subject. A perceptible shift in teachers' attitudes is now apparent. The younger teachers, especially, recognize the futility of preaching chastity to young people who will in any case make up their own minds. The emphasis in teaching has shifted from the purely informational to discussions aimed at helping young adults to handle sexuality and its profound emotions. It is now widely recognized that the subject, with or without scientific approach, will remain special.

VI

WHETHER THIS LONG educational effort *has* already been the major influence in an acceptance of greater sexual equality is difficult to say. Without benefit of sex education, young Americans, like young Scandinavians, appear to be easier in more egalitarian sexual relations than their elders are. In any case, the Swedes, by open discussion of sexual roles and sexual needs, have discovered some disturbing and complex difficulties.

The first set of problems relates to pornography. As is well known, pornographic materials, whether films to rent, or books, magazines, and equipment to buy are readily available in Swedish as well as in Danish cities—especially in Copenhagen and Stockholm where the sex-shops have become an important tourist industry. One would expect as much in sexually liberated countries. (The United States does not seem to be very far behind the Scandinavians in this regard.) But does pornography really represent sexual liberation? This question is just beginning to occur to some Scandinavian and American critics. It is very notable that the sex-

---

[19] Linnér, "The Sexual Revolution in Sweden," *Impact of Science on Society,* XVIII (October–December, 1968), 233–242; and interview, June 8, 1970.

clubs of Copenhagen are service-stations of a kind for the frustrated male. They deal in female performances and services for male customers. But perhaps most significantly of all, pornography usually offers women as *merchandise*—quite dehumanized—and it is questionable whether this constitutes any real sexual liberation.

In the famous adult sex education films with "Sven and Inge," the Swedes frequently discuss pornography and the goods in the sex-shops as if they were more of Sweden's fine and advanced social services. Nevertheless, the Scandinavian feminists have not missed the significance of the American and Scandinavian girlie industries. In her book, *As I Understand It*, Eva Moberg has provided some reverse Swedish on a similar, although less extreme, American product.

"In . . . (a playgirl's) eyes, a man is above all the *male of the species*. And she knows that, in their heart of hearts, this is how the majority of men want to be thought of. She doesn't expect much of them in the way of intellect or education—she's got enough for two herself. No, what she looks for in them is recreation and stimulation. . . ."

At last we have reached the highlight of the entire magazine, a magnificent panorama pull-out supplement featuring the Playmate of the Month. We find that Mr. September is a superb brunette of nineteen summers, Svante Lindgren from Sundsvall: . . . Says Svante, "I think being nominated Playmate of the Month is about the biggest thing that can happen to a fellow."[20] The feminists have not attacked the pornography industry, largely because the allegiance to a free press and to free sexual expression is strong. But the demand market suggests that sexual frustrations are not quite of the past.

The sex-clubs have also raised crucial and difficult questions of privacy. As Stanley Kauffmann has observed in the *New Republic*, revolutionary changes in a culture are implied when acts which have always been private are performed for audiences.[21] How do such performances influence the character of sexuality itself?

Another related difficulty arises in connection with sex-education. It is in the very nature of classroom teaching to present material in a reasonable, unemotional, and fairly formal manner. Are the most important aspects of sexual life really teachable, reasonable, and formal? Does the public presentation of sexual matters contain an inevitable distortion in that emotions discussed become emotions defused and generalized?

---

[20] Selection by Eva Moberg, "Playgirl," *Hertha* (no. 5, 1969), p. 29.
[21] Stanley Kauffmann, "Public Privates," *New Republic* (July 11, 1970), pp. 22, 32.

Perhaps the most difficult and troublesome question to feminists are not in this area, however, but in the area of economic opportunity and sex-role attitudes. The persistence of sex-role choices of occupation in countries whose teachers and officials have long been committed to sex-role equality, remains very disturbing. Presumably in a nation with so many attractive and feminine women in public life, girls would grow up believing that one can become an engineer, politician, or architect, and yet remain a charming woman. But Swedish girls still cut their educational opportunities short, and still eschew certain professions. Even to this day the great majority look to marriage for security as well as for love. The depth of sex-role commitment is literally from the cradle to the grave. If girls are *fated* to choose secretarial work, nursing and teaching, and all as spare-time work, from the moment mother says, "Oh what a little doll she is," the feminist organizations have an unending struggle ahead. This is what the Fredrika Bremer members have recently realized. For almost half a century the society has integrated economic and political goals. It has worked for changes in law, in political arrangements, and in the educational and job opportunities. Yet its most fundamental difficulties are not legal or even economic, but cultural and psychological. An advanced social welfare state, supporting woman's employment, has not yet converted minds from the association of femininity and dependence. The Swedish government assumes that changing institutions all the way from the handicraft classes to the tax structure may help. And the new education, the new taxation, promise to accomplish a great deal. As the young men and women share family responsibilities more evenly, as they experiment with new family forms and a more androgynous occupational balance, the cultural lag between the needs of a technological society and the present inequality may disappear.

No one has any idea, however, whether those Swedes who have stayed out of the debate all these years are indifferent or fearful. Does masculine confidence wane, even in Scandinavia, at the thought of male nurses and female business executives? Do those women, remaining silent, *want* to enter the job-market and meet the pressures and responsibilities that decision entails? Perhaps certain fears concerning identity lie too deep for public debate, too deep for social solution. The Scandinavian editors, officials, and publicists have at least raised the crucial questions. And they have discussed them with the highest intelligence. If ever we find a way to reconcile sexual distinctiveness and sexual equality, Sweden's debate and example may well provide the needed enlightenment.

AM
I
NOT
A
WOMAN
AND
A
SISTER

DRAWINGS BY LISA UNGER BASKIN

1972

So while I do not pray for anybody or any party to commit outrages, still I do pray, and that earnestly and constantly, for some terrific shock to startle the women of this nation into a self-respect which will compel them to see the abject degradation of their present position; which will force them to break their yoke of bondage, and give them faith in themselves; which will make them proclaim their allegiance to woman first; which will enable them to see that man can no more feel, speak or act for woman than could the old slaveholder for his slave. The fact is, women are in chains, and their servitude is all the more debasing because they do not realize it. O, to compel them to see and feel, and to give them the courage and conscience to speak and act for their own freedom, though they face the scorn and contempt of all the world for doing it!

From a letter to a friend, Summer, 1870.

SUSAN B. ANTHONY

Considering the care and anxiety a woman must have about a child before it comes into the world, it seems to me, by a *natural right,* to belong to her. When men get immersed in the world, they seem to lose all sensations, excepting those necessary to continue or produce life!—Are these the privileges of reason? Amongst the feathered race, whilst the hen keeps the young warm, her mate stays by to cheer her; but it is sufficient for man to condescend to get a child, in order to claim it.—A man is a tyrant!

Mary Wollstonecraft to Gilbert Imlay, 1794

I had reasoned this out in my mind; there was one of two things I had a right to, liberty or death. If I could not have one, I would have the other, for no man should take me alive. I would fight for my liberty as long as my strength lasted, and when the time came for me to go, the Lord would let them take me. *Harriet Tubman*

SARAH GRIMKE

But I ask no favors for my sex. I surrender not our claim to equality. All I ask of our brethren is, that they will take their feet from off our necks, and permit us to stand upright on that ground which God designed us to occupy. Boston 1838

ANGELINA GRIMKE.

Whatever it is morally right for a man to do, it is morally right for a woman to do. I recognize no rights, I know nothing of men's rights and women's rights but human rights; for in Christ Jesus there is neither male nor female. Sure I am that woman is not to be, as she has been, a mere "second-hand agent" in the regeneration of a fallen world, but the acknowledged equal and co-worker with man in this glorious work.

Two Remarks to Elizabeth Cady Stanton

The wrongs of women have too long slumbered. They now begin to cry for redress. Let them be clearly pointed out in your Convention; and then, not *ask* as *favor,* but *demand as right,* that every civil and ecclesiastical obstacle be removed out of the way.

Rights are not dependent upon equality of mind; nor do we admit inferiority, leaving that question to be settled by future developments, when a fair opportunity shall be given for the equal cultivation of the intellect, and the stronger powers of the mind shall be called into action.

April 13, 1850. A response to an invitation to address the Ohio Convention for remodeling the state convention.

How thankful I am for these bright young women now ready to fill our soon-to-be-vacant places. I want to shake hands with them all before I go, and give them a few words of encouragement. I do hope they will not be spoiled with too much praise.

July 19, 1878. A remark at the thirtieth anniversary of the first women's rights convention.

LUCRETIA MOTT

DELIVERANCE

And if any man should ask me
If I would sell my vote,
I'd tell him I was not the one
To change and turn my coat . . . .

But when John Thomas Reder brought
His wife some flour and meat,
And told her he had sold his vote,
For something good to eat,

You ought to see Aunt Kitty raise,
And heard her blaze away;
She gave the meat and flour a toss,
And said they should not stay . . . .

You'd laughed to seen Lucinda Grange
Upon her husband's track
When he sold his vote for rations
She made him take 'em back.

Day after day did Milly Green
Just follow after Joe,
And told him if he voted wrong
To take his rags and go.

I think that Curnel Johnson said
His side had won the day,
Had not we women radicals
Just got right in the way . . . .

FRANCES ELLEN WATKINS HARPER

On Sunday last, February 23rd, 1913, I was forcibly fed in Holloway Prison. There were two doctors, Dr. Forward, and another, tall and dark, without beard or moustache, and about seven wardresses. I struggled with the wardresses, but was overpowered and tied into a chair. But I went on struggling the whole time after that. They pulled my head backward across the back of the chair by my hair, which I resisted by wriggling my head about. Finally the doctor got the nasal tube partly down, but I managed to get it up out of the nose, before they poured anything down. Then it was introduced again and immediately my breathing became very rattling and noisy, so that the doctor told me to breathe more quietly. I was myself worried with the fear that my fellow-prisoner might hear this loud noise and be alarmed at it. I could not help it, indeed I was breathing only with great difficulty and could not speak. They poured in food twice, but it came back at once through my mouth and I coughed very much. The whole time the tube was really in I was coughing violently and continuously and made this queer noise in breathing. A voice said something I did not catch, to which a man's voice answered, "Yes, go on," then something was poured in again and came straight back by my mouth, I coughing ever so much meanwhile. Then they took out the tube, untied me and I got up, but fell against the wall. Three wardresses remained in the cell and one fetched in the bed (one mattress and a pillow on the floor), and helped me on to the bed and soon after left me. I continued to cough but not with cessation. I began to be in pain from the waist upwards.

I tottered to and fro and then lay down again and was left alone. The pain became intense; I rang the bell and first one Dr. came and examined my chest, warning me not to sit up. He told the wardress to bring blankets and a hot water bottle, which they did. Dr. Forward then went away and came back and said he was authorized to tell me I should be released as soon as possible if I promised to appear at the Police Court, Richmond, on the following Thursday.

Unidentified prison letter,
Sophia Smith Collection

EMMELINE PANKHURST

Nowhere is woman treated according to the merit of her work, but rather as a sex. It is therefore almost inevitable that she should pay for her right to exist, to keep a position in whatever line, with sex favors. Thus it is merely a question of degree whether she sells herself to one man, in or out of marriage, or to many men. Whether our reformers admit it or not, the economic and social inferiority of woman is responsible for prostitution.

Just at present our good people are shocked by the disclosures that in New York City alone one out of every ten women works in a factory, that the average wage received by women is six dollars per week for forty-eight to sixty hours of work, and that the majority of female wage workers face many months of idleness which leaves the average wage about $280 a year. In view of these economic horrors, is it to be wondered at that prostitution and the white slave trade have become such dominant factors?

Emma Goldman, *The Traffic in Women*

ANGELA Y. DAVIS

REFLECTIONS ON THE BLACK WOMAN'S ROLE IN THE COMMUNITY OF SLAVES

Angela Davis

T HE PAUCITY OF LITERATURE on the black woman is outrageous on its face. But we must also contend with the fact that too many of these rare studies must claim as their signal achievement the reinforcement of fictitious clichés. They have given credence to grossly distorted categories through which the black woman continues to be perceived. In the words of Nathan and Julia Hare, ". . . she has been labeled 'aggressive' or 'matriarchal' by white scholars and 'castrating female' by [some] blacks." (*Transaction*, Nov.-Dec., 1970) Many have recently sought to remedy this situation. But for the time being, at least, we are still confronted with these reified images of ourselves. And for now, we must still assume the responsibility of shattering them.

Initially, I did not envision this paper as strictly confined to the era of slavery. Yet, as I began to think through the issue of the black matriarch, I came to the conclusion that it had to be refuted at its presumed historical inception.

The chief problem I encountered stemmed from the conditions of my incarceration: opportunities for researching the issue I wanted to explore were extremely limited. I chose, therefore, to entitle this piece "Reflections . . ." It does not pretend to be more than a collection of ideas which would constitute a starting point—a framework within which to conduct a rigorous reinvestigation of the black woman as she interacted with her people and with her oppressive environment during slavery.

I would like to dedicate these reflections to one of the most admirable black leaders to emerge from the ranks of our liberation movement—to George Jackson, whom I loved and respected in every way. As I came to know and love him, I saw him developing an acute sensitivity to the real problems facing black women and thus refining his ability to distinguish these from their mythical transpositions. George was uniquely aware of the need to extricate himself and other black men from the remnants of divisive and destructive myths purporting to represent the black woman. If his

Reprinted from *The Black Scholar*, December 1971 with permission. © 1971 *The Black Scholar*.

81

life had not been so precipitously and savagely extinguished, he would have surely accomplished a task he had already outlined some time ago: a systematic critique of his past misconceptions about black women and of their roots in the ideology of the established order. He wanted to appeal to other black men, still similarly disoriented, to likewise correct themselves through self-criticism. George viewed this obligation as a revolutionary duty, but also, and equally important, as an expression of his boundless love for all black women.

II

The matriarchal black woman has been repeatedly invoked as one of the fatal by-products of slavery. When the Moynihan Report consecrated this myth with Washington's stamp of approval, its spurious content and propagandistic mission should have become apparent. Yet even outside the established ideological apparatus, and also among black people, unfortunate references to the matriarchate can still be encountered. Occasionally, there is even acknowledgement of the "tangle of pathology" it supposedly engendered. (This black matriarchate, according to Moynihan *et al.* defines the roots of our oppression as a people.) An accurate portrait of the African woman in bondage must debunk the myth of the matriarchate. Such a portrait must simultaneously attempt to illuminate the historical matrix of her oppression and must evoke her varied, often heroic, responses to the slaveholder's domination.

Lingering beneath the notion of the black matriarch is an unspoken indictment of our female forebears as having actively assented to slavery. The notorious cliché, the "emasculating female," has its roots in the fallacious inference that in playing a central part in the slave "family," the black woman related to the slaveholding class as collaborator. Nothing could be further from the truth. In the most fundamental sense, the slave system did not—and could not—engender and recognize a matriarchal family structure. Inherent in the very concept of the matriarchy is "power." It would have been exceedingly risky for the slaveholding class to openly acknowledge symbols of authority—female symbols no less than male. Such legitimized concentrations of authority might eventually unleash their "power" against the slave system itself.

The American brand of slavery strove toward a rigidified disorganization in family life, just as it had to proscribe all potential social structures within which black people might forge a collective and conscious existence.[1] Mothers and fathers were brutally separated; children, when they became of age, were branded and frequently severed from their mothers. That the mother was "the only legitimate parent of her child" did not therefore mean that she was even permitted to guide it to maturity.

Those who lived under a common roof were often unrelated through blood. Frederick Douglass, for instance, had no recollection of his father. He only vaguely recalled having seen his mother —and then on extremely rare occasions. Moreover, at the age of seven, he was forced to abandon the dwelling of his grandmother, of whom he would later say: "She was to me a mother and a father."[2] The strong personal bonds between immediate family members which oftentimes persisted despite coerced separation bore witness to the remarkable capacity of black people for resisting the disorder so violently imposed on their lives.

Where families were allowed to thrive, they were, for the most part, external fabrications serving the designs of an avaricious, profit-seeking slaveholder.

> The strong hand of the slave owner dominated the Negro family, which existed at his mercy and often at his own personal instigation. An ex-slave has told of getting married on one plantation: 'When you married, you had to jump over a broom three times.'[3]

This slave went on to describe the various ways in which his master forcibly coupled men and women with the aim of producing the maximum number of healthy child-slaves. In the words of John Henrik Clarke,

> The family as a functional entity was outlawed and permitted to exist only when it benefited the slave-master. Maintenance of the slave family as a family unit benefited the slave owners only when, and to the extent that such unions created new slaves who could be exploited.[4]

---

[1] It is interesting to note a parallel in Nazi Germany: with all its ranting and raving about motherhood and the family, Hitler's regime made a conscious attempt to strip the family of virtually all its social functions. The thrust of their unspoken program for the family was to reduce it to a biological unit and to force its members to relate in an unmediated fashion to the fascist bureaucracy. Clearly the Nazis endeavored to crush the family in order to ensure that it could not become a center from which oppositional activity might originate.

[2] Herbert Aptheker, ed., *A Documentary History of the Negro People in the United States,* New York: The Citadel Press, 1969 (1st ed., 1951), p. 272.

[3] Andrew Billingsley, *Black Families in White America,* Englewood, New Jersey: Prentice-Hall, Inc., 1968, p. 61.

[4] John Henrik Clarke, "The Black Woman: A Figure in World History," Part III, *Essence,* New York: July, 1971.

The designation of the black woman as a matriarch is a cruel misnomer. It is a misnomer because it implies stable kinship structures within which the mother exercises decisive authority. It is cruel because it ignores the profound traumas the black woman must have experienced when she had to surrender her child-bearing to alien and predatory economic interests.

Even the broadest construction of the matriarch concept would not render it applicable to the black slave woman. But it should not be inferred that she therefore played no significant role in the community of slaves. Her indispensable efforts to ensure the survival of her people can hardly be contested. Even if she had done no more, her deeds would still be laudable. But her concern and struggles for physical survival, while clearly important, did not constitute her most outstanding contributions. It will be submitted that by virtue of the brutal force of circumstances, the black woman was assigned the mission of promoting the consciousness and practice of resistance. A great deal has been said about the black *man* and resistance, but very little about the unique relationship black women bore to the resistance struggles during slavery. To understand the part she played in developing and sharpening the thrust towards freedom, the broader meaning of slavery and of American slavery in particular must be explored.

Slavery is an ancient human institution. Of slave labor in its traditional form and of serfdom as well, Karl Marx had the following to say:

> The slave stands in absolutely no relation to the objective conditions of his labor; it is rather the *labor* itself, in the form of the slave as of the serf, which is placed in the category of *inorganic condition* of production alongside the other natural beings, *e.g.* cattle, or regarded as an appendage of the earth.[5]

The bondsman's existence as a natural condition of production is complemented and reinforced, according to Marx, by his membership in a social grouping which he perceives to be an extension of nature. Enmeshed in what appears to be a natural state of affairs, the attitude of the slave, to a greater or lesser degree, would be an acquiescence in his subjugation. Engels points out that in Athens, the state could depend on a police force consisting entirely of slaves.[6]

[5] Karl Marx, *Grundrisse der Kritik der Politischen Oekonomie*, Berlin: Dietz Verlag, 1953, p. 389.
[6] Friedrich Engels, *Origin of the Family, Private Property and The State*, New York: International Publishers, 1942, p. 107.

The Black Woman's Role

The fabric of American slavery differed significantly from ancient slavery and feudalism. True, black people were forced to act as if they were "inorganic conditions of production." For slavery was "personality swallowed up in the sordid idea of property—manhood lost in chattelhood."[7] But there were no pre-existent social structures or cultural dictates which might induce reconciliation to the circumstances of their bondage. On the contrary, Africans had been uprooted from their natural environment, their social relations, their culture. No legitimate socio-cultural surroundings would be permitted to develop and flourish, for, in all likelihood, they would be utterly incompatible with the demands of slavery.

Yet another fact would militate against harmony and equilibrium in the slave's relation to his bondage: slavery was enclosed in a society otherwise characterized by "free" wage-labor. Black men and women could always contrast their chains with the nominally free status of white working people. This was quite literally true in such cases where, like Frederick Douglass, they were contracted out as wage-laborers. Unlike the "free" white men alongside whom they worked, they had no right to the meager wages they earned. Such were some of the many contradictions unloosed by the effort to forcibly inject slavery into the early stages of American capitalism.

The combination of a historically superceded slave labor system based almost exclusively on race and the drive to strip black people of all their social and cultural bonds would create a fateful rupture at the heart of the slave system itself. The slaves would not readily adopt fatalistic attitudes towards the conditions surrounding and ensnaring their lives. They were a people who had been violently thrust into a patently "unnatural" subjugation. If the slaveholders had not maintained an absolute monopoly of violence, if they had not been able to rely on large numbers of their fellow white men—indeed the entire ruling class as well as misled working people—to assist them in their terrorist machinations, slavery would have been far less feasible than it actually proved to be.

The magnitude and effects of the black people's defiant rejection of slavery has not yet been fully documented and illuminated. But there is more than ample evidence that they consistently refused to succumb to the all-encompassing dehumanization objectively demanded by the slave system. Comparatively recent studies have

---

[7] Frederick Douglass, *Life and Times of Frederick Douglass*, New York: Collier Books, 1962, p. 96.

demonstrated that the few slave uprisings—too spectacular to be relegated to oblivion by the racism of ruling class historians—were not isolated occurrences, as the latter would have had us believe. The reality, we know now, was that these open rebellions erupted with such a frequency that they were as much a part of the texture of slavery as the conditions of servitude themselves. And these revolts were only the tip of an iceberg: resistance expressed itself in other grand modes and also in the seemingly trivial forms of feigned illness and studied indolence.

If resistance was an organic ingredient of slave life, it had to be directly nurtured by the social organization which the slaves themselves improvised. The consciousness of their oppression, the conscious thrust towards its abolition could not have been sustained without impetus from the community they pulled together through the sheer force of their own strength. Of necessity, this community would revolve around the realm which was furthermost removed from the immediate arena of domination. It could only be located in and around the living quarters, the area where the basic needs of physical life were met.

In the area of production, the slaves—pressed into the mold of beasts of burden—were forcibly deprived of their humanity. (And a human being thoroughly dehumanized, has no desire for freedom.) But the community gravitating around the domestic quarters might possibly permit a retrieval of the man and the woman in their fundamental humanity. We can assume that in a very real material sense, it was only in domestic life—away from the eyes and whip of the overseer—that the slaves could attempt to assert the modicum of freedom they still retained. It was only there that they might be inspired to project techniques of expanding it further by leveling what few weapons they had against the slaveholding class whose unmitigated drive for profit was the source of their misery.

Via this path, we return to the African slave woman: in the living quarters, the major responsibilities "naturally" fell to her. It was the woman who was charged with keeping the "home" in order. This role was dictated by the male supremacist ideology of white society in America; it was also woven into the patriarchal traditions of Africa. As her biological destiny, the woman bore the fruits of procreation; as her social destiny, she cooked, sewed, washed, cleaned house, raised the children. Traditionally the labor of females, domestic work is supposed to complement and confirm their inferiority.

The Black Woman's Role

But with the black slave woman, there is a strange twist of affairs: in the infinite anguish of ministering to the needs of the men and children around her (who were not necessarily members of her immediate family), she was performing the *only* labor of the slave community which could not be directly and immediately claimed by the oppressor. There was no compensation for work in the fields; it served no useful purpose for the slaves. Domestic labor was the only meaningful labor for the slave community as a whole (discounting as negligible the exceptional situations where slaves received some pay for their work).

Precisely through performing the drudgery which has long been a central expression of the socially conditioned inferiority of women, the black woman in chains could help to lay the foundation for some degree of autonomy, both for herself and her men. Even as she was suffering under her unique oppression as female, she was thrust by the force of circumstances into the center of the slave community. She was, therefore, essential to the *survival* of the community. Not all people have survived enslavement; hence her survival-oriented activities were themselves a form of resistance. Survival, moreover, was the prerequisite of all higher levels of struggle.

But much more remains to be said of the black woman during slavery. The dialectics of her oppression will become far more complex. It is true that she was a victim of the myth that only the woman, with her diminished capacity for mental and physical labor, should do degrading household work. Yet, the alleged benefits of the ideology of feminity did not accrue to her. She was not sheltered or protected; she would not remain oblivious to the desperate struggle for existence unfolding outside the "home." She was also there in the fields, alongside the man, toiling under the lash from sun-up to sun-down.

This was one of the supreme ironies of slavery: in order to approach its strategic goal—to extract the greatest possible surplus from the labor of the slaves—the black woman had to be released from the chains of the myth of feminity. In the words of W.E.B. Du Bois, ". . . our women in black had freedom contemptuously thrust upon them."[8] In order to function as slave, the black woman had to be annulled as woman, that is, as woman in her historical stance of wardship under the entire male hierarchy. The sheer force of things rendered her equal to her man.

---

[8] W.E.B. Du Bois, *Darkwater, Voices from Within the Veil*, New York: AMS Press, 1969, p. 185.

Excepting the woman's role as caretaker of the household, male supremacist structures could not become deeply embedded in the internal workings of the slave system. Though the ruling class was male and rabidly chauvinistic, the slave system could not confer upon the black man the appearance of a privileged position vis-à-vis the black woman. The man-slave could not be the unquestioned superior within the "family" or community, for there was no such thing as the "family provided" among the slaves. The attainment of slavery's intrinsic goals was contingent upon the fullest and most brutal utilization of the productive capacities of every man, woman and child. They all had to "provide" for the master. The black woman was therefore wholly integrated into the productive force.

> The bell rings at four o'clock in the morning and they have half an hour to get ready. Men and women start together, and the women must work as steadily as the men and perform the same tasks as the men.[9]

Even in the posture of motherhood—otherwise the occasion for hypocritical adoration—the black woman was treated with not greater compassion and with no less severity than her man. As one slave related in a narrative of his life:

> . . . women who had sucking children suffered much from their breasts becoming full of milk, the infants being left at home; they therefore could not keep up with the other hands: I have seen the overseer beat them with raw hide so that the blood and the milk flew mingled from their breasts.[10]

Moses Grandy, ex-slave, continues his description with an account of a typical form of field punishment reserved for the black woman with child:

> She is compelled to lie down over a hole made to receive her corpulency, and is flogged with the whip, or beat with a paddle, which has holes in it; at every stroke comes a blister.[11]

The unbridled cruelty of this leveling process whereby the black woman was forced into equality with the black man requires no

---

[9] Lewis Clarke, *Narrative of the Sufferings of Lewis and Milton Clarke, Sons of a Soldier of the Revolution*, Boston: 1846, p. 127 [Quoted by E. Franklin Frazier, *The Negro Family in the United States*].
[10] Moses Grandy, *Narrative of the Life of Moses Grandy; Late a Slave in the United States of America*, Boston: 1844, p. 18 [Quoted by Frazier].
[11] *Ibid.*

The Black Woman's Role

further explanation. She shared in the deformed equality of equal oppression.

But out of this deformed equality was forged quite undeliberately, yet inexorably, a state of affairs which could unharness an immense potential in the black woman. Expending indispensable labor for the enrichment of her oppressor, she could attain a practical awareness of the oppressor's utter dependence on her—for the master needs the slave far more than the slave needs the master. At the same time she could realize that while her productive activity was wholly subordinated to the will of the master, it was nevertheless proof of her ability to transform things. For "labor is the living, shaping fire; it represents the impermanence of thing, their temporality . . ."[12]

The black woman's consciousness of the oppression suffered by her people was honed in the bestial realities of daily experience. It would not be the stunted awareness of a woman confined to the home. She would be prepared to ascend to the same levels of resistance which were accessible to her men. Even as she performed her housework, the black woman's role in the slave community could not be identical to the historically evolved female role. Stripped of the palliative feminine veneer which might have encouraged a passive performance of domestic tasks, she was now uniquely capable of weaving into the warp and woof of domestic life a profound consciousness of resistance.

With the contributions of strong black women, the slave community as a whole could achieve heights unscaleable within the families of the white oppressed or even within the patriarchal kinship groups of Africa. Latently or actively it was always a community of resistance. It frequently erupted in insurgency, but was daily animated by the minor acts of sabotage which harassed the slave master to no end. Had the black woman failed to rise to the occasion, the community of slaves could not have fully developed in this direction. The slave system would have to deal with the black woman as the custodian of a house of resistance.

The oppression of black women during the era of slavery, therefore, had to be buttressed by a level of overt ruling-class repression. Her routine oppression had to assume an unconcealed dimension of outright counter-insurgency.

III

To say that the oppression of black slave women necessarily incorporated open forms of counter-insurgency is not as extrava-

---

[12] Marx, *Grundrisse*, p. 266.

89

gant as it might initially appear. The penetration of counter-insurgency into the day to day routine of the slave master's domination will be considered towards the end of this paper. First, the participation of black women in the overt and explosive upheavals which constantly rocked the slave system must be confirmed. This will be an indication of the magnitude of her role as caretaker of a household of resistance—of the degree to which she could concretely encourage those around her to keep their eyes on freedom. It will also confirm the objective circumstances to which the slave master's counter-insurgency was a response.

With the sole exceptions of Harriet Tubman and Sojourner Truth, black women of the slave era remain more or less enshrouded in unrevealed history. And, as Earl Conrad has demonstrated, even "General Tubman's" role has been consistently and grossly minimized. She was a far greater warrior against slavery than is suggested by the prevalent misconception that her only outstanding contribution was to make nineteen trips into the South, bringing over 300 slaves to their freedom.

> [She] was head of the Intelligence Service in the Department of the South throughout the Civil War; she is the only American woman to lead troops black and white on the field of battle, as she did in the Department of the South . . . She was a compelling and stirring orator in the councils of the abolitionists and the anti-slavers, a favorite of the antislavery conferences. She was the fellow planner with Douglass, Martin Delany, Wendell Phillips, Gerrit Smith and other leaders of the antislavery movement.[13]

No extensive and systematic study of the role of black women in resisting slavery has come to my attention. It has been noted that large numbers of freed black women worked towards the purchase of their relatives' and friends' freedom. About the participation of women in both the well-known and more obscure slave revolts, only casual remarks have been made. It has been observed, for instance, that Gabriel's wife was active in planning the rebellion spearheaded by her husband, but little else has been said about her.

The sketch which follows is based in its entirety on the works of Herbert Aptheker, the only resources available to me at the time of this writing.[14] These facts, gleaned from Aptheker's works on slave revolts and other forms of resistance, should signal the

---

[13] Earl Conrad, "I Bring You General Tubman," *The Black Scholar*, Vol. 1, No. 3-4, Jan.-Feb., 1970, p. 4.

[14] In February, 1949, Herbert Aptheker published an essay in *Masses and Mainstream* entitled "The Negro Woman." As yet, however, I have been unable to obtain it.

urgency to undertake a thorough study of the black woman as anti-slavery rebel. In 1971 this work is far overdue.

Aptheker's research has disclosed the widespread existence of communities of blacks who were neither free nor in bondage. Throughout the South (in South and North Carolina, Virginia, Louisiana, Florida, Georgia, Mississippi and Alabama), maroon communities consisting of fugitive slaves and their descendants were "an ever present feature"—from 1642 to 1864—of slavery. They provided ". . . havens for fugitives, served as bases for marauding expeditions against nearby plantations and, at times, supplied leadership to planned uprisings."[15]

Every detail of these communities was invariably determined by and steeped in resistance, for their raison d'être emanated from their perpetual assault on slavery. Only in a fighting stance could the maroons hope to secure their constantly imperiled freedom. As a matter of necessity, the women of those communities were compelled to define themselves—no less than the men—through their many acts of resistance. Hence, throughout this brief survey the counter-attacks and heroic efforts at defense assisted by maroon women will be a recurring motif.

As it will be seen, black women often poisoned the food and set fire to the houses of their masters. For those who were also employed as domestics these particular overt forms of resistance were especially available.

The vast majority of the incidents to be related involve either tactically unsuccessful assaults or eventually thwarted attempts at defense. In all likelihood, numerous successes were achieved, even against the formidable obstacles posed by the slave system. Many of these were probably unpublicized even at the time of their occurrence, lest they provide encouragement to the rebellious proclivities of other slaves and, for other slaveholders, an occasion for fear and despair.

During the early years of the slave era (1708) a rebellion broke out in New York. Among its participants were surely many women, for one, along with three men, was executed in retaliation for the killing of seven whites. It may not be entirely insignificant that while the men were hanged, she was heinously burned alive.[16] In the same colony, women played an active role in a 1712 uprising in the course of which slaves, with their guns, clubs and knives, killed

---

[15] Herbert Aptheker, "Slave Guerrilla Warfare" in *To Be Free, Studies in American Negro History*, New York: International Publishers, 1969 (1st ed., 1948), p. 11.

[16] Herbert Aptheker, *American Negro Slave Revolts*, New York: International Publishers, 1970 (1st ed., 1943), p. 169.

members of the slaveholding class and managed to wound others. While some of the insurgents—among them a pregnant woman—were captured, others—including a woman—committed suicide rather than surrender.[17]

"In New Orleans one day in 1730 a woman slave received 'a violent blow from a French soldier for refusing to obey him' and in her anger shouted 'that the French should not long insult Negroes'."[18] As it was later disclosed, she and undoubtedly many other women, had joined in a vast plan to destroy slaveholders. Along with eight men, this dauntless woman was executed. Two years later, Louisiana pronounced a woman and four men leaders of a planned rebellion. They were all executed and, in a typically savage gesture, their heads publicly displayed on poles.[19]

Charleston, South Carolina condemned a black woman to die in 1740 for arson,[20] a form of sabotage, as earlier noted, frequently carried out by women. In Maryland, for instance, a slave woman was executed in 1776 for having destroyed by fire her master's house, his outhouses and tobacco house.[21]

In the thick of the Colonies' war with England, a group of defiant slave women and men were arrested in Saint Andrew's Parish, Georgia in 1774. But before they were captured, they had already brought a number of slave owners to their death.[22]

The maroon communities have been briefly described; from 1782 to 1784, Louisiana was a constant target of maroon attacks. When twenty-five of this community's members were finally taken prisoner, men and women alike were all severely punished.[23]

As can be inferred from previous example, the North did not escape the tremendous impact of fighting black women. In Albany, New York, two women were among three slaves executed for antislavery activities in 1794.[24] The respect and admiration accorded the black woman fighter by her people is strikingly illustrated by an incident which transpired in York, Pennsylvania: when, during the early months of 1803, Margaret Bradley was convicted of attempting to poison two white people, the black inhabitants of the area revolted en masse.

---

[17] *Ibid.*, p. 173.
[18] *Ibid.*, p. 181.
[19] *Ibid.*, p. 182.
[20] *Ibid.*, p. 190.
[21] *Ibid.*, p. 145.
[22] *Ibid.*, p. 201.
[23] *Ibid.*, p. 207.
[24] *Ibid.*, p. 215.

The Black Woman's Role

They made several attempts to destroy the town by fire and succeeded, within a period of three weeks, in burning eleven buildings. Patrols were established, strong guards set up, the militia dispatched to the scene of the unrest . . . and a reward of three hundred dollars offered for the capture of the insurrectionists.[25]

A successful elimination by poisoning of several "of our respectable men" (said a letter to the governor of North Carolina) was met by the execution of four or five slaves. One was a woman who was burned alive.[26] In 1810, two women and a man were accused of arson in Virginia.[27]

In 1811 North Carolina was the scene of a confrontation between a maroon community and a slave-catching posse. Local newspapers reported that its members "had bid defiance to any force whatever and were resolved to stand their ground." Of the entire community, two were killed, one wounded and two—both women—were captured.[28]

Aptheker's *Documentary History of the Negro People in the United States* contains a portion of the transcript of an 1812 confession of a slave rebel in Virginia. The latter divulged the information that a black woman brought him into a plan to kill their master and that yet another black woman had been charged with concealing him after the killing occurred.[29]

In 1816 it was discovered that a community of three hundred escaped slaves—men, women, children—had occupied a fort in Florida. After the U.S. Army was dispatched with instructions to destroy the community, a ten-day siege terminated with all but forty of the three hundred dead. All the slaves fought to the very end.[30] In the course of a similar, though smaller confrontation between maroons and a militia group (in South Carolina, 1826), a woman and a child were killed.[31] Still another maroon community was attacked in Mobile, Alabama in 1837. Its inhabitants, men and women alike, resisted fiercely—according to local newspapers, "fighting like Spartans."[32]

Convicted of having been among those who, in 1829, had been the cause of a devastating fire in Augusta, Georgia, a black woman was "executed, dissected, and exposed" (according to an English

---

[25] *Ibid.*, p. 239.
[26] *Ibid.*, pp. 241–242.
[27] *Ibid.*, p. 247.
[28] *Ibid.*, p. 251.
[29] Aptheker, *Documentary History*, pp. 55–57.
[30] Aptheker, *Slave Revolts*, p. 259.
[31] *Ibid.*, p. 277.
[32] *Ibid.*, p. 259.

93

visitor). Moreover, the execution of yet another woman, about to give birth, was imminent.[33] During the same year, a group of slaves, being led from Maryland to be sold in the South, had apparently planned to kill the traders and make their way to freedom. One of the traders was successfully done away with, but eventually a posse captured all the slaves. Of the six leaders sentenced to death, one was a woman. She was first permitted, for reasons of economy, to give birth to her child.[34] Afterwards, she was publicly hanged.

The slave class in Louisiana, as noted earlier, was not unaware of the formidable threat posed by the black woman who chose to fight. It responded accordingly: in 1846 a posse of slave owners ambushed a community of maroons, killing one woman and wounding two others. A black man was also assassinated.[35] Neither could the border states escape the recognition that slave women were eager to battle for their freedom. In 1850 in the state of Missouri, "about thirty slaves, men and women, of four different owners, had armed themselves with knives, clubs and three guns and set out for a free state." Their pursuers, who could unleash a far more powerful violence than they, eventually thwarted their plans.[36]

This factual survey of but a few of the open acts of resistance in which black women played major roles will close with two further events. When a maroon camp in Mississippi was destroyed in 1857, four of its members did not manage to elude capture, one of whom was a fugitive slave woman.[37] All of them, women as well as men, must have waged a valiant fight. Finally, there occurred in October, 1862 a skirmish between maroons and a scouting party of Confederate soldiers in the state of Virginia.[38] This time, however, the maroons were the victors and it may well have been that some of the many women helped to put the soldiers to death.

IV

The oppression of slave women had to assume dimensions of open counter-insurgency. Against the background of the facts presented above, it would be difficult indeed to refute this contention. As for those who engaged in open battle, they were no less ruth-

---

[33] *Ibid.*, p. 281.
[34] *Ibid.*, p. 487.
[35] Aptheker, "Guerrilla Warfare," p. 27.
[36] Aptheker, *Slave Revolts*, p. 342.
[37] Aptheker, "Guerrilla Warfare," p. 28.
[38] *Ibid.*, p. 29.

lessly punished than slave men. It would even appear that in many cases they may have suffered penalties which were more excessive than those meted out to the men. On occasion, when men were hanged, the women were burned alive. If such practices were widespread, their logic would be clear. They would be terrorist methods designed to dissuade other black women from following the examples of their fighting sisters. If all black women rose up alongside their men, the institution of slavery would be in difficult straits.

It is against the backdrop of her role as fighter that the routine oppression of the slave woman must be explored once more. If she was burned, hanged, broken on the wheel, her head paraded on poles before her oppressed brothers and sisters, she must have also felt the edge of this counter-insurgency as a fact of her daily existence. The slave system would not only have to make conscious efforts to stifle the tendencies towards acts of the kind described above; it would be no less necessary to stave off escape attempts (escapes to maroon country!) and all the various forms of sabotage within the system. Feigning illness was also resistance as were work slowdowns and actions destructive to the crops. The more extensive these acts, the more the slaveholder's profits would tend to diminish.

While a detailed study of the myriad modes in which this counter-insurgency was manifested can and should be conducted, the following reflections will focus on a single aspect of the slave woman's oppression, particularly prominent in its brutality.

Much has been said about the sexual abuses to which the black woman was forced to submit. They are generally explained as an outgrowth of the male supremacy of Southern culture: the purity of white womanhood could not be violated by the aggressive sexual activity desired by the white male. His instinctual urges would find expression in his relationships with his property—the black slave woman, who would have to become his unwilling concubine. No doubt there is an element of truth in these statements, but it is equally important to unearth the meaning of these sexual abuses from the vantage point of the woman who was assaulted.

In keeping with the theme of these reflections, it will be submitted that the slave master's sexual domination of the black woman contained an unveiled element of counter-insurgency. To understand the basis for this assertion, the dialectical moments of the slave woman's oppression must be restated and their movement recaptured. The prime factor, it has been said, was the total and violent expropriation of her labor with no compensation save the pittance necessary for bare existence.

Secondly, as female, she was the housekeeper of the living quarters. In this sense, she was already doubly oppressed. However, having been wrested from passive, "feminine" existence by the sheer force of things—literally by forced labor—confining domestic tasks were incommensurable with what she had become. That is to say, by virtue of her participation in production, she would not act the part of the passive female, but could experience the same need as her men to challenge the conditions of her subjugation. As the center of domestic life, the only life at all removed from the arena of exploitation, and thus as an important source of survival, the black woman could play a pivotal role in nurturing the thrust towards freedom.

The slave master would attempt to thwart this process. He knew that as female, this slave woman could be particularly vulnerable in her sexual existence. Although he would not pet her and deck her out in frills, the white master could endeavor to reestablish her femaleness by reducing her to the level of her *biological* being. Aspiring with his sexual assaults to establish her as a female *animal,* he would be striving to destroy her proclivities towards resistance. Of the sexual relations of animals, taken at their abstract biological level (and not in terms of their quite different social potential for human beings), Simone de Beauvoir says the following:

> It is unquestionably the male who *takes* the female—she is *taken.* Often the word applies literally, for whether by means of special organs or through superior strength, the male seizes her and holds her in place; he performs the copulatory movements; and, among insects, birds, and mammals, he penetrates . . . Her body becomes a resistance to be broken through . . .[39]

The act of copulation, reduced by the white man to an animal-like act, would be symbolic of the effort to conquer the resistance the black woman could unloose.

In confronting the black woman as adversary in a sexual contest, the master would be subjecting her to the most elemental form of terrorism distinctively suited for the female: rape. Given the already terroristic texture of plantation life, it would be as potential victim of rape that the slave woman would be most unguarded. Further, she might be most conveniently manipulable if the master contrived a ransom system of sorts, forcing her to pay with her body for food, diminished severity in treatment, the safety of her children, etc.

The integration of rape into the sparsely furnished legitimate social life of the slaves harks back to the feudal "right of the first night," the *jus primae noctis.* The feudal lord manifested and rein-

---

[39] Simone de Beauvoir, *The Second Sex,* New York: Bantam Books, 1961, pp. 18–19.

forced his domination over the serfs by asserting his authority to have sexual intercourse with all the females. The right itself referred specifically to all freshly married women. But while the right to the first night eventually evolved into the institutionalized "virgin tax,"[40] the American slaveholder's sexual domination never lost its openly terroristic character.

As a direct attack on the black female as potential insurgent, this sexual repression finds its parallels in virtually every historical situation where the woman actively challenges oppression. Thus, Franz Fanon could say of the Algerian woman: "A woman led away by soldiers who comes back a week later—it is not necessary to question her to understand that she has been violated dozens of times."[41]

In its political contours, the rape of the black woman was not exclusively an attack upon her. Indirectly, its target was also the slave community as a whole. In launching the sexual war on the woman, the master would not only assert his sovereignty over a critically important figure of the slave community, he would also be aiming a blow against the black man. The latter's instinct to protect his female relations and comrades (now stripped of its male supremacist implications) would be frustrated and violated to the extreme. Placing the white male's sexual barbarity in bold relief, Du Bois cries out in a rhetorical vein:

> I shall forgive the South much in its final judgement day: I shall forgive its slavery, for slavery is a world-old habit; I shall forgive its fighting for a well-lost cause, and for remembering that struggle with tender tears; I shall forgive its so-called 'pride of race,' the passion of its hot blood, and even its dear, old, laughable strutting and posing; but one thing I shall never forgive, neither in this world nor the world to come: its wanton and continued and persistent insulting of the black womanhood which it sought and seeks to prostitute to its lust.[42]

The retaliatory import of the rape for the black man would be entrapment in an untenable situation. Clearly the master hoped that once the black man was struck by his manifest inability to rescue his women from sexual assaults of the master, he would begin to experience deep-seated doubts about his ability to resist at all.

Certainly the wholesale rape of slave women must have had a profound impact on the slave community. Yet it could not succeed in its intrinsic aim of stifling the impetus towards struggle. Countless black women did not passively submit to these abuses, as the

---

[40] August Bebel, *Women and Socialism,* New York: Socialist Literature Co., 1910, p. 66–69.

[41] Franz Fanon, *A Dying Colonialism,* New York: Grove Press, 1967, p. 119.

[42] Du Bois, *Darkwater,* p. 172.

slaves in general refused to passively accept their bondage. The
struggles of the slave woman in the sexual realm were a continuation of the resistance interlaced in the slave's daily existence. As
such, this was yet another form of insurgency, a response to a
politically tinged sexual repression.

Even E. Franklin Frazier (who goes out of his way to defend
the thesis that "the master in his mansion and his colored mistress
in her special house nearby represented the final triumph of social
ritual in the presence of the deepest feelings of human solidarity"[43])
could not entirely ignore the black woman who fought back. He
notes: "That physical compulsion was necessary at times to secure
submission on the part of black women . . . is supported by historical evidence and has been preserved in the tradition of Negro
families."[44]

The sexual contest was one of many arenas in which the black
woman had to prove herself as a warrior against oppression. What
Frazier unwillingly concedes would mean that countless children
brutally fathered by whites were conceived in the thick of battle.
Frazier himself cites the story of a black woman whose great-grand-
mother, a former slave, would describe with great zest the battles
behind all her numerous scars—that is, all save one. In response to
questions concerning the unexplained scar, she had always simply
said: "White men are as low as dogs, child, stay away from them."
The mystery was not unveiled until after the death of this brave
woman: "She received that scar at the hands of her master's youngest son, a boy of about eighteen years at the time she conceived
their child, my grandmother Ellen."[45]

An intricate and savage web of oppression intruded at every moment into the black woman's life during slavery. Yet a single theme
appears at every juncture: the woman transcending, refusing, fighting back, asserting herself over and against terrifying obstacles. It
was not her comrade brother against whom her incredible strength
was directed. She fought alongside her man, accepting or providing guidance according to her talents and the nature of their tasks.
She was in no sense an authoritarian figure; neither her domestic
role nor her acts of resistance could relegate the man to the shadows. On the contrary, she herself had just been forced to leave
behind the shadowy realm of female passivity in order to assume
her rightful place beside the insurgent male.

[43] E. Franklin Frazier, *The Negro Family in the United States,* Chicago: U.
of Chicago Press, 1966 (1st ed., 1939), p. 69.
[44] *Ibid.,* p. 53.
[45] *Ibid.,* pp. 53–54.

The Black Woman's Role

This portrait cannot, of course, presume to represent every individual slave woman. It is rather a portrait of the potentials and possibilities inherent in the situation to which slave women were anchored. Invariably there were those who did not realize this potential. There were those who were indifferent and a few who were outright traitors. But certainly they were not the vast majority. The image of black women enchaining their men, cultivating relationships with the oppressor is a cruel fabrication which must be called by its right name. It is a dastardly ideological weapon designed to impair our capacity for resistance today by foisting upon us the ideal of male supremacy.

According to a time-honored principle, advanced by Marx, Lenin, Fanon and numerous other theorists, the status of women in any given society is a barometer measuring the overall level of social development. As Fanon has masterfully shown, the strength and efficacy of social struggles—and especially revolutionary movements —bear an immediate relationship to the range and quality of female participation.

The meaning of this principle is strikingly illustrated by the role of the black woman during slavery. Attendant to the indiscriminant brutal pursuit of profit, the slave woman attained a correspondingly brutal status of equality. But in practice, she could work up a fresh content for this deformed equality by inspiring and participating in acts of resistance of every form and color. She could turn the weapon of equality in struggle against the avaricious slave system which had engendered the mere caricature of equality in oppression. The black woman's activities increased the total incidence of anti-slavery assaults. But most important, without consciously rebellious black women, the theme of resistance could not have become so thoroughly intertwined in the fabric of daily existence. The status of black women within the community of slaves was definitely a barometer indicating the overall potential for resistance.

This process did not end with the formal dissolution of slavery. Under the impact of racism, the black woman has been continually constrained to inject herself into the desperate struggle for existence. She—like her man—has been compelled to work for wages, providing for her family as she was previously forced to provide for the slaveholding class. The infinitely onerous nature of this equality should never be overlooked. For the black woman has always also remained harnessed to the chores of the household. Yet, she could never be exhaustively defined by her uniquely "female" responsibilities.

As a result, black women have made significant contributions to struggles against the racism and the dehumanizing exploitation of a wrongly organized society. In fact, it would appear that the intense levels of resistance historically maintained by black people and thus the historical function of the Black Liberation Struggle as harbinger of change throughout the society are due in part to the greater *objective* equality between the black man and the black woman. Du Bois put it this way:

> In the great rank and file of our five million women, we have the up-working of new revolutionary ideals, which must in time have vast influence on the thought and action of this land.[46]

Official and unofficial attempts to blunt the effects of the egalitarian tendencies as between the black man and woman should come as no surprise. The matriarch concept, embracing the clichéd "female castrator," is, in the last instance, an open weapon of ideological warfare. Black men and women alike remain its potential victims—men unconsciously lunging at the woman, equating her with the myth; women sinking back into the shadows, lest an aggressive posture resurrect the myth in themselves.

The myth must be consciously repudiated as myth and the black woman in her true historical contours must be resurrected. We, the black women of today, must accept the full weight of a legacy wrought in blood by our mothers in chains. Our fight, while identical in spirit, reflects different conditions and thus implies different paths of struggle. But as heirs to a tradition of supreme perseverance and heroic resistance, we must hasten to take our place wherever our people are forging on towards freedom.

AFFIRMATION OF RESISTANCE:
A RESPONSE TO ANGELA DAVIS

Johnnetta Cole

ANGELA DAVIS's "Reflections on the Black Woman's Role in the Community of Slaves" is a masterful attack on prevailing misconceptions about the role of Black women within their families and against an oppressive system during slavery. Professor Davis's

---

[46] Du Bois, *Darkwater*, p. 185.

article is also a positive affirmation of Black people's determined resistance, revolutionary spirit, and creativity under severely adverse conditions—qualities and conditions powerfully demonstrated in Sister Davis's own life. This brief response cannot sum up the arguments so carefully developed in the article. To do so would be an offense to the richness and insight of her thoughts. Neither can it detail the qualities of Blackness, womanhood, and revolutionary radicalism which infuse her life and work. It can, however, emphasize the significance of her essay and suggest a few of the many parallels between her own struggle and that of the Black women who are her subjects.

The prime significance of the article is that it strikes at the heart of the so-called Black matriarchy issue through a refutation of its falsely assumed basis in slavery. The myth of the Black matriarchy, perpetuated in its fullest form by the "Moynihan Report," is, however, only one example of a widespread pattern in which Black folks are accused of being the cause of their own oppression. Stripped of academic jargon and political rhetoric, common assumptions in American society are that aggressive, domineering Black women are the cause of "broken" homes and "illegitimate" children; the laziness and sexual promiscuity of Black folks are the cause of heavy welfare rolls; and the general deterioration of Black American life is caused by the deterioration of the Black family.

Another myth (as long-lived as that of the Black matriarchy and, in fact, related to it) is the notion of Black slaves as relatively satisfied individuals who might have had a few grievances, but who never substantially questioned the concept of slavery through either individual acts of rebellion or organized attempts at revolt. Professor Davis successfully challenges the insidious assumption that Black women not only failed to resist slavery, but were collaborators of the slave class. Although the conditions of her imprisonment forced her to draw on secondary sources exclusively, Professor Davis nevertheless managed to present a number of cases of Black women participating in conspiracies against slave masters and engaging in individual acts of resistance and rebellion. If Professor Davis were able to work with primary sources and without the threat of life imprisonment, she would surely have extended the documentation of Black female resistance during slavery.

Additionally—and significantly—"Reflections on the Black Woman's Role . . ." also demonstrates the compatibility of a revolutionary perspective with excellence in academic scholarship. It is a well established, although seldom acknowledged fact that the questions one asks grow out of one's ideological position. For example, Moynihan's involvement in and commitment to the basic power arrangements in the United States lead him to advance an hypothesis which blames the victim rather than the victimizing society. Miss Davis's moral sentiments are quite different and lead her to examine the society itself and movements by which it might be changed. Indeed, it is tempting to suggest that it was Angela Davis's own spirit of resistance which encouraged her to see the roles a Black woman might play in a captive situation. Although Professor Davis exercises all the rigor of academic research, it is her revolutionary perspective which leads her to question the entrenched assumptions about Black women and Black society under slavery.

There is an important lesson here. Academic work is unlikely to contribute to liberation of Black people in the context of a new and healthier society until it is pursued by those who have deep commitments to such goals. In the absence of such sentiments, intellectual efforts are likely to be directed towards controlling Black and other oppressed people and perpetuating America as it now exists.

Professor Davis's life and thoughts represent a continuation of both individual and organized Black struggles for freedom and equity. Like the Black women she describes in her article, Angela Davis has taken upon herself the responsibility of helping to liberate those whom America oppresses. And, like Black women under slavery, her job and her work were not necessarily the same. Just as Black women under slavery were assigned jobs in the fields and in the houses of slave owners, their work was to nurture resistance to slavery; so in the case of Angela Davis, her job was as a teacher of philosophy, but her work was and is about the use of philosophy in the interest of correcting the human condition. As she states in *Lectures on Liberation:* "My idea of philosophy is that . . . if it does not tell us how we can go about eradicating some of the misery in this world, then it is not worth the name of philosophy."[1] The conditions she would change, the miseries she would eradicate are those which she identifies as fundamental to American or any capitalist society: the penal system, poor health facilities, a war-oriented economy, serious unemployment, poverty in the midst of affluence.

Like the Black women she writes of, Angela Davis has resisted the advantages which the oppressing class offers for acquiescence. She could have surrounded herself with the rewards which most of us academicians strive for, but refused to remain silent and ignore the misery of others. Instead, she maintained her revolution-

---

[1] (New York, n.d.), p. 14.

ary spirit despite the physical and mental anguish to which her jailers subjected her, and like her people was creative and productive under the worst of conditions. Out of racism and exploitation, Black Americans have produced a musical tradition, a wealth of folklore and expressive culture, and an adaptive family organization and structure. In the cell of a California prison, Angela Davis produced the essay reprinted here, as well as the recently published book *If They Come in the Morning*. These works constitute a part of that massive movement of resistance, which now, as a century ago, is required if Black people are ever to be free.

La Compiuta Donzella

IN THE SEASON WHEN THE EARTH

Translated by Giuliana Mutti

In the season when the earth greens and flowers
joy swells in all the fair lovers:
together they go to the gardens at that hour
when the love-birds make sweet songs;

all the gentle people fall in love,
eager to fulfill each other,
and each young woman lives in delight;
but as for me, I am filled with tears and sorrow.

For my father has wronged me,
and often keeps me in great pain:
he wants to give me a master against my will,

and I have neither need nor desire to marry,
and I live in constant torment;
so that flowers and leaves do not delight me.

[This sonnet was written by a Florentine woman in the 13th century,
when few women were literate. What is remarkable about La Compiuta
Donzella (The Most Perfect Young Woman) is that she developed her
poetic vision and so used it to challenge the oppression of her sex.]

A la stagion che 'l mondo foglia e fiora
acresce gioia a tutti fin' amanti:
vanno insieme a li giardini alora
che li auscelletti fanno dolzi canti;

la franca gente tutta s'inamora,
e di servir ciascun tragges' inanti,
ed ogni damigella in gioia dimora;
e me, n'abondan marrimenti e pianti.

Ca lo mio padre m'ha messa 'n errore,
e tenemi sovente in forte doglia:
donar mi vole a mia forza segnore,

ed io di ciò non ho disio né voglia
e 'n gran tormento vivo a tutte l'ore;
però non mi ralegra fior né foglia.

Lucille Clifton

TURNING

turning into my own
turning on in
to my own self
at last
turning out of the
white cage turning out of the
lady cage
turning at last
on a stem like a black fruit
in my own season
at last

WALKING THROUGH WALLS

(report to mama)

walking through walls
bumped by young girls
pushing me through through

hair on my head
curled up like children
words coming easy easy

rolling in black
rolling in nigger
everytruth music music

walking through walls
white women say they're not free and
i tell them your name

Sonia Sanchez

THREE X THREE

1.

a blk / woman / speaks

i am deep / blk / soil
they have tried to pollute me
wid a poison called America
they have tried to
          scorch my roots
wid dope
          they have tried to
drown my dreams wid alcohol
wid too many men who spit
their foam on top of my fruit
til it drops
          rotten in America's
parks.
      but. i am deeeeeeEEEp
blue / blk / soil
          and u can hear the
sound of my walken
as i bring forth green songs
from a seasoned breast
as i burn on our evening bed
of revolution.
        i, be/en   blk
           woooOOOOMAN
Know only the way of the womb
fo i am deep/red/soil
      fo our emergen blk nation

2.

i have walked a long time

i have walked a long time
much longer than death that splinters

106

wid her innuendos.
my life, ah my alien life,
is like an echo of nostalgia
bringen blue screens to bury clouds
rinsen wite stones stretched among the sea.

> you, Man, will you remember me when i die?
> will you stare and stain my death and say
> i saw her dancen among swallows
> far from the world's obscenities?
> you, Man, will you remember and cry?

And i have not loved.
always
while the body prowls
the soul catalogues each step;
while the unconscious unbridles feasts
the flesh knots toward the shore.
ah, i have not loved
wid legs stretched like stalks against sheets
wid stomachs drainen the piracy of oceans
wid mouths discarden the gelatin
to shake the sharp self.

i have walked by memory of others
between the blood night
and twilights
i have lived in tunnels
and fed the bloodless fish;
between the yellow rain
and ash,
i have heard the rattle
of my seed.
so time, like some pearl necklace embracen
a superior whore, converges
and the swift spider binds my breast.

> You, Man, will you remember me when i die?
> will you stare and stain my death and say
> i saw her applauden suns
> far from the grandiose audience?
> you, Man, will you remember and cry?

3.

welcome home. my prince

welcome home. my prince
into my wite/season of no u.
welcome home
to my songs
that touch yo/head
and rain green laughter
in greeting
welcome home
to this monday
that has grown up
wid the sound of yo/name
fo i have chanted to yesterday's sun
to hurry back wid
his belly full of morning.
and u have
come.
and i cannot look up at you.
my body
trembles and i mumble things as u
stand tall and sacred
so easily in yo/self.
but i am here
to love u
to carry yo/name on my
ankles like bells.
to dance in
yo/arena of love.
u are tatooed on the round/soft/
parts of me.
and yo/smell
is always wid me.

THE ROLE OF WOMEN
IN LIBERATION STRUGGLES

Amy Jacques Garvey

WHAT IS THE CREATIVE purpose of women in the world? Immediately one answers—"to bear children." And on this assumption alone men of Africa and Asia, up to the early part of this century kept their women uneducated, veiled in public, and closeted in harems and women's quarters. Because these men knew nothing of pre-natal influence, they stupidly thought that because they were sheiks, rajahs, chiefs and rich men their sons would grow up to be the same—strong and powerful.

Woman Power. Modern science has taught us that a woman's thoughts during pregnancy, her behavior and outlook on life, and confrontation with it, have a great emotional stamp on her offspring. With love, care and training in a home a child's character is molded. What it inherits from its father can be overcome or enhanced by an intelligent, disciplined mother. This is WOMAN POWER, which has been greatly overlooked.

Because of the exigencies of two world wars, and the Age of the Common Man in Europe—a leveling of class distinctions—women of Africa and Asia have been perforce "liberated" to help in every field of endeavor to free their respective countries from the domination of the rapacious exploiters, and to develop same. Within a few decades we see them in industry, scientific agriculture, legislative bodies and even filling the highest posts in governments. For example Mrs. Indira Gandhi of India and Mrs. Bandaranaike of Ceylon.

Fathers' influence on girls far-reaching. Mrs. Gandhi was trained by her father Pandit Nehru, so politics and public administration were nothing new to her when he died. In fact, they were family talk.

As a Black woman I was trained by my father, who lived in Cuba for years and spoke Spanish fluently; he also lived in Baltimore. He married my mother, and settled down in Jamaica, West Indies. For five years they had no children; so my mother prayed for a "son and heir." I came a girl, but my Dad trained me as if I were a boy. He took me around the property, explained to me how tobacco was grown and cured, taught me to use a gun to shoot stray goats. On Sundays, after dinner, he would collect his foreign newspapers, and

I had to get a dictionary, and read editorials and news items; he would explain everything to me and answer all my questions. Sometimes he would give me an essay to write on a news item or article. This made me learn to think independently on world affairs and to analyze situations. So when I met Marcus Garvey the International Black mass Leader, he found in me an understanding and dedicated partner.

Woman's abilities are not limited because she is a female. On the contrary she is more versatile than man; she has more staying power in poverty and adversity than the he-male. She has charm, wit, intuition, humor and ingenuity; she can balance a home budget on a few dollars, and make the food "stretch" to feed her hungry household. She is noted for paying attention to details, and this skill enables her to contribute greatly to big projects in the community, state and nation. There is nothing more noble than a good woman, and nothing more vile than a bad one.

Twenty million Africans and six million Jews exterminated. When the European settlers came to the New World they could not capture the Indians and reduce them to slavery, so they gradually killed them off. They sent for Africans—men and women whom they used for centuries clearing the forests, bridging the rivers, fighting their wars, building towns, then cities, while the house servants looked after the frail white women and nursed their children.

It is said that over twenty million Africans—men and women—lost their lives during the Middle Passage—the voyage over. Some were thrown overboard to lighten human cargo in stormy weather, others died writhing from brutal whippings, hunger, thirst, chained to each other, wallowing in their vomit and filth.

During the last World War Hitler ordered six million Jews—men, women, and children, even babies—exterminated scientifically, mostly in gas chambers. These mass murders were motivated by GREED AND HATE.

Men in power do not yield to prayers or appeals to conscience. They only respect FORCE equal to theirs or superior. That is why Communist China now having nuclear weapons and missiles is given a seat in the United Nations, and the President of Racist America visits the President of Yellow China—tinted Red—to TALK. About what? The leadership of Asia, which is copartnered with industrialized Japan.

The exploitation of Africa's wealth and her peoples. After physical emancipation in America, without any compensation for their labors, African freedmen, called Negroes, were forced to work as serfs, peons and share-croppers. They were robbed and exploited, reduced to a state of grinding poverty; even today, the industrial north does not offer them economic security. The known fact is that "they are the last to be hired and the first to be fired."

In the Caribbean areas African slaves were used on the plantations to produce "green gold" for their Spanish, Dutch, French and English masters. After emancipation Chinese and Indians were imported as indentured laborers. Most of them remained after serving their term of servitude. The hot climate and tropical diseases prevented white women from living in numbers and bearing children; so the Planters forced black women to satisfy their lust and produce mulatto offspring.

On the continent of Africa—rich in minerals—Missionaries were used to make overtures to the Africans under the guise of "civilizing and christianizing them." After them came the soldiers and the Explorers and Exploiters, who occupied the whole continent of nearly twelve million square miles and partitioned it among the Spanish, Portuguese, Belgians, Germans, French and English. They extracted the minerals, using Africans under forced labor conditions —inhuman and despicable. Thus the cities and towns of these European Metropolitan countries were built, and their industries were fed by the raw materials obtained mainly from Africa and India.

In the last two World Wars when white nations fought among themselves on a "scientific" scale, they exhausted themselves, and had to conscript brown and black men to help them; these saw that white superiority was a physical myth and that white power was based on the exploitation of the resources of other peoples' lands and their labors. So they determined to return to their homelands and liberate themselves. Today all Asia and nearly all of Africa is independent, except the Southern tip, where a minority of whites aided by European capitalists and Industrialists are keeping their "kith and kin" in power over millions of oppressed and brutalized Africans.

Women more humane than men. Women's Liberation Movements are demanding equal rights with men. Perhaps if there were more women in the Courts and Legislative Councils of the nations of the world (especially the big powerful ones) there would be a more humane approach to world conditions. If the American Cabinet was made up of a majority of women, it is hardly likely that they would appropriate billions of dollars to fight a war in Korea and Indo-China, and send 18 and 19 year old Americans to die. For what?

Sojourner Truth, Harriet Tubman, and Angela Davis symbolize noble Black women. Because of the brutal necessity for human exploitation from slavery Black women have been "liberated," because, even during pregnancy, they were made to work on the plantations like men. Their babies were sometimes strapped to their backs or put under a tree in a little box. After nursing them, they had to take up the hoe again.

At that period among the Black martyred women were Harriet Tubman and Sojourner Truth, who (like all slaves) were not taught to read and write, yet they exhibited all the noble qualities of women. Harriet Tubman risked her life for years leading slaves from the South to freedom in the North. At present Angela Davis symbolizes the educated Black woman who has not allowed white philosophies to prevent her from seeing and feeling the oppression and injustices meted out to her race, and thus becoming an Activist in the Cause of freedom for all. For this she has been victimized, jailed and is now before the courts on many charges. If only she would agree to give up her Crusade and confine herself to the lecture halls of Universities and Colleges she would be free; but she has chosen to follow her conscience, and her life hangs in the balance.

Black women are not traitors, they are not cowards, they are truly the "better half" of Black men. If Angela goes to prison that will not deter the educated women from using their intelligence in a righteous Cause. In fact it would be an incentive to many to fill the breach, and fight on as never before, for the masses need intelligent dedicated leadership.

Women do not want to jostle men for jobs. They want what they merit, and to which they can contribute their God-given qualities in trying to liberate this civilization from GREED AND HATE.

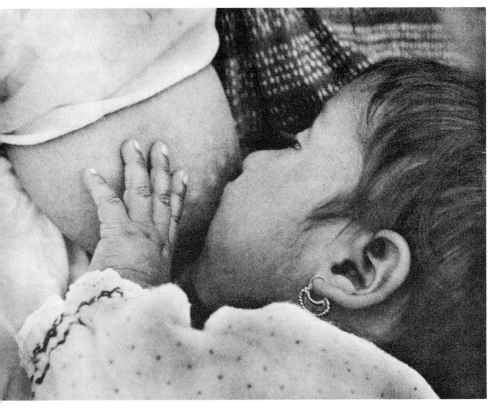

Untitled,

TINA
MODOTTI
SOME PHOTOGRAPHS

Tina Modotti, 1924, by Edward Weston

A NOTE

"I consider myself a photographer, nothing more."

For many years it was impossible to obtain Modotti photographs for publication. Although during her lifetime she was published in *International Literature*, a Soviet publication, and was a frequent contributor to *Mexican Folkways*, following her death her name and her works were shrouded in mystery. But there has always been a group of people interested in the work of this great woman photographer. With the publication of the *Daybooks* of Edward Weston, her name, her face, and her body broke through the veil that kept her from our sight. The Museum of Modern Art, which had received anonymously a group of her photographs are now at last willing to share them. With their help and that of the Philadelphia Museum of Art, we are thus able to present this small gathering of her work. The political as well as the human quality of Tina Modotti's photographs are paramount in her work. She has stated: *"Photography, precisely because it can only be produced in the present and because it is based on what exists objectively before the camera, takes its place as the most satisfactory medium of registering objective life in all its aspects, and from this comes its documental value. If to this is added sensibility and understanding above all, a clear orientation as to the place it should have in the field of historical development, I believe that the result is something worthy of a place in social production, to which we should all contribute."* Mexican Folkways, 5 (1929), 198. The photographs in this tiny selection record forever the Mexican people in the coils of social change, burdened with poverty but full of remarkable dignity. Born in Udine, Italy, in August, 1896, Tina Modotti spent her adult life in anti-fascist activities, moving from Italy to the United States, to Mexico, to Spain during the Spanish Civil war; she eventually returned to Mexico where, in 1942, she died a tragic and mysterious death.

L·U·B

Roses, Mexico, 1924,   Museum of Modern Art. Gift of E. Weston

Woman Carrying Naked Baby, Mexico, 1929,   Philadelphia Museum of Art

Untitled,   Museum of Modern Art, Anonymous g

ntitled,   Museum of Modern Art, Anonymous gift

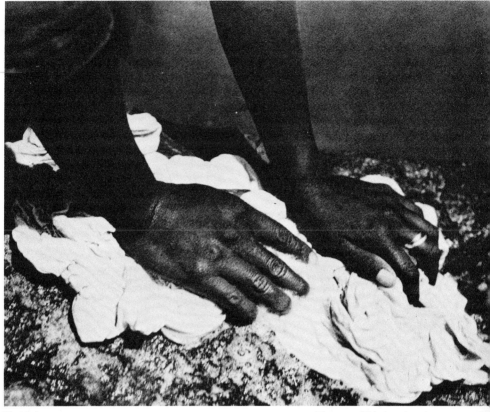

Untitled,   Museum of Modern Art, Anonymous gift

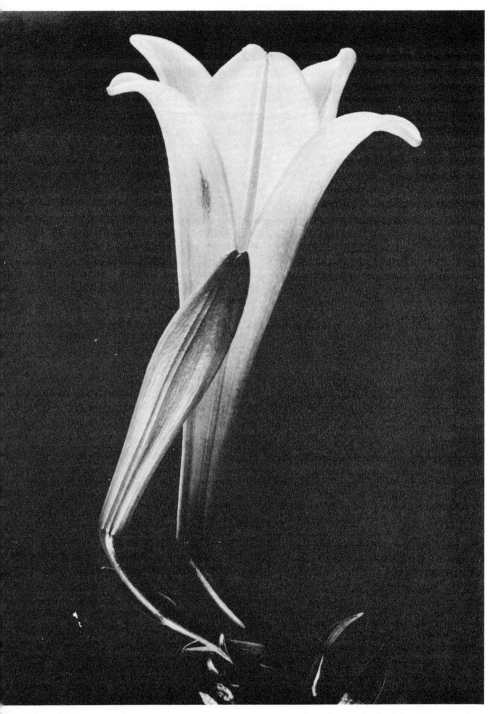

aster Lily and Bud,   Museum of Modern Art. Gift of Dorothy M. Haskins

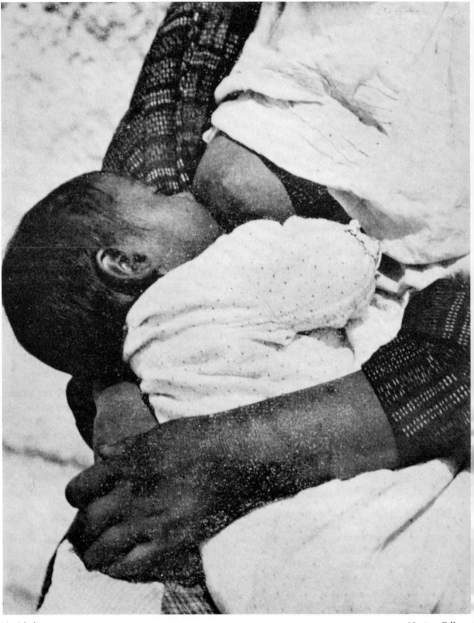

Untitled,   *Mexican Folkway*

xican Woman, Elisa, 1924,   Museum of Modern Art. Gift of Edward Weston

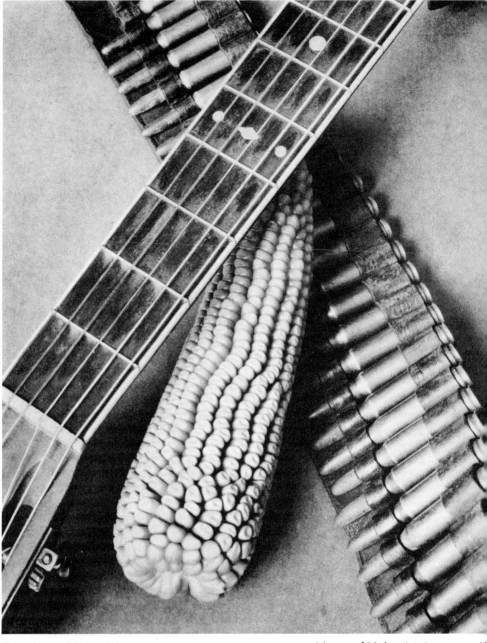

Illustration to a Mexican Song,   Museum of Modern Art. Anonymous gi

MARY BEARD'S
WOMAN AS FORCE IN HISTORY: A CRITIQUE

Berenice A. Carroll

WHEN *Woman as Force in History* appeared in 1946, it was greeted with mixed reviews, and it has had an equally mixed fate. Reviews written for the lay public appear to have been generally sympathetic, calling the book "scholarly," "bright and learned," "delightful," and "only occasionally tiresome and talky." Sometimes it was felt to be "ponderous in content" or "a trifle oppressive" in argument, but on the whole these reviewers found it persuasive. R. A. Brown, writing for the *Christian Science Monitor* (April 17, 1946), thought its impact would be so significant that it seemed "reasonable to prophesy that no sound historian of the future will neglect the role of women, as was done in the past." When Mary Beard died in 1958, the general press recalled *Woman as Force in History*. The *New York Times* provided a full-column obituary, much of it devoted to Mary Beard's efforts to develop the field of women's history. Even the brief notices in *Time* and *Newsweek* made reference to this book in particular, *Time* with its characteristic tongue-in-cheek,[1] *Newsweek* with a quotation.

But professional historians met the book with attitudes ranging from marked caution[2] to outright hostility,[3] and within a decade they

---

This paper was read at New Orleans on April 16, 1971, for the annual convention of the Organization of American Historians.

[1] "Mary Beard argued that, between the sexes, women hold the lesser place in history because men write the history books." *Time*, August 25, 1958, p. 66. *New York Times* obituary: August 15, 1958, p. 22; *Newsweek*, August 25, 1958, p. 61.

[2] See the review by Jeannette P. Nichols in the *American Historical Review*, vol. 52, no. 2 (January 1947), pp. 292–4. Professor Nichols opened her review by remarking that "more than one male historian has expressed doubt whether [this book] should be reviewed by a woman," thus "warning the reviewer that any comments will meet piercing scrutiny." As a consequence her comments on the book seem strangely involuted, though basically sympathetic. Ultimately she concludes that "this book is not a rash challenge but is couched in constructive rather than denunciatory terms"; and that it "has demonstrated sound historical techniques and its indictment holds against a great many historians." Nevertheless, Professor Nichols is uncomfortable with this indictment of historians, and ends by arguing that Mary Beard had addressed the wrong

had seemingly consigned it to oblivion. In the few lines which the *American Historical Review* (January 1959) accorded Mary Beard by way of obituary, she was identified first as Charles A. Beard's wife, next by the works she co-authored with him, finally by a few of the books which the A.H.R. noted—as though by surprise—came "from her own pen;" the A.H.R. had no comment on her work. Two decades after R. A. Brown had prophesied that "no sound historian" would henceforth neglect the role of women in history, the Chicago University historian William H. McNeill capped the irony of this remark by publishing *A World History*, a college textbook published by Oxford University Press, (1967) which features exactly one woman's name in the index, Catherine the Great of Russia, and no general index entry for "women."[4]

Yet in recent years Mary Beard's book has experienced a curious rebirth. It never achieved a second printing in hard-cover, and one wonders a little what moved Macmillan to reissue it in 1962 (rather before the "new feminist" wave) as a Collier paper-bound. But in the past two or three years it has won increasing attention, primarily in the women's movement; the paperbound edition is now in its second printing, and it is being used in a number of college courses on women's history or women's liberation. It even begins to seem possible that R. A. Brown's prophesy might yet be fulfilled, if only after two or three decades' delay.

---

audience—that instead of addressing herself to historians, in such a "sober treatise," written for a "reading level which is not common," she should have written a popular paperback book designed "to interest many thousands of women" readers. For that time, Professor Nichols may have been right; neither historians nor the female public was ready for the book Mary Beard wrote. Perhaps the recent growth in interest in the book is witness both to the increased numbers of women to whom the reading level of the book is now common, and to significant changes in the ranks of historians.

[3] See the review by Jack H. Hexter in the *New York Times Book Review*, March 17, 1946, p. 5. This review can only be described as condescending and derogatory in tone, yet in its hostility it strikes closer to the real importance of the book than do many more sympathetic reviews. Substantive points raised by Hexter are discussed below.

[4] McNeill's earlier and larger work, *The Rise of the West: A History of the Human Community*, is a little better; it mentions four women (Jane Austen, Catherine II, Fatima, and Isabella of Castile); three female deities (Athena, Isis, and Mary); and *Alice in Wonderland!* Some authors of course, do better than McNeill. Gordon Craig's *Europe Since 1815* (1961) has the ratio of women to men up to about 1:40; on the other hand some do worse: Herbert Heaton's *Economic History of Europe* (1948, 769 pages) has not a single woman's name in the index. See also below, notes 8-9.

Woman as Force in History

As we read *Woman as Force in History* carefully today, we can hardly deny that it was in many ways a failure—a failure in design, in execution, in conception, and (until recently) in impact. Yet we can as little deny that this is a unique and important book, a work of complexity and subtlety, which raises, even if it fails to answer, a number of significant questions for contemporary historiography. It is these contrasting characteristics, of failure on the one hand, and significance on the other, I wish to explore here.

Woman as Force in History may be read as an effort to reconstruct the history of women, from prehistoric to modern times, and to interpret its significance. But this reconstruction of women's history is set in a complex polemic: first, against a "myth" of female subjection in history; second, against feminists who adopted and propagated the myth; third, against historians—mostly male— who have contributed to the myth either directly or by minimization or sheer neglect of women in the writing of history; finally, against the slogan of "equality" as escape from that mythical subjection of women. And this polemical setting is at once responsible for many of the defects of the book and for some of its most provocative and significant features.

The core of the polemic is the argument that contemporary ideas about the relations between men and women are deeply influenced by the notion that women have been "members of a subject sex throughout history," and that this notion is easily shown to be a myth by reference to historical realities. The treatment of this argument is in some respects heavy-handed and ill-designed, giving rise to some of the complaints of reviewers already noted, and to the more ample complaint of J. H. Hexter that some "rather simple points" are proved "well past the hilt, with a copiousness of repetitious quotation that suggests a positive aversion to condensation and conciseness in the author."

Hexter here refers to a portion of the book which presents a subordinate line of argument, namely that the myth of subjection must be attributed largely to Sir William Blackstone and to the easy acceptance of his common law bias by American lawyers and American feminists in the nineteenth century. Common law doctrines, as formulated by Blackstone, appeared to extinguish the very person of the married women before the law, but Mary Beard argues that besides the common law there existed a "vast" body of other law, composed of equity, legislative acts, and customary law and practice, in which such common law doctrines had no force, and under which the married woman was a fully competent legal person.

127

To these subordinate aspects of her main theme, Mary Beard devoted five of the twelve chapters of her book—over one-third of its length—not including shorter passages in other chapters. The rest of the material is dealt with in approximately reverse chronological order, beginning with an examination of contemporary attitudes of women and men and concluding with a survey chapter, much of which is devoted to prehistory and the ancient world.

This scheme of organization, dictated in part by the structure of the polemic, was undoubtedly an unfortunate choice, for it is the main source of that repetitiousness or oppressiveness of which the critics complain. On close examination, there is actually very little repetition of content, but the argument doubles back on itself again and again, each time taking up a different aspect, or a different chronological slice of the subject—now focusing on Blackstone's time in England, now on colonial America, now on medieval England, now on classical Rome; now dealing with equity, elsewhere with legislative or customary law, now with the education of women, elsewhere with their economic or social status. With each doubling-back, Mary Beard is obliged to repeat some part of the connective tissue of the polemic. The argument thus repeats itself, but the historical content, the information communicated, is for the most part different in each case.

In fact, had Hexter not let himself become so impatient with the apparent repetitiousness, he might not have been so ready to concede that Mary Beard had proved her points—least of all "well past the hilt." For what those "repetitious quotations" really show is that the legal subjection of women was no myth invented by Blackstone and American feminists, but was a very real and substantial part of the "historical reality" in which women lived, at least from the early medieval period in England to the nineteenth century in America. If we are to credit the quotations from Maitland, the legal position of women in England was at best equivocal in the thirteenth century, and probably became rather worse with the development of the common law in subsequent centuries.

Mary Beard herself is obliged to remark that "had it not been for the growth of equity, the position of women before the law in the eighteenth century would have been lower in many respects than it had been in the thirteenth century." (208)[5] And when we examine the effects of equity, we must recognize that what this statement implies is that the position of many women, perhaps most

---

[5] Numbers in parentheses refer to pages in the Collier edition of *Woman as Force in History: A Study in Traditions and Realities*, New York: Collier Books, 1971.

women, before the law *was* "lower in many respects" in the eighteenth century than it had been before. For no matter how large a body of law relating to property equity became, with respect to married women it protected *only those* whose affluence, knowledge, prudence, or careful relatives led them to make special contractual provisions, before and after marriage, for the protection of their property and legal rights:

> Informed men and women of property [Mary Beard tells us] . . . knew that the disabilities of married women in respect of property under common law could be avoided by a resort to trusts, and that equity, liberally construing the rights of such women, would proect them and their heirs in the enjoyment of the rights so vested. (213)

Thus equity provided only a limited avenue of escape through specified rights vested by contract or trust in particular individuals. It did nothing for women in general, nothing for unpropertied women, ignorant women, imprudent women, or women of ill-disposed families—and of all these one can hardly doubt that there must be large numbers in all times and places. For all these, then, it was the disabilities of the common law which defined their legal status, not the liberal advantages of equity.

III

Similarly, with respect to the "myth" of subjection in general, we may say that Mary Beard has proved a point—a point of considerable significance—but she has not disposed of the notion that women have been a "subject sex." (To the latter we return below.) The point she has proved is that history will not support "the dogma of women's complete historic subjection to man," nor "the image of woman throughout long ages of the past as a being always and everywhere subject to *male* man or as a ghostly creature too shadowy to be even that real." (155, 87) On the contrary, what *Woman as Force in History* shows most clearly is women active, competent and recognized in their own time in a wide range of occupations and endeavors. In some places the examples are packed in so tightly that one reviewer remarked: "At moments the listing of individual women and their achievements suggests a catalogue overmuch."[6] In the concluding chapter, which is something like an abridged version of Mary Beard's earlier book, *On Understanding Women* (Longmans, 1931), the compression is so great that it struck Hexter

---

[6] Mary S. Benson, *Political Science Quarterly*, vol. 61, June 1946, p. 299.

as "one of the great historical grab-bags of all time." Grab-bag, catalogue, or whatever, one thing is certainly clear from this material:
women were far from being totally passive, inactive, ignorant, submissive, uncreative, unassertive, subordinate, and invisible through
the course of human history.

But can we really call this point significant? Isn't it positively
superfluous? Would anyone seriously maintain the contrary? Unfortunately, yes.

The worst offender in recent times, perhaps, is Simone de Beauvoir. In *The Second Sex*, which first appeared in 1949, three years
after *Woman as Force in History* and nearly twenty years after *On
Understanding Women*, which had already made similar points,
Simone de Beauvoir wrote boldly:

> Throughout history [women] have always been subordinated to men,
> and hence their dependency is not the result of a historical event or a
> social change—it was not something that *occurred*.[7]

The proletarians, she continues (not stopping to ask whether there
were any women among them, nor what role they played), have
accomplished the revolution in some countries and are battling for
it in others,

> but the women's effort has never been anything more than a symbolic
> agitation. They have gained only what men have been willing to grant;
> they have taken nothing, they have only received. . . . They have no
> past history . . . of their own . . . woman has always been man's de-
> pendent, if not his slave.

Worse still: "in the past all history has been made by men."[8]

While one may not find such bald assertions of this notion in the
work of professional historians, they are not without responsibility

---

[7] *The Second Sex*, New York: Bantam Books, 1961, p. xviii.

[8] *Ibid.*, pp. xix, xx. The historical section of Simone de Beauvoir's book, however, fails to bear out these generalizations, despite the fact that the opening
words of that section reiterate: "This has always been a man's world. . . ."
Though one may argue that there is some sense in which this may be true,
Simone de Beauvoir herself shows women active, demanding, independent,
even commanding, and certainly in no way bearing out the assertion that
"they have no past." It is Simone de Beauvoir, not Mary Beard, who writes
of Mme. de Pompadour and Mme. du Barry that they "really controlled the
State." This contradiction is one very frequently encountered in dealing with
women's history, a part of the extraordinary phenomenon by which, no matter
what women actually do in history, they continue to be perceived—even by
those who have extensive information to the contrary—as having done nothing.

for propagating the idea. Certainly that is the inference one is bound to draw, if only unconsciously, from the numerous textbooks, readers, and even more specialized works which conform closely to the example of McNeill's *A World History*. In a recent study of twenty-seven textbooks currently in use in college courses in American history, Earl and Dolores Schmidt found that the space devoted to women in the textual material of these works ranged from a low of .05% to a *high* of 2%.[9] Jack Hexter, in his review of *Woman as Force in History*, was at pains to deny that the omission of women from the history books should be attributed to the bias of male historians.[10] But in defending the historians, Hexter resorted to arguing, in effect, that women are not mentioned by historians because they weren't there to mention—not, anyway, in the places worth looking at, the places in which history is made. (We return to this point below.)

We also find this view expressed from time to time among the writings of the women's liberation movement today. Shulamith Firestone, in her recent book, *The Dialectic of Sex*, adopts not only the subjection theory, but Simone de Beauvoir's biological explanation of it as well: "Women throughout history before the advent of birth control were at the continual mercy of their biology—menstruation, menopause, and 'female ills,' constant painful childbirth, wetnursing, and care of infants, all of which made them dependent on males (whether brother, father, husband, lover, or clan, government, community-at-large) for physical survival."[11] Thus not only government but even clan and "community-at-large" become *male* in character, and one wonders how women so described ever could or did find the resources to invent agriculture and most of the primitive industrial arts, to do most of the heavy labor in many so-called

---

[9] "The Invisible Women: The Historian as Professional Magician; An analysis, quantitative and qualitative, of 27 textbooks designed for college survey courses in American history," by Earl R. and Dolores Barracano Schmidt, dittoed, 1971. The high figure of 2% was for Charles and Mary Beard's own *Basic History of the United States*, which according to the Schmidts is now out of print.

[10] To some extent, Mary Beard agreed that the blame should not be laid only to *male* historians, though she held them primarily responsible, if only because they write most of the history books. In *On Understanding Women*, however, she also had some acerbic comments on women historians, who, once permitted "to study with the high priests in Clio's temple, . . . easily slid into the grooves worn smooth by tradition, assuming with humility and without thought the garb of the disciple." (p. 14)

[11] Shulamith Firestone, *The Dialectic of Sex*, Wm. Morrow, 1970, pp. 8–9.

primitive societies, to acquire learning, property, and independence at least for some of their number throughout the history of literate societies, to engage in military exploits, and to become rulers in their own right, regents, or the "power behind the throne" at various times in the history of almost every nation in the world (the United States being perhaps the pre-eminent exception).

A similar view of women's subjection is reflected in the "Redstockings Manifesto," which declares:

> Male supremacy is the oldest, most basic form of domination. . . . All power structures throughout history have been male-dominated and male-oriented. Men have controlled all political, economic and cultural institutions and backed up this control with physical force. They have used their power to keep women in an inferior position.[12]

This kind of rhetoric is cited by Gerda Lerner in concluding of the radical feminists today that "the essence of their concept is that all women are oppressed and have been throughout all history."[13]

In short, the myth of "complete historic subjection of women," which Mary Beard sought to overthrow, is still very much with us today, and still presents the same problems. In its extreme forms it is not only irreconcilable with the verifiable data of history, but as Gerda Lerner points out, it is "politically counter-productive, since it lends the authority of time and tradition to the practice of treating women as inferiors."[14] And as Mary Beard recognizes (with her usual fidelity to facts even when inconvenient to her argument), those very feminists whom she holds largely responsible for the myth of subjection were also quite conscious that women had played an active role in history. Thus she writes that the authors of the *History of Woman Suffrage* (Elizabeth Cady Stanton *et aliae*):

> confronted with the question as to how a creature who had been nothing or nearly nothing in all history could suddenly, if ever, become something—something like a man, his equal— . . . used history to show what force women had displayed in history. (168)

On the other hand, the myth of subjection can also be politically useful. Mary Beard concedes this herself, though she seems to view it rather as an accusation:

---

[12] "Redstockings Manifesto," in: *Sisterhood Is Powerful,* edited by Robin Morgan, Vintage, 1970, p. 534.
[13] Gerda Lerner, "The Feminists: A Second Look," *Columbia Forum,* vol. XIII, no. 3 (Fall, 1970), p. 26.
[14] *Ibid.,* p. 27.

Woman as Force in History

Each construct or version of this doctrine fitted into the requirements of some political party or faction as a convenient instrument of agitation for the vindication of traditions or for the reform or overthrow of social and economic institutions. The doctrine in its totality or special phases of it were utilized in all media of literary expression. . . . It haunted the dreams of Freudian disciples and incited women to brave police and prison in passionate struggles for equality with their historic 'masters.' (115)

This passage, we may note in passing, illustrates nicely one of the virtues of Mary Beard's work—an unwillingness to cling to over-simplification for the sake of consistency. Having attributed primarily to the feminists the formulation and propagation of what she regards as a damaging myth, she does not hesitate ultimately to present a rather different and rather more valid conclusion: namely, that the myth of subjection was one which suited the interests and purposes of a variety of groups, male and female, political and intellectual; that it was developed, modified, and used in a variety of ways accordingly; and that among its many functions it did serve to inspire some of the energy of struggle of the early feminists and the suffrage movement—not surely an entirely negative consequence, even in the eyes of Mary Beard.

IV

The last two passages quoted from *Woman as Force in History* touch tangentially on another target of Mary Beard's polemical fire: the feminist goal of "equality" with men. This is one of the most obscure and least successful aspects of the book, yet it too raises interesting questions.

The attack on the feminists in the matter of "equality" is unmistakable by its tone (which Hexter calls "waspish" in another context), but it is indirect, and not easy to pinpoint, even though a separate chapter is devoted to "Equality as the Escape from Subjection." As well as I am able to discern, Mary Beard's main objections to the slogan of "equality" lie in its vagueness, its links with egalitarian socialism or communism, and its inadequacy in application to real circumstances. In her brief review of the history of the ideal of equality, she shows how variously it was conceived, how little it represented a clearly understood principle, and how easily it could lead to contradictory programs—for example, as between the libertarian ideal of equality, which was "atomistic in its social effects" and which exalted the individual and the competitive urge, and the communistic ideal of equality, quite the contrary in character. She concedes that the feminists did try to define their objectives more narrowly in terms of political and legal rights:

equal protection of the laws; equal opportunity in all 'fields of endeavor'; equal suffrage; and equal privileges and immunities, including the right to hold public offices. (169)

But even these she refers to as "formulas" and "phrases," and she adds that

> the favorite line of assertion was simplified to the absolute and unconditional demand for 'equal rights' and 'no discrimination on account of sex' anywhere in any relation. (169)

Her chief objection to these formulas and demands, beyond their vagueness, appears to center on what she regards as their inapplicability in practice. Here she considers primarily the difficulties arising from the married women's property acts which were passed in many states in the late 19th century. Here too, by implication, she admits the disabilities which had prevailed for most women before the passage of such acts:

> Such an act meant the abolition of numerous common-law rules respecting the right of the husband to control his wife's real estate and take possession of her personal property, in case no pre-nuptial or post-nuptial settlements or arrangements intervened. Rights which prudent parents had long secured for daughters under Equity were now to be extended to all married women as a matter of written law . . . and special precautions in the form of elaborate legal documents, drawn by skilled lawyers, were no longer necessary to assure the possession of property to the married woman as against her husband and his creditors. (170)

There is nothing in this to suggest that Mary Beard opposed the married women's property acts; nevertheless she did emphasize the difficulties they raised in practice. In particular, she devoted a number of pages to raising questions and describing particular cases which came to be adjudicated under the new laws: May the wife require the husband to pay rent to her for the house she owns separately, in which the family lives? Is the wife's property liable for payment of domestic servants engaged in doing the household work of the family? And so forth. The questions are left unanswered and unanalyzed, but one point is clear: Mary Beard is certain that no abstract principle of "equality" can answer such questions. From her point of view, wife and husband are caught up in a network of social, emotional and economic entanglements to which no legislative act, designed to protect the rights of married women, could hope to do justice.

This is undoubtedly true, particularly where the legislative acts impose only a somewhat artificial and limited equality in property rights upon a system of much more basic inequality, a system which expects and even tends to enforce the dependence of wife upon husband for support. But is there an alternative? The answer is less than explicit, but it does appear that Mary Beard saw an alternative in equity, as principle, and as practice. And what is equity? Mary Beard describes it here mainly in institutional terms, or by contrast with the common law: "a body of precedents and law which was concerned with 'justice' rather than prescriptions of the feudal State." (209) John of Salisbury, centuries before, had offered a more general definition, of which Mary Beard would surely have approved:

> Now equity, as the learned jurists define it, is a certain fitness of things which compares all things rationally, and seeks to apply like rules of right and wrong to like cases, being impartially disposed toward all persons, and allotting to each that which belongs to him.
> (*The Statesman's Book*, 1159)

But is this principle, which in itself presents many difficulties, really a practical alternative? Even John of Salisbury added that "of this equity, the interpreter is the law"; and the Courts of Equity were after all courts of law, though more flexible than the common law. In this context, it seems doubtful that even Mary Beard would deny that the married women's property acts were an improvement in equity over the common law, that women's suffrage was an improvement in equity over manhood suffrage alone, and that "equal privileges and immunities" would be an improvement in equity over the exclusion of women from public offices. And if the slogan of equality helped to secure these improvements, as Mary Beard does not deny, then it may be a valuable slogan to hang onto, despite its vagueness and inadequacy.

v

But we must note one other aspect of Mary Beard's attack on the slogan of equality: one which hits curiously close to the rhetoric of women's liberationists today, and which has important implications with respect to the study of women's history. This is the charge that for many women "equality" means "taking the stature of man as the measure of excellence and endowing woman with his qualities, aims, and chances in the world for personal advantages." (163)

Taken seriously, this challenge to "taking *man* as the measure" has a double thrust. On the one hand it challenges all prevailing standards of excellence, honor, and authority (which today clearly do accord to men the lion's share of both material and intellectual rewards, privileges, and "power" in society). On the other hand it challenges the value premises and principles of selection by which historians have been guided in writing histories devoid of women.

To this extent, Jack Hexter missed the point of *Woman as Force in History* in his argument in defense of the historians. What he argued was that historians are primarily interested in the processes of change in "the framework of society" or in "the pattern of culture" from one period to another, and that accordingly they have looked mainly "where the power to make change" is, namely:

> in the councils of the princes, in the magistracies of the towns, in the membership of the great leagues of traders, in the faculties of the universities—and they found men. On the occasions on which they happened to find women they usually noted the exception[15]; but through no conspiracy of the historians the College of Cardinals, the Consistory of Geneva, the Parliament of England, the Faculty of the Sorbonne, the Directorate of the Bank of England and the expeditions of Columbus, Vasco da Gama and Drake have been pretty much stag affairs.

Now there can be no doubt that the institutions which Hexter mentions have indeed been "pretty much stag affairs"; and there can be almost as little doubt that these types of institutions are those we conventionally regard as authoritative, influential, and "powerful."

Moreover, by virtue of their exclusion (not total, but certainly general) from such institutions, women have certainly been deprived of access—at least direct access—to the opportunities, rewards, privileges, honor, authority, and "power" available to the men who did have entry into these institutions. From this point of view, the idea that women have been a subject sex, through much if not all of "civilized" history, appears to be no myth. Mary Beard has demonstrated that women have been active participants in a much wider range of economic and social pursuits than is usually recognized, that some won acclaim from contemporaries, and some reached even the highest positions of governing authority and material rewards. The demonstration is essential and non-trivial, and insofar as it is incomplete or inadequate, it needs to be expanded and reinforced. But it is doubtful that any amount of expansion and reinforcement will do away with the historical reality of the subjection of women in this sense, that is, the exclusion of most women from the honorific statuses and ruling positions of the societies in which they lived.

---

[15] "Usually" seems dubious here, if not excessive.

Woman as Force in History

VI

But it may be that "subjection" is a phenomenon as little understood as "power," and Mary Beard, while aiming at the wrong words, may have been striking at the right target in deliberately turning her eyes away from those institutions which do preoccupy historians, and urging them to look elsewhere. For, looking back at Hexter's remarks, we may well feel that they raise more questions than they answer: *Why* were the institutions he mentions "pretty much stag affairs"? *Does* the power to make change in society lie wholly—even mainly—in the hands of the men who predominated in those institutions? What kind of change *is* change "in the framework of society" or in "the pattern of culture"? Or—what *kinds*? Are all kinds of significant social and cultural change in the same hands? What is "power" anyway?—in particular "power to make change"? Are the kinds of institutions which are ordinarily said to hold "power" generally much disposed towards making fundamental changes in society? If and when they are, from what sources does the initiative for change come? Does it never come from "subject" people? (Some today might ask: does it *ever* come from anyone but "subject" people?) *Are* historians anyway so completely preoccupied with *change* rather than with continuity, inertia, reversions, comparisons across time or across cultures, or simply trying, on occasion, to reconstruct "wie es eigentlich gewesen war"? (J. P. Nettl's biography of Rosa Luxemburg suddenly springs to mind here.) And finally, *should* historians focus their attention so heavily on the kinds of institutions Hexter mentions?

Mary Beard answers the last question explicitly, in the negative. She suggests in her Preface that she means to outline in the book "the kind of studying, writing and teaching which I believe to be mandatory if a genuine interest in understanding human life is to be cultivated," and that for such an understanding, "the personalities, interests, ideas and activities of women must receive an attention commensurate with their energy in history." Thus for example in discussing the historians' treatment of medieval education, she argues that they have been too preoccupied with *formal* education, particularly in the universities, as a consequence of which they have overlooked or ignored the fact of women "receiving an education by some process, pursuing intellectual interests, reading, writing, expounding, and corresponding with one another and with learned men." (257) Finally, she asserts that

> being men as a rule, [the historians] tend to confine their search for the truth to their own sex in history. This is in accord no doubt with the caution of their professional training. Yet the caution which eliminates

the quest for truth about women in long and universal history may in
fact limit the ideas of such scholars about long and universal history or
any of its features. . . . (282)

And she adds:

While exaggerating the force of men [*read* "rulers"? or "the powerful"?] in the making of history, they miss the force of women [*read* "the
subject"?] which entered into the making of history and gave it important directions. (282)

VII

Unfortunately, it must be said that the major failure of *Woman
as Force in History* is the failure to develop these points coherently.
There are hints, but no more than hints (and sometimes mutually
contradictory hints), as to what consequences would follow from
the broadening of the historians' perspective which Mary Beard
calls for here. And there are hints, but no more than hints (and
again sometimes mutually contradictory hints), as to what "important directions" were contributed by women in the making of
history. Nor is it at all clear, upon setting down this book, wherein
lies the distinctive "force" of women in history.

Sometimes it appears that Mary Beard conceives woman's "force"
in history as a civilizing mission. This idea is set in a discussion of
various theories of history with which she opens the chapter on
"Woman as Force in Long History." She begins with a brief run-
down of some generalizations of the "all history proves" variety,
such as: "Universal history . . . is at bottom the history of the
Great Men who have worked here" (Thomas Carlyle); "The history of the world is none other than the progress of the consciousness of freedom" (Hegal); "The history of all hitherto existing
society is the history of class struggles" (Marx and Engels); and
so forth. She dismisses each of these with a rapidity which undoubtedly contributes to Hexter's feeling that he is confronted with
a "grab-bag." But the selection is neither random nor pointless. Her
purpose is to contrast these theories, which she regards as too
dogmatic and limited—as well as the less dogmatic but even more
narrow forms of specialization pursued by professional historians—
with a theory which she attributes to Condorcet and Guizot, and
with which she later associates herself more directly.

This is an approach to history rather unfashionable to state today,
yet probably still more widely held by historians—even those who
count themselves sophisticated—than they might care to admit:
namely, the idea of history as progress in "the human struggle for
civilization against barbarism in different ages and places, from the
beginning of human societies." (281)

Woman as Force in History

In the concluding paragraphs, Mary Beard spells out more fully what is meant by this idea of history as the progress of civilization:

> In its composite formulation it embraces a conception of history as the struggle of human beings for individual and social perfection—for the good, the true, and the beautiful—against ignorance, disease, the harshness of physical nature, the forces of barbarism in individuals and in society. . . . Inherent in the idea is the social principle. That is to say, the civilization of men and women occurs in society, and all the agencies used in the process—language, ideas, knowledge, institutions, property, arts, and inventions, are social products, the work of men and women indissolubly united by the very nature of life, in a struggle for a decent and wholesome existence against the forces of barbarism and pessimism wrestling for the possession of the human spirit. (339)

But she goes beyond the assertion that, as social products, the agencies of civilization are the work of "men and women indissolubly united by the very nature of life," to claim further that women play a special role in the civilizing process:

> Despite the barbaric and power-hungry propensities and activities in long history, to which their sex was by no means immune, women were engaged in the main in the promotion of civilian interests. Hence they were in the main on the side of *civili*zation in the struggle with barbarism. (339)

This sounds rather like a bad pun, but that it is meant seriously is suggested not only by the context, but by the fact that the theme had already been set in the chapter on "Women in the Age of Faith—the 'Judge of Equity',"where Mary Beard devotes considerable space to Henry Adams' interest in the influence of women in medieval France—the preeminent influence of the Virgin Mary, and that of her earthly counterparts in politics and literature:

> Thus the Virgin signified to the people moral, human or humane power as against the stern mandates of God's law taught and enforced by the Church. As such, her position made trouble for the Church; but the Papacy, if it had been so minded, could scarcely have suppressed the urge of the people to Virgin worship, however successful it was in excluding women from the priesthood and the . . . choir. In the popular devotion to Mary was asserted a passionate attachment to the feminine qualities so directive in the long history of the human race. (216)

Yet it still remains somewhat unclear just what these "feminine qualities" were, or in what way they are specifically feminine, or in what ways they exerted their "force." Partly through the words of Henry Adams, partly through her own, Mary Beard here leads us to understand that the qualities she has in mind are qualities of

mercy, morality, humanity, and pity—qualities upon which suppli-
ants could rely in hoping for the Virgin's intercession in their behalf
before the stern judgment of God the Father and the Son (i.e., the
male principle). This then is woman the Mother, comforting, protecting, helping, indulgent. (While man plays the conventional role
of authority.)

On the other hand, it appears that "civilizing" qualities *per se*
were something else. For Mary Beard suggests that the Virgin's
power sprang not only from her role as advocate and intercessor
for sinning humanity. "An immense, if immeasurable, portion of it
sprang from the fact that she was regarded as the most convincing
expression of civilized aspirations and ways of life. . . ." (223) She
represented in this regard: intelligence, calm, strength, emotional
stability, inspiration and the standard of refined taste. (221)[16]

But still we are not on sure ground, for it is clear in this same
chapter, and even from the same source—Henry Adams—that Mary
(or woman in general) was not all sweetness and light. Mary is a
Queen, imperial and imperious, able to do as she pleases, above
earthly judgment. Woman was a power, often an evil power:

> The idea that she was weak [wrote Henry Adams] revolted all history;
> it was a paleontological falsehood that even an Eocene female monkey
> would have laughed at. . . . One's studies in the twelfth century, like
> one's studies in the fourth, as in Homeric and archaic time, showed her
> always busy in the illusions of heaven or of hell—ambition, intrigue,
> jealousy, magic. (218)

And as Mary Beard added:

> If on the whole [medieval women] were more Christian in habits, they
> could be even more perfidious in the arts of crime. (221)

Moreover, she herself questions designating some human qualities
as "feminine," others as "masculine." She objects to the tendency to
ascribe the energies and power of Eleanor of Aquitaine or Blanche
of Castile to "their 'masculine' qualities, as the sensibility of men
is often ascribed to their 'feminine' qualities." (226)

VIII

We are thus left entirely at sea with respect to woman's civilizing
force in history, and those "feminine qualities so directive in the
long history of the human race." And in general it appears that

---

[16] For amplification, see Henry Adams, *Mont St.-Michel and Chartres*.

Woman as Force in History

when Mary Beard refers to the force of woman in history, she has in mind simply the active presence and participation of women engaged in all the same kinds of activities as men:

> From modern times running back into and through the medieval ages of Western feudalism and Christian contests with barbarism, the force of woman was a powerful factor in all the infamies, tyrannies, liberties, activities, and aspirations that constituted the history of this stage of humanity's self-expression. (282)

The bulk of the contents of the book surely leans in this direction, seeking to show women active in buying and selling, contracting, laboring, joining in or forming guilds, patronizing the arts and fine craft industries, founding churches and hospitals, negotiating diplomatic agreements between states, going into battle with men, directing armies, directing governments, drafting political programs, agitating for change, writing and engaging in all intellectual pursuits, competing (via Mary) for dominance in the Church, etc.

Unfortunately, this interpretation of woman's force in history also has its problems. To begin with, it does not suggest any "important directions" contributed specifically by women as distinct from men. And if it is intended to show that women are simply persons, *like men*, it falls into a double trap: first, it is a retreat into "taking man as the measure"; second, in so doing it leads back to the admission that, by that measure, women by and large don't come out very well. If women were simply doing—or trying to do—the same things as men, and failing to achieve equal success, at least in terms of recognition, rewards, status and authority—then it might seem difficult to escape Hexter's conclusion that it is history itself, not the prejudice of male historians, which warrants looking mainly at men, acting in the predominant, and predominantly male, institutions of their societies.

The dilemma is a hard one, at least to anyone who does not feel comfortable with that conclusion—and that includes not only women interested in women's history, but blacks interested in black history, radicals interested in heretical and revolutionary movements and in the history of the "inarticulate" or in "street history," people anywhere interested in the "losers" or the "subject" of the earth, people interested in the role of mass action in social change—as well as in the nature and sources of mass consent as the foundation of social stability—and a host of others who, in some way, reject the view that in the College of Cardinals, the Consistory of Geneva, the Parliament of England, the Faculty of the Sorbonne, the Directorate of the Bank of England, and all like institutions, lie all the qualities worthy of the attention and admiration of historians.

But however much one may reject this view, however much one may want to look elsewhere, it is not easy to do so. This is manifested even in Mary Beard's work. She raises one of the key questions, in discussing the three queens: Eleanor, Blanche and Mary of Champagne. "How could the force of the three queens in the private and public affairs of Western Europe be measured or appraised? That it was pronounced and wide in its ramifications was scarcely to be questioned. But measurement was difficult." (225) Mary Beard neither spells out the difficulties nor provides us with an answer to her question. What she does in practice is to take man as the measure: to suggest the power of these women over states or over men. This is generally true in other parts of the book as well: a woman's significance is measured by her influence on men, or by the recognition she won from men. In what seems like one of his nastier moments, Hexter notes that even in *Woman as Force in History,* men outnumber women in the index (by a ratio of 13:10)—but the point is significant after all, though not in the way Hexter intended, for it reflects the continued practice of "taking man as the measure."

In fact, Mary Beard is remarkably uninterested in the influence of women upon each other, or their judgment of each other. She notes the great interest of Queen Isabella of Spain in learning, and how she "watched with eagle eyes and sharp ears the progress of this education among her retinue. She collected texts for the courtiers to read and for students to use in the universities." She adds that "one woman was commissioned to lecture in classics at Salamanca; another on rhetoric at Alcalá," but she does not find it worthwhile to mention their names, and their importance seems defined not by what they did or were, but by their appointment to those male sanctuaries, the universities. She does not mention the pains taken by Isabella for the education of her daughters—of which we know more from Garrett Mattingly's biography of Catherine of Aragon, Isabella's daughter. (Mattingly also names the two distinguished women: Doña Lucia de Medrano in classics at Salamanca, and Doña Francisca de Lebrija in rhetoric at Alcalá.) Hexter may smile in triumph: the male historian outdoes the female proponent of women's history—at least in this instance—in a faithful portrayal of women and their influence upon each other, as a matter of importance in itself!

ıx

In sum, *Woman as Force in History* surely failed in many respects. It failed in design and execution by its involuted, unbalanced

Woman as Force in History

organization, which weakens the argument and makes the book seem "repetitious" and "oppressive," sometimes confused or superficial. It failed in appeal and persuasiveness partly also by its method—strangely scholarly and unscholarly at once: relying all-too-heavily on long excerpts from scholarly works, demanding of the reader a level of knowledge and sophistication "not common," yet without the trappings of rigorous historical scholarship, without the footnotes sometimes really needed to identify sources, and without much recourse to "original sources." It failed in conception by its contradictions and aborted beginnings, hints of big ideas left undeveloped, polemics left unfinished. And it failed in impact not only by these defects, and by its appearance on the very edge of the post-war anti-feminist wave, but also because it alienated its two main potential sources of support by sharply attacking both: the feminists, and the historians.

Yet today it must be said that *Woman as Force in History* is an important book. This is in part because of significant changes in education and outlook in the reading public, which make Mary Beard's ideas and her subject more welcome and more congenial than they were in 1946. It is more particularly because of the growth of the women's movement, and the outlook of that movement, which on the whole today is more likely to cry "our history has been taken from us!" than to subscribe to the myth of subjection in its extreme forms.

But it is essentially because of the richness and inherent virtues of the book that it has come to life again in this changed climate. Certainly it provides an essential resource, in the information packed into its pages, the references in its long bibliography, and the interpretations—however full of difficulties—of the material. But beyond that, much more can still be said. I do not know of another book in the field of women's history which has the sweep, the depth, the mastery of detail, and the grasp of complexities that this one has. I do not know of many books in any field of history which pose challenges as fundamental to the preconceptions and practices of professional historians. There are few books which attempt as much and emerge as full of life and force, as free of bombast as of sterilized textbook style, and as provocative and readable after twenty-five years, as this one. At the risk of seeming as foolish as R. A. Brown might have seemed, I will prophesy that *Woman as Force in History* will prove as significant and enduring a work of history as any which appeared in that quarter-century.

143

Maxine Kumin

LIFE'S WORK

Mother my good girl
I remember this old story:
you fresh out of the Conservatory
at eighteen a Bach specialist
in a starched shirtwaist
begging permission to go on tour
with the nimble violinist you were
never to accompany and he
flinging his music down
the rosin from his bow
flaking line by line
like grace notes on the treble clef
and my grandfather
that estimable man I never met
scrubbing your mouth with a handkerchief
saying no daughter of mine
tearing loose the gold locket
you wore with no one's picture in it
and the whole German house on 15th Street
at righteous whiteheat . . .

At eighteen I chose to be a swimmer.
My long hair dripped through dinner
onto the china plate.
My fingers wrinkled like Sunsweet
yellow raisins from the afternoon workout.
My mouth chewed but I was doing laps.
I entered the water like a knife.
I was all muscle and seven doors.
A frog on the turning board.
King of the Eels and the Eel's wife.
I swallowed and prayed
to be allowed to join the Aquacade

and my perfect daddy
who carried you off to elope
after the fingerboard snapped
and the violinist lost his case
my daddy wearing gravy on his face
swore on the carrots and the boiled beef
that I would come to nothing
that I would come to grief . . .

Well, the firm old fathers are dead
and I didn't come to grief.
I came to words instead
to tell the little tale that's left:
the midnights of my childhood still go on
the stairs speak again under your foot
the heavy parlor door folds shut
and *Au Clair de la Lune*
puckers from the obedient keys
plain as a schoolroom clock ticking
and what I hear more clearly than Debussy's
lovesong is the dry aftersound
of your long nails clicking.

THE HORSEWOMAN

It is said to begin with the father
who is strong with a mustache
and a full mouth as bright as a semaphore
mixing up kisses with rages.
Nothing contains his breathing.
The triphammer of his chest
strains even the best suitcloth.
Hairs grow from his knuckles.
The crop is stuck in his right boot.

And here comes the loving cup lady
leading her thoroughbred.
They are a perfect fit.

She loves his sweat.
Sweetly she wheels his manure
down the barn floor
and sweetly into the ring
he lifts the proud startle
of his great feet
highest of all the flyers
over the spines of fences.

All this for her daddy—
the scrape of the curry
the sweat strap, the hoofpick
the pyramid droppings.
All this for her daddy—
the banging on iron
the foaming on leather.

She returns at a trot for her ribbon
with her slim neck and good teeth
with her hair wayward in the wind.
Reins slack, leaning back in the saddle
she comes on like a messenger
to the king.

All this for the fantasy daddy
that princely blackboot
when in fact the bona fide father
hunkered over his bourbon
and never went out of doors
except to dry out on the cure
or begin again with AA
on coke and straight water
and kept his indifferent eyes away
from his wishbone of a daughter.

MY MOTHER AND POLITICS

Mary Doyle Curran

M Y MOTHER was a wild Democrat, my father a rigid Republican. Our dinners were one long argument. Very early I was introduced to the political scene.

I woke one morning to hear my father grumbling about the polls, a word that was entirely mysterious to me. My mother, up earlier than usual, was sitting on the side of the bed undoing her braids. She answered my father's grumbling with "Oh, go scratch." I knew something was up because she put on her best dress, a blue silk. She dressed very carefully and said "Well, I'm off to the polls." My father turned his back on her.

It wasn't long, however, before the words "polls" and "politics" were very familiar to me. I couldn't have been more than six when my mother, who was head-checker at the polls, had my brother and me stationed outside the polling place, distributing flyers. She was very canny. She knew that the policeman would allow kids close to the entrance to the polls, although it was illegal. I can remember standing out in front of those places, rain or snow, passing out pieces of paper with strange men's faces on them. People would pat me on the head according to their political affiliations. I'd go into the crowded basement to get more flyers from my mother. She'd be sitting at a long table with a long list of names before her. She politicked even at the polls with "Good morning, Mrs. Cassidy. How's your John? Has he a job yet? You know our man is for the unemployed."

When I was just slightly older, I attended committee meetings and rallies. Most of the time the committee meetings were held at our house because my mother was chairman of the Democratic party in Ward seven. My father would retreat in disgust to John McHarp's pub. The doorbell rang constantly as both men and women crowded into our parlor. The room would fill with cigar smoke. There was a roar of conversation. I'd retreat to the corner with my dolls while my mother argued, cajoled and ordered people around.

My mother had the perfect strategy for getting votes: the most-

These pages comprise one chapter from Ms. Curran's present work in progress.

147

liked woman on a street, the woman with the most relatives. She chose women to do the doorbell ringing and to deliver the relatives' votes because, she said, "A man is off to a pub or the committee room where there's warmth and beer. Women will stick to their jobs without any temptation." There was no beer at committee meetings at our house, and when the cigar smoke got too dense, my mother would open a window and order the men to throw their cigars out. The men would do so, complaining about the lack of a good shot and the loss of their cigars. But no one disobeyed because my mother was the best organizer and best vote getter in the precinct. It wasn't that she was against drinking. My father always brought her back two bottles of Porter every Saturday night. I could hear the bottles being rolled under the bed when she finished them. But there was no drinking at her committee meetings because, she said, "Anyone who comes for the booze is not a serious vote getter."

I watched her one evening. She had a map of every street in the precinct before her. She pointed her finger at a street and said "That's Mary Sullivan's street." Turning to Mary Sullivan, a fat jolly woman with seventeen children, she said "Who can you deliver?" Every house on the street was marked with the name of an occupant or occupants. Mary Sullivan, standing beside my mother, said "Well, I sat with the Delaneys' child while she was sick. They're for us, and George Meaney got his job through my husband going to the Mayor. He'll be for us. Then there's the Clearys—I helped wash their dead mother, and I know she was for us, God rest her soul, but I'm not sure of him. Maybe if we offered him fifteen dollars to be a poll watcher, he'd be for us. God knows he needs the money badly." Every house was marked with a star if the vote was sure. Others were marked with a question, and my mother did this very carefully. Then she said to Mary Sullivan, "The questions are the ones to work on. Never mind the Robinsons, they're strict Protestants. But you can get the Kellys' grandmother's vote. Tell them we'll send a car for her."

My mother's greatest defeat was the Old Woman's Home on Pearl Street. She even went and canvassed herself, dragging me by the hand. I was required to sing for the old ladies who stared at me blankly, clapped politely and went to the polls and voted Republican.

I didn't mind the rallies. They were fun—the halls all decorated with posters of the candidates—red, white and blue bunting surrounding them. There was always some Irish tenor who started the evening off with "The Star-Spangled Banner," and there was always a priest who ended the rally with a prayer. In between, there were endless political speeches, but also there were paper hats and popcorn.

I rarely listened to the speeches except when Mayor Curley from Boston spoke. He had a voice like a silver-tongued flute. It rose and fell rhythmically. I found myself carried away by the sound, paying no attention to the rhetoric. My mother adored him, and her proudest moment came when he shook her by the hand and said "Mary O'Leary, a gem of a Democrat. And this is your little girl. I understand she's a true Democrat, too," and he patted me fondly on the head.

Mayor Curley was her idol, and she could always get money for her precinct from him. "You see," she'd say when someone attacked him as a crook, "he may be a crook (which she didn't believe), but he has his hand out to you and he passes it around. Let no one make a mistake. He's for the poor man." She liked Honey Fitz, too, but I preferred Mayor Curley's delivery. The rallies were like religious devotions, but they were noisy—everyone worked up to a pitch by the oratory. I heard the shouting and clapping in my dreams all night.

But it was best of all if our candidate won. The extras would be out in the street about ten o'clock. We all sat in the living room, waiting for the boy's shout of "extra, extra." My mother would rush down for one and the words "Sullivan Wins" would be spelled out in huge black headlines. There were no Hiroshimas in those days, so they saved the big print for elections. Then off we would all go to Headquarters and the torchlight parade would begin. Hundreds of people carrying torches wound through the streets, usually ending up at the candidate's house where he would appear to be cheered and cheered. Then the parade would walk back to Headquarters for the acceptance speech and free drinks. The party would go on and on. My mother usually found me curled up in some corner asleep. We'd be driven home about three in the morning to my furious father who'd shout, "You're ruining that child's health." My mother's invariable answer was, "Well, it's her soul I'm after."

And this was true. Politics for my mother was a religion, closely connected with her own faith. But when the first Catholic President, John F. Kennedy, was elected, she said, "They'll crucify him."

The most exciting election I remember in connection with my mother was the first Roosevelt election. There were constant fights at the dinner table. My father was staunchly for Hoover, because Hoover was going to maintain a high tariff and not undercut the American working man—this, despite the fact that my father had been out of work for two years. "Besides," he'd shout, "that Roosevelt is no better than a Communist." I've never seen my mother work harder for any candidate. She was going night and day, and the blanket of gloom that had spread over our house because of poverty seemed to vanish. She was gay and tireless, and she laughed away my father's tirades with, "For the working man is it? Well, may you starve under him."

The rallies were even wilder, the campaigning more intense. My mother was murderous against Hoover. "A chicken in every pot. There's only his own pot filled with chicken these days." Every time Roosevelt spoke, she read reports of it carefully. She even went as far as Boston to shake his hand. When Roosevelt was elected, she went wild. My father sat in his chair, gloomily predicting doom. She was so elated that she even allowed me to be in a church minstrel show, where I sang with a full heart and an empty stomach "Happy Days Are Here Again."

Her interest in politics has never abated, and she is almost always uncannily right. During the Eisenhower administration, when the trouble at Little Rock broke out, my mother wrote me "that P Eisenhower better get down to L Rock and quit playing golf." She always knows what's going on, but she learns it from newspapers, not from television which she hates. When the first astronauts went up, she announced firmly, "I will not go to the moon." She prays devoutly for Roosevelt, John and Bobby, and her name for Nixon is "Tricky Dicky."

She made me into a political animal. All my boundaries expanded. I moved rapidly from Seven Thorpe Avenue and Hampden Street to the city, the country, the world, but not to the universe.

Ruth Whitman

THE PASSION OF LIZZIE BORDEN

ON THE MORNING OF AUGUST 4, 1892, DURING AN IN-
TENSE HEAT WAVE, LIZZIE BORDEN'S FATHER AND STEP-
MOTHER WERE FOUND BRUTALLY MURDERED IN THEIR
HOUSE IN FALL RIVER, MASSACHUSETTS. THEIR DAUGHTER
LIZZIE, A THIRTY-THREE YEAR OLD SPINSTER, SECRETARY
OF THE YOUNG PEOPLE'S SOCIETY FOR CHRISTIAN EN-
DEAVOR AND ACTIVE IN THE FRUIT AND FLOWER MISSION,
WAS ARRESTED FOR THE MURDER, TRIED, AND ACQUITTED.

Q. *I ask you again to explain to me why you took those pears from the
pear tree.* A. *I did not take them from the pear tree.* Q. *From the ground.
Wherever you took them from. I thank you for correcting me; going into
the barn, going upstairs into the hottest place in the barn, in the rear of
the barn, the hottest place, and there standing and eating those pears
that morning?* Inquest, Fall River, August 9–11, 1892

*We were talking in the afternoon, me and Lizzie Borden, and I says, "I
can tell you one thing you can't do," and she says, "Tell me what it is,
Mrs. Reagan." I says, "Break an egg, Miss Borden," and she says, "Break
an egg?" I says, "Yes." "Well," she says, "I can break an egg." I says,
"Not the way I would tell you to break it. . . ." And she did get the egg,
and she got it in her hands, and she couldn't break it, and she says,
"There," she says, "that is the first thing that I undertook to do that I
never could."* Mrs. Hannah Reagan, police matron, New Bedford, June
14, 1893

*It is innate in the female psyche to bring blood, conception, birth and
death into close connection with one another. . . .* Helene Deutsch

1

Heat cracks the skin of Fall River.
Soot hangs flat
over the moist city.

Pears
sweat in the backyard.
Sitting alone in the kitchen

151

Lizzie feels
chunks of leftover mutton
heavy in her

belly. Her father
has left for the bank. The ring
he gave her long ago

pinches her finger.

2

Openeyed last night she felt
her blood pounding
the back of her neck,

    tidal waves from the sea
    that poured up the Taunton river,
    tore open the breakwater,
    ripped apart her corsets
    and pumped breath, air,
    sealife into her,

sunstorms, volcanoes, astral debris,
until she was pregnant with a pregnancy
that puts an end to wishing.

3

She woke, thicker around the shoulders, heavier
under the jaw. The birds
had left the burning pear tree.

This house has killed the girl she was.
Narrow, gray, grudging in windows,
bare of guests or laughing,

the parlor's only pleasure is to lay out
corpses or tell tales of each new
disease, step by fatal step.

What holds her here, eating pears?

4

In the August heat
she irons handkerchiefs for her stepmother,
heating the iron on the kitchen fire
in the black stove.
The center of the earth is always boiling,
and she must have the trick of eye to see
how she can liquefy
stones, trees,
slash air so she can breathe,
take life to make life, break
the blind wall open with her fist.

5

She'll hurl this pear against the door
until its ripe meat splatters,
like flesh torn in handfuls from the bone.

She'll trap rage in her like a cage
trapping a bear. Not only where
her sex is, but where her veins
become its bars.

She'll think, as it draws her juice
to her nipples: *that channel is why
I was made.
My roots curl under me
where they suck life
(I'll find the sun
I'll husband a flowering bough)*

6

this sprung and spiralled wrath
won't uncoil till she's invented death

Her father is napping in the parlor,
her stepmother is sitting
at the vanity upstairs.

7

Shake the murderous mountains and dance
a step or two before you turn to rain.

Then in the sky that gives you lightning,
in that same sky
your meteor will hurl;
will singe the tops of trees and bring
spring to the dry hedges of the moon
and set a clanging in the world
and break
by twos
the timbrels of the stars.

> *Who's to judge me? When I sleep I sleep*
> *curled on the shoulder of God*

8

> *At last*
> *I feel hallelujah in my hips*
> *my son the day comes out of me the morning*

She raises the ax.

Priscilla Gibson

FRAYINGS

> **WARREN GIBBS**
>
> *died by arsenic poison*
>
> Mar. 23, 1860.
>
> AE 36 yrs. 5 mos.
> 23 dys.
>
> *Think my friends when this you see*
> *How my wife hath dealt by me.*
> *She in some oysters did prepare*
> *Some poison for my lot and share*
> *Then of the same I did partake*
> *And nature yielded to its fate*
> *Before she my wife became*
> *Mary Felton was her name.*
>
> Erected by his Brother
>
> **WM. GIBBS**

Her shadow, in report of her, fell
Familiarly, like other hill-wives men have sung
Praise of laconically. To tell
Acts alone and stunning silences
Among too small graves of periodic birth
Makes potent calumny.

Rent cloak, dry cheek, wandering eye,
These tableaux, these fabled absences
Astound only husbands and sons,
Lovers who measure themselves by response,
Recorders seeking their anima.
Strayed glance, the sculpted margins
Of lips whose sap has all flowed
Instantly from trembling,
The mad girl in the marble woman,
Celebrated as monstrously pitiful, pitifully merciless.

Those unheard-from matter-of-fact hill-wives I know
By hearing men tell their silence, the threat in it.
Sharper still
The steeled posture of their heartbreak warns
How deep the figure annoys, and reassures.
For some emergencies
Repression is the sole specific. Let Her,
Who can be half for him, display it ceremoniously
If she can. Simples can aid, for instance, the Other Woman.

Familiar like them this grave's report.
Mary Felton on stone erected by his brother,
Indicted, thrills us. For she is Passion
Transformed from helpmeet in this upland country.
Yet (since his craft pays her cunning) become
A puckish fury, a domestic humor.
Put arsenic in his chowder, oyster too!
We were in the habit of chuckling, a little gravely,
At his green mound. She
Would not be planted near, and had her whim.
The yard can spread his rumor.

Rhyme spells her.
Yet where *is* her tomb, this Mary's
Who walks among the hill-women
Into our terror of them, part mirror
Reversal of their quiet, part fey
Seasoning her own charm? The laugh-laced brew
We swallow casually. I speak of
Her shadow, neglecting substance. All: report.
As in the wives' edges traced by those who mingle
Praise for silences with blame.

Silences might just as well have shouted
Neither acceptance nor rejection—a queerer mixture
We have not heard yet.
All: silhouettes, the too familiar
Shapes of all need, outlines brittled
Because fragility is our glass.
Man need, woman need
To search self by fission, by Other.
Resented, oh resented this strait;
But welcomed, chiefly in images of Her.
Bodied in them our Sphinx: Alternatives.
Paths always crosspoints; the ways split, uncoupled.
Even in species' forms imagination faces
The excluded cosmos; in the gained niche, the missed one.
—How not in our closest riddles, primal separations?

These rumors of Her plait a homespun swaddling
To bind the animal-who-foretells-his-death.
In various report
Woman combines ambiguous powers,
Virtues of mending, tearing the weave.
Each country daughter
Knew stitches-in-time a lie;
Hands pierced, nevertheless, the fabric
(Reckless to patch that knowledge)
In work that kept the thread,
Pulling it taut to knot again.
                    Penelope or Mary
Each celebrates our glimpse
Of constant accident,
Of the uncommon dailiness of kind.

All fatal sicknesses nursed,

Yes, wilfully
By these strange figures—stepmothers, Fates,
Dark ladies, snow maidens, witch, silent wife,
By stitchers and hemmers against frayings,
I know you.
I do not know what ravels
In bands and shrouds now

Now when grave robbers, murderers, false accusers
Obliterate pastness to memorialize
Their Instant. Look, the stone is sheared
Clumsily near the base that named *Mary*.
They cease to skulk by night, lift by day
All that belongs to noone,
To signal a taking.
I fear the shapes that shadow this deed.
My vandal ghouls who slice stone
For decoration, found object in an unfound room.
They mark no grave, accuse no longer any
Mystery of poisoner, mender, domesticated Other.

Now when I accuse too, project ciphers,
Confront only my phantoms.
Say
Shall they then,
Then shall they, shall they,
Who tell no slander, cease to praise in terror,
Who cast no shadow selves,
They exorcise to forgive,
Shall they then know her?

This voice I speak in
Is it not like hers?
Is it her witching stitches,
Her crazy darning?

CONFESSIONS OF MOTHER GOOSE

Anne Halley

A WICKED WITCH turned two beautiful princesses into geese, because of a grudge she had long borne the king, their father.
A Miller had a youngest son whom everyone thought a little simple. He used to drop stones into the millpond and let grains of corn run slowly through his fingers for long minutes at a time. Nevertheless, though he often wore an absent, meditative smile, he added up what the farmers owed correctly and quickly in his head —much before they could figure it in crayon on the edges of their meal-sacks. They paid him, but afterwards at the inn always considered that there was something not quite right about him. Until, angrily, he came to half-believe it.

Some geese thought they were enchanted. Goose-like, they mistook the simple Miller's son for a prince (he had the meditative smile) and, cackling excitedly and waving their silly necks, they waddled up to him across the millyard. But he who was, after all, a Miller's son, thought they wanted only the corn in his hand. Which he held out to them gladly because, as people said, he may have been a little simple in certain ways. And they, who were geese and not princesses, gobbled up the corn. But when the corn was gone they grew angry with him for not recognizing their enchantment and pecked at his hand and hurt him rather badly.

And once upon a time a youngest son went out to seek his fortune and won the fat goose at the Fair.

And now, a quite different now. These may be a morning's cautionary tales—or all that is left of last night's dreaming. Eggshell, coffee grounds, red-eyed morning delusions and toots and sneezes and the vestiges of dream and urgent appointments and bursts of song and rush of small piss waters and the mechanical roar and flush—down the drain, down the stairs, out the doors and windows.
Gone.

Gone?

A Miller's jolly wife may say, Thank Goodness, and, Now it is for me. Let's say she ties on a dry blue apron, carefully hangs up her damp one beside the kitchen towels. And, sitting then among her rosemary, chives, philodendron, telephone, peeling a mound of potatoes (for all her sons and the Miller too were strong and great eaters) she fell into a reverie. The day is coming. She let the potatoes fall, one by one, splash and splat, into the basin of salted water that stood ready for them, and she considered the while. And

159

if jolly Miller's wives did—and do—she considered like this:

I am coming to a new phase in the cycles of child-bearing wom-en—a lull or promise of a lull, when the clanking enameled pails, the cries of night-feeding infants, quiet, and only the youngest child—at odd moments—still runs up to pat my breast, but without meeting my eyes with his new self-knowledge. When the menstrual stain neither startles nor proclaims emptiness, disappointment, but can be dealt with simply, like any other waste. A wife could change with the born children now: look forward thankfully to the less hectic, dryer life of the village—the school, the clubs with admirable aims—in streetclothes again, she could be like the children, bright in new-buttoned proprieties. But some of us have come to the private, violent satisfactions of childbearing from an equally private doubling of self, from a previous withdrawal with one not other, that seemed to wipe out town and group, sometimes made marriage impossible. So that there will surely come uncertain times; it may be rough for the matron—even for this jolly wife so well-situated among her flowering pots—to shrink and subside into a middle phase: to put magic behind her and become what she was at ten, some variety of girl scout doing the world's business.

The time of near-quiet, of approaching change, can be the time for divorce, crying jags and black depression, for a last (or first) willful lover—at the very least for confrontations. Often enough I see signs in acquaintances: the long distance phonecalls to unforgotten but long ago disconnected numbers, the flying visit to some long-gone friend or love, undertaken at great inconvenience to the family and perhaps in slippers, after midnight, when all houses are locked-up tight. In the other direction, they send after catalogues to study medicine or the law, to become painter or poet at last. And what about the girl graduates of forty smiled on by decently retired husbands as they move down the aisle wedded to Pomp and Circumstance? A mild case will end in another baby, conceived after a weepy class reunion or its equivalent; a new girlish haircut and a manly paycheck may soothe the ache for some; with a bad case you will have to change your life.

So if now I begin to feel the impulse, the pull, to go back to go forward to go—to forget these conjured-up, emblematic props (what were they? yes, my peeled-close-to-the-skin potatoes, my blue apron)—to hope by going to meet again a separable self, I think I know better than to begin with real projects, real letters, telephones, railway cars. I remind myself, only for instance, that the present Jenny in her present life and choices is no different from any of my present neighbors—all Miller's wives, more or less, in a world of Jolly Millers—and can have no special knowledge for me. It is only some quality in our lives that for a while ran parallel, that continues to sound in me, but that I need neither to renew nor exorcise.

Or so I say to myself, often.

There are two stories that occur to me now. For me they explain a good deal. But to tell them we must leave the Miller's wife there at her window—a still point far in the future, she will wait, half-realized and insufficiently rehearsed as she is, until we need to push her on stage again. There will be ground to cover first.

For I—about to tell the stories—have not only the part of the Miller's wife waiting for me, I must first (you guessed it) be the goose. Downy neck straining for the hatchet—or so it was. That the goose only rarely, by moonlight by star by the twitch of an eyelid, turned into Queen of the May was not for want of trying, if firm expectation, faith, and a willingness to wait can go by that name. A special goose belonging to a special, expensively nurtured group: general American, female, A.B., so many hours intermittently analyzed, group therapized (Help!), so many pages anatomized in the Sunday Press, the Alumna News Letter. And Jenny—Geneva—girlfriend, amanuensis, blood brother, emotional catch-all, dormitory sweetheart—she may have been another. So that—according to the chattering nature which I fondly deplore—and as I am shy, repressive but also—given or seizing the chance—garrulous, an endless beginner and modifier—here and now I begin again.

Jenny and I were odd.

Peculiar not so much in the ways which we—like anyone else—easily recognized, but possibly in one more significant. That we were covered with psychic bumps and scabs; that we may have borne these a little more exaggeratedly and self-consciously than some; that we were lumpy, carried around our infancies crookedly bulging with growing pains and birth bruises, unmatched, is not the queerness I mean. It is of little general importance, for instance, that the afternoooon tea served once a week in the sundusty Hall of Crenellate Towers regularly turned us into tragedians and slobs. I suppose the same silver urns, the gruff maternal maids rushing about with hot water, the institutional cups, the gracious enunciating smile of the lady who poured, still comfort and confuse undergraduates wearing a modernized gym costume. What if we could not approach our tea without spasms of self hate, and mutterings of Non Serviam, could not get away without having mauled the Hydrox cookies, grabbed and elbowed like ten-year-olds too long unsupervised. What if we were congruently backward in other areas of normal human female praxis. No, more importantly, we were—and it may be that our class is—notably peculiar in those expectations least known to us, yet most central to our being.

I mean:

There was nothing, from afternoon tea to the Yalta agreement, towards which we did not feel it necessary to have an attitude; nothing about which we were not required to pose and posture and emote. Too simple and too fearful to ask the mirror the only true mirror question, we stared—nevertheless—at our doughfaces, saying, Felix Culpa close to the heart: this angle for Heraclitus: Oh, how would the Rights of Man look on me?

We conceived of human history simply as the evolution, the progress, which had produced us: of its purpose as our complete development. City of God or Classless Society, Utopia or Republic, Categorical Imperative, Social Contract, Monad Electrode Orgon—life, liberty, and the pursuit of happiness (all painful and painstaking thought and action, all work pursued doggedly and against fantastic odds) seemed to us daisies for the picking, petals for He loves me, He loves me not. We had always made the same mistake, of course, about our physical parents' works and days, hopes and pleasures. So with intense seriousness, with suffering of a kind, we still in all our education never learned to believe in a reality which might include us, but not exist for our self-aggrandizement, our ends. Consumers in the market place of ideas—half debutante agonizing over fit and color, half housewife snuffling and fingering her noontime soupgreens—privately educated, incapable of thought we began and, I fear, we have in the main self-indulgently remained.

We expected to marry.

(Grammatical foolishness—yet a truth. Surely not each other? But someone, something—purpose and definition, romance and subjection, freedom necessity and love: some great stoneface warm smile —unimaginable.)

Our oddness, then, is the merest commonplace. We shared it with all the other cause-and-effect fictions who, once upon a time, set out on stories. I think so. Listen.

ONCE UPON A TIME there lived a powerful King with his beautiful Queen. They had everything their hearts desired—riches and many servants and men-at-arms, strong horses, a clever cook, and warm soft beds in their castle high on the hill, overlooking their green and flourishing peaceful kingdom. But the King and Queen grew sad as they looked out over the rolling countryside; neither the music of the lute and soft songs, nor trumpet flourishes, not the court peacocks nor the peasants' funny dances, any longer amused them. The cook's puddings and clever sauces—only a little unsettled on their plates and unfinished—were sent back to the cellar kitchen. The King had no heir.

Confessions of Mother Goose

So they sent for all the wise men and doctors of the kingdom—and for a few from beyond the borders—and held many councils, some in the Great Audience Hall and some secret ones, at night in the King and Queen's private chambers.

After many months one wise old doctor, who wore a black cloak covered with magic signs, revealed to them a way. He said that if the King would go on a long journey—seven nights and seven days—by a difficult way and in darkness to the very center of the earth, and bring back what he should find there, the Queen would bear a child. But there was one prohibition, because it would be a child called up with the help of a powerful and perhaps dangerous magic: whatever the King brought back must be given to the doctor, to be kept safe until the child's maturity. Neither the King nor the Queen must desire the magic object or even be curious about it, if they wished to ensure their child's happiness and wellbeing.

So it was done. The King indeed had a long dark journey. He slept afterwards for seven days and seven nights and the clever cook's cordials and eggnogs restored him only slowly. In due time the Queen conceived. The magic object—a simple but beautifully-wrought golden pin—was carefully put away in an iron box that locked with a heavy key. But instead of giving the box to the wise man, the proud King who now blamed this advisor for all his hard labors and subsequent fatigue, sent the doctor away. And the Queen, fretful as women are and heavy with the child, wept and said, I must have the pin, for without it I cannot bear to live. So she sent her lady in waiting to get the box and herself stole the key from the King's dressing table.

That night in the banquet hall the golden pin shone and sparkled between her breasts.

The King, who had begun to love her more and more because she was with child, forgave her greedy selfishness and she wore the pin every day. Then, shortly before she was to be brought to bed, the King presented her with many new jewels and other precious ornaments. Also spices, silks, wooly rugs, earrings, necklaces, and toe-bells arrived from the rulers of the east, both to honor the heir and for the Queen herself. In the confusion and general joy the simple golden pin was lost and no one noticed it.

A healthy child, a daughter, was born to them, although the Queen's labor lasted seven days and seven nights and was very painful to her. The Queen remained fat and fruitful for many years and ultimately gave birth to three sons and another daughter besides. They all lived happily ever after, and the children married other princes and princesses. They would feast together, while the King's noisy grandchildren played with his crown and scepter under the dais. The wise man was never heard from again.

Only. Until?

Let it stand; it is a fairy tale so far and familiar enough. We have an alternate text, no doubt dating from the same period. It remains for research and comparative analysis to establish whether the variations are of real significance. Let us assume that they may indicate a somewhat different geographical origin and climate, perhaps also variant religious practices within the same general cultural configuration. Be with me: Listen.

Once upon a time (imagine now, the deer in the park, the clever cook, the finches caged in the Queen's bower, and the view from the turret) a King and Queen had two beautiful infant children: a boy and a girl. So they were well content. But during the winter, while the boy grew fat—he already guzzled porridge from a wide-mouthed bottle and had learned to kick away the furlined blanket with his strong pink feet—the baby daughter took sick. She lay still and blue-lipped among the white bunnyskins and only whimpered faintly when the old nurse tried to feed her.

Seven days and seven nights the nurse, and the Queen too, and the learned doctors, watched with the child and did what they could to revive her: warm baths and cold baths, rocking and singing, drops of bitter medicine, sugar water, suppositories, magic incantations, vigils and prayers and candles and a clove of garlic tied to the basket's side, all did no good, and the time came when the Queen was exhausted, miserable from lack of sleep and from eating almost nothing in her distracted state. The King, who of course had to rule some of the time, was with them as often as he could be, and would pace around the baby's basket several times each day.

Finally, on the seventh day, with a wet snow darkening the castle windows and a damp wind whistling in the chimneys, the King said, Something else must be done. And quickly. But the Queen, looking at her sick cold child, whose breath only fluttered irregularly now, felt discouraged and very sick herself. Let the poor child die, she said. It has suffered enough.

But the King had heard of one more powerful doctor who lived far on the outskirts of an ancient city, and he sent for him by special courier, saying, It is my duty as a King and as a Father to leave nothing untried. The doctor came—hurriedly brought away from his dinner, his napkin stuck in his pocket. And he said, We must give the child a magic injection.

No one except the King was allowed in the room with doctor and child. The old nurse said, afterwards, that the King too must have been afraid to watch, for he never told anyone what was said and done. But we all know that an injection is painful, and the baby did, suddenly, give a great scream. (Some of the servants—as far

away as the kitchen—reported that they heard a huge rush of wind
and saw the flames in the stove flare and sputter.) The baby's face
which before was cold and white, turned purple and then bright
red; her breathing grew steadier; almost at once she was able to
take some drops of weak milk.

By spring both babies were fat and healthy and no one but the
Queen remembered those terrible days. She, however, always worried that her children might be taken sick again, and warned her
daughter every day never to run down the winding stair, nor lean
too far over the parapet. The wise doctor died unexpectedly of gout
that same year, without having taught anyone his magic. But for
the rest: they all lived ever after. One way or the other.

WELL. Who has not known the sleeping beauties, dreamwalkers
enveloped in a spell, frozen and waiting, and the many angry boy
and girl children who walk the earth, grey-faced, looking for the
doctor who may yet keep the lost talisman, the magic. Absence of
God, dessication, the dark night of the soul—impotence, frigidity,
the lockjaw of the heart; lack of self-esteem it says in the weekly
supplements, no love. Weak ego—was that what Jenny and I suffered from the afternoon Jenny's eyes skittered so wildly and ab-
sently; why she tossed her head from side to side, moved bluish
lips, talked so seriously to herself and swung her arms in short
tensely rigid arcs, as she crossed at University and Fourth? Or only
the perfectly ordinary burden of choice into which I—her old and
never objective friend—might project irrelevant desperations? I did
not run after her, take hold of her arm, say, Come home love, come
home. We were young women then, working out our separate des-
tinies and waiting for prince and potentate; no longer the babes
in the woods who could hold to each other, hang on for warmth.
Nor had it ever been our style to speak directly; not even to touch
that much, but by indirection to find direction out and to read
many volumes into small bits of evidence.

Jenny now walked directly past me: her look was unfocused, unwilling or unable to know me. So that I felt I had reason to be
angry besides. We don't really want even our crazy friends to cut
us. But by then I thought I had learned—begun to learn, this much,
which is all I wish and hope sometime to be able to unlearn. People
either make it or they don't. Lightning will or won't strike. Friends
don't answer. With luck you get time off for the funeral or the tense
wedding; to visit the madhouse once or—in a setting so new that
it has all the homey confusion of an old country band concert—to

165

attend the childbed. Whatever joy or disaster comes to stand for someone's word, I have chosen. It has happened, chosen me. Usually you will then have to line up far at the back, behind the proper relatives and eager neighbors. More likely life or death, the distant job—Africa?—the newest marriage will be something you hear about, by the way and on the telephone from some chance voice, an outsider's, suddenly become hateful and real.

Of course, Jenny no more than I collapsed weeping and wailing— not that day, there on the Lake City sidewalk, grainy with old snow, intricately marked by rubber-treaded bootsoles and out-of-season bicycle tires through the thrown-up little walls of dirty white, where I watched her, fifteen years ago, stomp by in what looked like a private agony. She plays bridge these days; she sends children to school with bag lunches (does she?); she opens cans and attends museum film series. To each age its congruent activities. But I judge that she died once or twice too. That the dying continues around us.

Something may have died, the last time I really saw Jenny. She stayed over, pacing the three-room apartment, taking quinine and other pills on an around-the-clock schedule; she was grim and pale and silent, as I had come to know her in earlier crises, but while she was taking one of the hot baths required by that particular regimen, I must have fallen asleep. When I woke, feeling thickheaded and cruddy and hot with the milk that pounded and rose in damp circles through the Army shirt I then affected, I heard my baby crying for his early morning feeding, and saw Jenny just getting into her clothes. Whatever had happened to her in her night of dizzy hour-counting, I had missed it. We didn't say much to each other, then, except that she would let me know and I thought that, of course, I had failed her, but more, that it could not be helped. And I thought, in something like despair—before I settled back with the steaming-wet baby into a willing doze—that it had taken me seven years to lose a friend, that I had neither toiled nor spun, that I was twenty-four and married and a mother and fell asleep, unwashed, on a wretched iron cot (Klaeber's *Beowulf* kicked under the table) while the overhead light faded into the morning, that I would certainly waken the husband, who lay naked, tangled in our trousseau sheets and that I would certainly quarrel with him. That Jenny, no matter what made her desperately haggard, would brush her teeth faithfully, morning and night. And for all I knew, say a Presbyterian prayer. So I gave her up, that morning, but she had given me up long before.

Some days after that dim night, Jenny menstruated, but I always doubted that it was the quinine. And not much later she too married and went to live in an apartment with ivy-print wallpaper in a section of the city far away from campus. The month before the wedding—the sidewalks were streaked with brown slush so it must have been getting on to spring—I ran into Francis Donovan, who had been Jenny's true love these four long years of winter. This burly, portly man, going grey under his hat brim, had—as far as I knew—only one thing to recommend him. That thing at first had been experience. Older, divorced, determined never to marry again, and working on some indescribably dreary thesis which was neither critical nor modern, nor scholarly in the old-fashioned gentlemanly way, but had something to do with statistics and word-counts, he had always seemed impossible to me. None of my other friends had wished to talk with him more than five minutes and, as a matter of truth, Francis never showed the slightest interest in any of us—not in our poems, our theories, our gossip, or subsequently in our politics and babies. I had come to respect the idea of Francis: four years ago he had taken Jenny's virginity under the sacred heart in Mrs. Mecklenburg's sitting room. Jenny had flowered with his monumental fucking and served him cocoa with marshmallow fluff and taken to wearing ruffled blouses. I had had to think Jenny well repaid for these tastes, for those unimaginable evenings of "working on her thesis" with Francis, for their two collections of notecards, her brave acceptance of his wish to remain single. In my simple-minded way, I had never doubted that she would bring him round, marry her true love at last. And even get rid of his hat and fuzz-linted overcoat when he got his degree: they would go off to be happy, literary after their fashion.

When Francis left to teach in a far-western college, I thought that Jenny had played her cards wrong, but that she would love him forever. Six months later, there he was. I want to marry Geneva, he said to me, there on the corner—where two drugstores and a fishbowl lunchroom and the First National signal SPECIALS to each other. For the first time since we had known each other, he seemed to look at me as if I existed and so—naturally—I began to prickle with interest in him. I have come back to marry Geneva, he said in that old, dreary Francis way—which suddenly seemed manly, almost attractive. You're her friend. Why won't she? My God, I said. (She had wanted to long enough.) And tried to persuade him that Jenny was only coy, that he might not have used the right words. Though what words he ever used with her before must have been unambiguous enough. Yes or no, he used to say, and Jenny said yes. Yet here he was, come back, turned down. So wellbeloved against such odds (I had thought) that it must surely come to something. That it didn't, still worries me, and that Jenny married a more social, smiling man who—like the rest of us—drinks vodka and lime, or whatever is the going thing instead of cocoa, comforts me not at all.

Although it turned out that she was not pregnant, Jenny must have had enough. She married and moved away. We were invited once or twice, I think, but it was a long drive through featureless city streets, past two and three-family houses, garages, seat-cover salesrooms, grocery basements, home beauty parlors. We never spoke of Francis: I believe I talked at length about my baby's feeding, while we ate spinach creamed in mushroom soup. We saw a wooden file, recently refinished and enormous, which contained data for a sociological dissertation. Except for its pretty surface, the file might have been Francis'—more particularly since all the data was said to be "practical," gained by doorbell ringing and interviews among the people. It was Francis who had always looked to me like some silenced, displaced precinct captain, an alderman, wandered by chance into the world of letters. That this was a wholly childish misconception can be shown by his now lengthy bibliography of publications in the learned journals. But the incumbent—I mean Jenny's—was younger and talkative and softer; smiled with a ready pleasant interest on her old friends and, unlike. Francis, soon abandoned the dissertation in the filing cabinet. I don't know what happened to Jenny's careful, compulsive copying of all the images in *The Blithesdale Romance* either. Perhaps, since Francis had never been a letter writer, she burned her notes in that charred and dented wire basket—stuffed foolishly with orange peel and eggshells—that used to sit in all our rented Lake City backyards. But this so much pleasanter Francis—I shall call him Frank—took my charming and witty friend out of that overwrought and underpaid student's world in which we had all floundered for so long and which led, it appears, inexorably—although we never guessed it—to committees, the typed *curriculum vitae*, turned shirt collars, and tenure. Today it is my husband who shakes hands with Francis Donovan at the MLA, next year they may listen to each other's papers, they may yet meet again as colleagues with adjoining offices, although it will be several years, I should think, before Francis shows up—more grizzled, but with the same pen and pencil set sticking out of his vest—as the new Chairman. When I, after all this time, will have my chance to peel potatoes or avocadoes for his dinner. Jenny's Frank has different meetings and committees, representing something electronic or detergent in a midwestern capital, and our lives are not likely to adjoin again.

NEVERTHELESS, there were once a Miss G. and Miss H. Classmates

Confessions of Mother Goose

at Crenellate College, they met and became friends during the Sophomore year. They shared a strong interest in literary studies; particularly the then fashionable, so-called metaphysical, poets aroused their excited concern. Upon graduation both young women set out for Lakeland University (a *solid* department), as they had been advised to do by at least one of their instructors.

At Lakeland they seem to have studied in a progressively more desultory manner for a few years longer, worn out their undergraduate wardrobes, become Candidates, perhaps taken degrees, ultimately married fellow students. Although both young women were registered in the Department of English, Miss G. married a Sociologist, while Miss H.'s future husband did file a dissertation (in the required quadruplicate) with the Lakeland University Department of English.

After a ten-year child-rearing hiatus one may, it seems clear, expect them to augment the lower ranks of the teaching profession.

Mmmmm, yes. Proceed.

Today G. and H. live thousands of miles apart. They have not met for many years, nor do they now correspond. During their undergraduate summers, however, it is believed that the young women exchanged letters written in both heroic couplets and poulter's measure. We know of no extant copies; all the same it seems unlikely that these bits of written work would have been purposefully destroyed. The mementoes of married women have a way of dropping out of sight; neither did both always live orderly. On those now increasingly rare occasions when either husband recalls, sentimentally, the common past, it must be noted that he entirely forgets this former friendship of his wife's—as well as its literary beginnings and the girlish aspirations around which it evolved. That part has come to bore him.

Understandably.

And were I to imagine Geneva today, whom would I see? (I have no second-sight, no caul lost somewhere along with manuscript, love note, term-paper, pencil stub, famous professor's *comment*.) And most mornings hardly see myself squinting around the edges of years and—what's more—blocking out a good deal of foreground noise by holding my ears. Is she cropped and greying, still bright-eyed, broadshouldered? Still inexorably gartered and girdled into the costume which then and (I realize) now alone means grown-up? Lapel-pin and tailored suit, nylons with seams, high-heels? Or marketing in sneakers, a braid down her back—her children grimy but chess-playing, guitar-strumming prodigies? You would not read to the blind, give parties for mental patients or Cub Scouts, would you? Neither can I see you chairing the Great Books discussion. But we all have, and must have, our *thing*, as we had majors and minors, fields, even specialties. Only last month I had word from Miss F., Recluse and Orthodox, beside a heated swimming pool in Ohio. Nearly 200 lbs., in black crepe. She leaves her landscaped enclave only to race the overloaded MG to daily prayers. We all have those possibilities. Though she must have married or inherited well; Miss G. and Miss H. know that a dignified contemplative requires money. And as most of us cannot decide to stink (it is too fiercely against our upbringing) and still lack the sheltered pool for solitude and immersion, we come to bargain for our share of—at least—stall-showers, deodorants, and may well teach Sunday school faintly scented by Guerlain.

What is the burden of your song?

When G. and H. left Crenellate they were sure that all their *problems* (which is what all the nebulous decisions, choices and grand gestures they hoped to meet, as well as the familial fantasies they hoped to grow out of, were then called) could and would be solved by simple fiat: an experience no more complicated nor mysterious than a close analysis of "The Good Morrow" and closely related to that. Simply by love. And by that they understood, in their enlightened way, sexual climax.

These young ladies were, perhaps, not so much miseducated as misread, and had gathered in several years of passionate literary study, some wildly divergent texts and data: Prufrock and Strether and Stephen Dedalus and the young Dylan Thomas haunted them as possible models for emulation; meanwhile the agony of the shipwrecked nuns was superimposed on the "Mistress Going to Bed" and by their other poet's inelegant (who were *they* to argue?) location of love's mansion.

Unlike those of their contemporaries who hailed from more *engagé* urban institutions, they had managed to avoid The Working Day, but considered themselves influenced by the Modern Library Freud. They assumed that they could become Milly Theales, Maude Gonnes *and* skinnier Gertrude Steins; they had had no lovers to speak to them or touch them in a language more meaningful than that of their English 202 instructor.

A lack of lovers, verbal and otherwise, was of course one real problem in these—after all physically maturated—young women's lives. Nor can they have been, in their hearts, fully confident about their abilities to both attract and be the poets of their generation. Still, at graduation, neither would have felt sympathy for a mute inglorious Milton of any sex. The Word Made Flesh was a story we read literally.

Immersed in that story, Jenny and I spent a summer in rented rooms near the University. It was a lush, leafy, green season, as I think of it now, with moist early mornings (summer session classes began at eight) and long evenings, like caves or underwater grassy hollows. We lived in a large wooden house with turrets and porches, many narrow hallways and steep stairs: my room had high windows almost up to the ceiling and down to the floor—the window sills were wide and old-fashioned, substantial shelves. At the windows, which were of course always open, the landlady had hung long skinny streamers of crepe-paper—these were pale green with large red poppies and darker green foliage. There was a bed, also, and I remember my books and papers stacked around the bare floor. The typewriter on a chair in front of the bed. In those days I never thought of rearranging or improving a rented room: I knew that whatever taste I had was only for taking away objects, for rejecting decorations and the impresses of personality on matter: having passed through college banners and cheap Braque reproductions, I now felt all décor equally shameful. But my windows in Mr. and Mrs. Shallup's tower-like second-story-front gave me, nevertheless, a great deal of pleasure: I used to lie on the bed and far away, across the room, the flowery crepe paper moved in the wind and changed texture with sunlight and the shadows of leaves from the trees outside.

Mr. and Mrs. Shallup, now, were a strange pair—at least to me, that summer. He, very white-skinned with an impressive lock of dark hair, a soft belly, taught a version of History at the Bible Institute and figured largely as HE in his tiny, handwringing wife's breathy and hurried conversation. It was my impression that HE was omnipresent, always having to mow the lawn or needing to be fed; that Mrs. Shallup was always ironing in the heat of the day, while she yearned to take her children on impossibly distant educational trips to Bunker Hill Monument and the Empire State Building. A daughter of eight meanwhile collected Bible picture cards, played daily-vacation-church bible-school on the porch swing, and stood in the front hall, her arms spread wide as wings, humming about Baby Jesus. They had a mean little boy too, whom I remember only as a thin frown above a striped jersey. All in all they were people whose concerns—mortgages and jungle gyms, groceries, laundry, and religion—struck me then as fantastic, wholly out of this world. I lowered my eyes when I met one or another of them, bought my own lightbulbs rather than penetrate with Mrs. Shallup to the cupboard where she thought HE must have stored them, after HIS breakfast before the children's lunch underneath the sprinkled or the drying-out or the folded away washing.

Encounters with people—Connors Shallup, for instance, telling

171

me it was a nice day—were intensely painful to me then. In my vanity I could not see how they could bear to live. I was ashamed, of course, whenever I caught this feeling in myself, and sometimes realized that they—in all probability—felt pity for me too: a shy grubby girl, drab and bookish, who did not even think to close windows against the rain, that the crepe paper drapes would run.

In a way, the Shallups controlled my perceptions that summer as they apparently could not affect Jenny's. She lived first-floor-back—to my horror—in the midst of them. And could pass the time of day—wide-eyed—in a riot of platitudes that set my teeth chattering. Then played them back to me so sincerely that I cannot now separate Geneva's performances from my own observations. Especially little Deanna; Jenny would appear above my typewriter, catch the sideseams of jeans between delicately stiffened fingers, curtsy, and—with little pursed lips and staring baby eyes, sing, Jesuth lovth me. Then, in quicker, curl-tossing rhythm,

> Do not WAIT until some DEED of greatness YOU MAY do
> Do not WAIT to spread your LIGHT afar
> To the many Dumdumsomethingsdumdum NOW be true
> BRIGHTen the CORNer WHERE you are.

That child will come to no good, we agree.

We share—at the Shallups—an upstairs kitchen and bath. Nor are Geneva and I the only tenants: the bathtub is always full of little wrung-out wads of washing—like worms; the kitchen stove always has bubbling stew pots and hissing pans of oil on it; the corners of the kitchen are filled with gallon bottles of red wine, vinegar, methyl alcohol—we don't quite know what. The Shallups, good people that they are, have rented two rooms to several families of Ukranians. So Nadia and Pola pad barefooted back and forth between bath and kitchen while I type; in the evenings there are two hairy-armed men in undershirts at the kitchen table. The child has its head shaved for the summer and last week, in an access of friendliness which I could neither foresee nor control, threw the keyboard out of joint, so that now I write poems without the letter O. An interesting discipline, maybe, but Albert—with whom I dally on the front steps—says he will see to it for me. For while Geneva spreads creamcheese on slices of chipped beef (you roll it up and fasten with a tooth pick!) and wrinkles her nose in outrage at Pola's cabbage that engulfs our kitchen, and waits for Francis Donovan to put his feet under a corner, at least, of the oilclothed table, I too have a gentleman caller.

It is Albert. He has come back, although last night—rather this morning—I feared I would never see him again. We argued so hopelessly. No, I whispered. No. How can you come upstairs! No. The Shallups. The Polas and Nadias. What are you thinking of? And he, so reasonably. They'll never hear or see. But I feel them, Oh Albert, like Grand Central Station. No. No and No. I want it to be right. Not all those other tossings and turnings, smell and prayers to be conscious of. Then his hands. Why be conscious of them? You won't be. I will. I mean, No Albert, No, I won't. Not here!

And just at that moment (we are entangled at the foot of the stairs) the back hall door opens, and out strides—oh horror—out capers and canters adjusting uncouthly the hang of his trousers—not a wrathful Mr. Shallup but a cheery Francis. Hi Kids.

So Albert left and I went upstairs alone.

He is back now; he will see to the portable; perhaps he sees my point. Walking down Fourth Avenue by the light of the dawn, he reports that Francis has asked him, Does she put out?

I promise myself never to tell Jenny and I wonder, of the four of us, who is dishonored? And how?

My friend my gentleman caller, that summer was Albert, whom I loved. For reasons. I had not, however—in reason or unreason—loved Albert at first sight: his small neat shoes, his richly shining black curls—much too long, too ornate, to jibe with my austere roundhead ideal, his breastpocket full of pale green Havanas, his russet tweeds and wine-dark turtleneck pullovers, were in a tradition I neither recognized nor felt in tune with. What I had responded to, negatively at the outset, were his manners and—more important—his eyes. Green eyes, clear as glass and very slightly bulging—I thought immediately there must be something behind them. When Albert first spoke to me—it had been after a late class—I already felt a challenge. It was close to six in the afternoon, I remember—the empty, inside-full-of-holes feeling, depletion almost ready to chew the eight dark blue and gold volumes of Grierson that shine substantial with organic varnish and glue; the emptied oppressive marble hallway; and Albert, all thickening twenty-seven years of him, someone I might have read about but had never yet met: the suitor, respectful troubador, who seemed to be spreading a carpet for me to step on as we loitered down the hall. As he spoke in his carefully lowered Little Theatre voice and took—or offered to take—some of the load of reserve books that I held against my chest, I knew I was honored and cherished, acknowledged as a group, a representative, suddenly, of womanhood.

And yet the eyes, as they said all that, said something else to me too. There is someone home here. Wait.

As it turned out, of course, Albert and I took turns waiting. That is, I waited and so did he—together and separately—and later on across half the continent—for signs and pledges that we either could, or would not give each other: we wasted a good deal of time, I have thought since, and perhaps emotion too—although, unlike the stricter moralists, I have never wanted to measure out fear and love—those stock responses—in accord with any object's intrinsic value. A sentimentalist, I wanted involvement—process in me, and progress—and if I came to wait, with hate and gritty longing, for Albert to reveal himself, to do willing battle with my self-important virginity, I would not now reject those empty, shivering nights and long afternoons—cannot altogether wish them to have been otherwise.

For things were not otherwise, but thus. Albert, to my amusement and later disappointment, was a Saturday night—and not even every Saturday night—man. So that all the previous winter semester, before we moved to the Shallup's and while Jenny had spent the long dark evenings with Francis Donovan in his room above the Minnehaha Drug Store, alternately (I imagined) making love and making notes in the kind of comradeship in which I, at least, supposed reality to reside, it came about that Albert and I, in gloves, would be taxied out of the student-mildewy cheap brown gravy sector of Lake City, to dine under bright lights and on white cloths among the Salesmen (Account Executives?), the furriers and rising young lawyers and their ladies. Cocktail Rings sparkled among the ice-filled water carafes and lipstick crescents and broken bread and lambchops in greenpaper frills: there were hotel dining rooms and the harmonica player straight from New York; chopped liver and freshfaced local talent to shout out Oklahoma! Bea Lillie or Edward G. Robinson on the road: Albert would have the taxi waiting outside and, while I deprecated such ostentation, would insist that he had spent enough of his life waiting for trains, and counting the cost. This was true, but meanwhile I was enamored of a kind of voluntary poverty—at least of a life with the appearance of poverty —that is, of a lack of external flourishes, comforts, appurtenances, and indulgences. The straight wooden chair, the pillowless bed, the unperfumed earlobe and the unshaded 200-watt light, were my chosen magic—I felt that somehow amidst such honest straightforward austerity I might better break through to my own especial pain or joy. I laughed at Albert, who had no intention of joining me in a dinner of bargain-high hamburger from the Great Northern; I was sure that in old clothes that kept their known folds, on greenlined fresh paper, I could catch and confront experience uncomplicated by any past. Actually, I had to spend a good deal of my parents' money, because it turned out that roaches, a hot plate, privacy and an absentee landlord cost more, by the week, than

Confessions of Mother Goose

dressing tables, and familial warmth. It is also possible that my prose and verse, during these months, began to luxuriate all the more intricately and artificially. That I rocked myself to sleep on billowing, wavering periods and pulled the froths of language up around my ears to find sleep, I remember; I indulged myself, shameless, in recitals of ornately decorative sounds; colons and semi-colons spawned on my pages and clauses slithered, like those coiled red-eyed bracelets in reptilian shape, down the strict green lines. And if Albert, who had come by his taste for simple, real luxuries honestly—I mean, had done without by necessity and learned, then, to relax and use—if Albert found my style of life hallucinatory or comic, he did not let on. But brought me a flower and, as I said, kept the taxi waiting while we kissed.

So let us wait too with the Lake City winter taxi driver (fur earflaps pulled to meet steamy glasses, car trunk full of snow-chains) while Albert and I—he only a ghost of a shade shorter—carefully kiss. The flower—it is a rose—is between us; I don't know how to receive flowers, nor how to hold them, once received. But the tobacco tickle of Albert's mustache, his little broad hands with manicured nails—somewhere in my belly something else I have not learned to count on flips over, thuds. Why doesn't he know? And while that ancient *contretemps* repeats itself, I can ask, How Albert (whom I loved) from Jenny (whom I lost) how this other not all so different structure of muscle and bone? Covered with its own springy curls of hair—hair that weaves itself into sheets, shows up on soap and on plates in the kitchen. We breathe in and out the air tempered between the same walls; last night—a black and gold fish—his mass displaced gallons of water splashing in the tub; then snoring, he filled the doors and windows with his dream. Who is he?

Why, the Miller's son.

Lillian S. Robinson

MISS AMERICA

In Harvard Square
three nights before
my twenty-ninth birthday
I broke my first
window: a bank;
It felt good—
like laughter—or like
the most touching poem
about the Condition
of Woman.

HEROINES

Elizabeth T. Pochoda

A FTER I FINISHED COLLEGE, I sent some money back to my institution for the Rosemond Tuve Memorial Library Fund. I did that
because Rosemond Tuve had been a great scholar, a remarkable
woman, and because, quite naturally, she approved of libraries.
After that I changed my address, avoiding further alumni requests
and communication for several years. This year somebody has
turned me in. My first communique was an alumni magazine an-
nouncing that the stately women's college which had granted me
a degree for my four years of near-celibacy was giving itself over
most fully and most eagerly to coeducation. I read on noting something almost obscene in the triumphal sigh with which the old
structure lay down before the inevitability of men in its midst. I
considered what Rosemond Tuve and the other grand old ladies
(now either dead or in retirement) would have made of this gleeful capitulation, and it gave me pause. I thought also about the
nearly universal suicide of the woman's college, and on the strength
of my ambivalence toward their demise, I suggested to a friend
that we go investigate some of those places currently in the throes of
sex change. We could have a last look at the dying breed, I thought,
and take note of the emergence of the new woman from the ashes.
She turned me down, insisting that the very buildings would be
sufficient to make her throat close in remembered anguish of the
years spent there. I anticipated a similar response, but went anyway, convinced that in death, if not in life, there was something
significant to be seen.

Now among my friends, if you were hip no matter whether you
went to Sarah Lawrence, Smith, or to Connecticut College as I
did, the thing you never did was to allude to the place later, and
above all you were never so crude as to return to the scene of the
crime. The reason for this was that these places had been for most
of us the occasions for acts of violence against ourselves—acts that
were best not remembered in the cool moments of life years afterwards. To break that silence was to acknowledge a dirty past un-
worthy of our elaborately created selves. I have a friend who
exists as the center of a very productive cultural set. Does she
enjoy remembering college years when she had to eat ten jelly
donuts before she could even get out of bed, and those days when
if her boyfriend neglected to call, she lay in bed all day warming

177

her behind with a hair dryer? Memories like these are only funny when one is no longer in danger of regression, which is to say that for many women I know, remembering is a repugnant activity. By mutual agreement we have tried to rewrite these years out of our histories, and I don't think my sample of women is entirely atypical. Of course there were other types of women emerging from these institutions, too. They were the ones who for the most part could be counted upon to give money, to keep the alumni magazine informed on their changes in status, and to diet strenuously each spring before going to class reunions. For them keeping in touch is like cross pollination; it perpetuates the species and not incidentally gives sanction to the lives of the devoted. We, on the other hand, have kept our distance from the tainted spot, and I expect, receive similar satisfactions for doing so.

Thinking that there was now a new lesson to be learned from the transformation of the women's college I managed to return by expecting that my intellectual purpose would immunize me from the guilt by association which I had avoided for so long. But even so armed I arrived in New London, Connecticut, and soon forgot exactly what it was I had come to see. I redid my paralysis of age seventeen when I had first been dropped at those same gates. I had no trouble remembering that sensation, but I could for the moment remember very little else that happened to me there. I had known at the time of my first day at college that I would retain little of it in the end, that everything was supposed to get past me if I was to survive "outside" afterwards, that I was entering a place which might like to do me over or do me in, but as for me, I would never touch it or see beyond the tiny rectangle of light which was my immediate share of its offerings. Even now, I don't remember college as much as I remember being sent to college. I recall the grayness of the buildings, and when I try certain unpleasant smells present themselves. Apart from that, much of the experience has to be reconstructed from inference, from what must have been there: grass, trees and some several hundred girls who were, I think, addressed as "women" without a shade of irony.

Forgetting for the moment my immediate purpose enabled me to remember a time when it was not conceivable to me that I would ever have any purpose at all. That was college as I experienced it. Finally remembering that, I was also able to remember that the first of my many aimless perversities was to pass my time on biology field trips. I sought out field trips simply because there was some organized movement there that would take me along, and not out of any attachment to the mysteries of the larch or the swamp mushroom. Very little remains in my memory of these outings—no flora, no fauna, not even the face of the man who plodded ahead of us focusing our vision on this or that, and we, like survey researchers interested in the neatness of detail, but not in the quickness of life did his bidding as he did ours. This relationship was as close as we were to come to nature. I might have called it symbiotic then; now it seems more unevenly parasitical as though we were in training for roles to come.

Occasionally, the biology field trips troubled my sense of propriety. They were not part of my routine; they were only part of the routines of students involved in the course of study called biology who now undoubtedly recall even less of those afternoons than I. I satisfied my conscience by indulging my fancy for the novelty of the landscape and keeping myself pure from the precision and rigors of specific plant life. After the first three or four of these outings we were often joined by Susanne Langer, eminent philosopher and aesthetician. She emerged mid-walk one day, and I remember thinking she looked like a part of that dramatic New England terrain which they might have had waiting to impress milk-fed girls from Chicago like me. Back home, I thought, no one would know what to do with a face like that—upturned and gaunt like a tercelet eagle, at once naked, childlike and old. I wondered, after I had accustomed myself to her beauty, about my family, which stood in those days for the world outside, and whether they could see the possibility of beauty in something as small, as self-contained, as intense as this figure which also called itself woman. Her books, *Philosophy in a New Key, Feeling and Form,* I knew already from the carefully selected bookshelves of my more adventurous friends (all male) at the University of Chicago. But the proximity of the woman herself provoked deeper issues for me than her philosophy was liable to do, at least in the beginning. For what reasons were women sent or disposed by themselves to go to women's colleges if not to carry on their education behind closed doors? For a very few women students four years of closed doors and sexual separation paid for the freedom and peace to work seriously. But for the rest, the great majority, sexual privacy was a temporary social maneuver, a geographical convenience and above all a persistent reminder of the unreality of intellectual pursuits and all other activities which required of women that they hold onto something of their own. Loneliness and serious study were discouraging bedfellows, and they had few progeny. I also knew women's colleges for places where although one was dressed in the very best the humanist tradition had to offer, the unspoken word among women was out: these were borrowed robes, and only a fool would wear them beyond the confines of the theatre.

Given this, what was this woman doing in our pantomime like a real toad in an imaginary garden?

Thinking these questions over was to become an absorbing activity. For the trouble it cost me I fully expected such absorption to be a one-time thing. It was strange that at a time when one's life was fully given over to the idea that there was almost infinite opportunity for such concentration, something siphoned off the energies of women, miraculously distracting them with nothing at all. In my case the joys of the terrain became more problematic on the biological afternoons. I had liked the landscape at first for its unaccountability. Illinois plants, Illinois flowers, none of which I could recall, all had the heavy predictability of their terrain. But here in New England it was possible to have your feet nastily embraced by bog or marsh, or to encounter a turtle with its guts hanging out and no assailant visible. And once Mrs. Langer's passion for biology made itself felt on our walks, the tiny mutations of plants and vines assumed significance, as did their Latin and popular names, which I wished to learn but never did. Indeed, their very survival and reappearance mattered now, and that was the inessential complication in my life which I had from my first paralysis at the gates of the college decided to do without.

I was not alone in sensing that the philosopher's presence had introduced an alien and dangerous element into our muffled lives. Famous philosopher notwithstanding, she was merely "that woman" to the rest of the students. They entered into a silent conspiracy to close out her presence, never addressing her or remarking on her existence except to complain derisively to each other when she held us up with exacting questions about some seemingly insignificant plant. And that she did frequently. Would men behave in this fashion, I ask myself now? Perhaps. But would they in similar circumstances behave this way out of fear, because something was knocking at the needless limitations of their lives? I think not, no, fear would not be necessary.

I took care not to speak to her either, not then nor in the next four years of chance encounters. And she continued asking questions about any unassuming fern, inquiring about its health, its environment, its disposition, its kin, and its chances to divide and multiply in the three hundred or so acres of arboretum which were its domain. Bent over her charge she was a solitary child in the grip of an adult's passion, looking occasionally to the professor who might give her the information she required and then raising up satisfied and, yes, in a biological word, *autonomous,* conforming to her own laws only, and absorbing those of the plant just to make the connection. How was it, then, that I feared her discovery of the scorn that my companions did not trouble to disguise? How was it that I imagined scorn from hearty redfaced men who did "the world's business?" It was, I thought at the time, because she was autonomous like the plants conforming to her own laws, and that made her every bit as fragile as those organisms. That was how I imagined it because even then I suspected that the price of being alone and a woman was the nagging sense of being wrong about what you were up to. *Wrong* was not a word a philosopher would use in such circumstances, I reflected, but it was a word that would come to mind if you allowed your father his say. It was a word that had to come to the minds of all those fathers' daughters who found themselves somehow on biology field trips when they knew that the only reality that mattered if they thought about it at all, was the reality of their emotional lives which they put almost entirely at the mercy of other organisms. Laughter at the philosopher's expense was simply protective coloring.

Not to laugh, not to see this woman as a hopeless eccentric or a disembodied mind left one exposed to the dangers of the environment. Education had already provided me with the easy tools for whacking apart the values of my mid-western pragmatism. That was child's play, and it did not lead me to much else. But here on the biology field trip I had encountered something that went beyond the facile dichotomies of aesthetics versus technology, something that did not so much take on the past as go a separate way. A woman alone, a woman self-contained, a woman with an intellectual turf of her own making which she had marked off and would defend; nothing had prepared me for this.

Soon after I gave up the field trips, only remembering them when I overheard complaints that Mrs. Langer had dawdled mercilessly over worthless sticks or had insisted upon the unique value of a dead blackbird. At these times I imagined her excitement at discovering anew the house centipede or the Early Meadow Rue, or even—and more likely—a philosophical idea which seemed to grow so effortlessly from her observation of such treasures. These were disquieting imaginings in that women's college atmosphere where the dangers of such tangible involvement, such assertion of self crowded out the admonitions of Mrs. Langer and other eminent women that we had better look to ourselves and our creations. Everything pulled the other way. Our sense of the unreality of our lives was immeasurably strong. It had to be strong if we were to be able to collapse the reality of those exceptional women who threatened to destroy the sustaining fantasy of our lives. Such women reappeared in those years at women's colleges playing the role of Spenser's Britomart to our Amoret. They attempted to destroy for us the mask of Cupid (or the fallacy of romanticism to be more exact) as Britomart does in the *Faerie Queene* when she releases poor Amoret from her imprisonment in Cupid's court. Our Britomarts were, alas, less successful. We didn't accept their legitimacy as women. There was always the "out" of seeing them with the eyes of society at large—eccentric creatures, emotional or physical cripples, outcasts by necessity we thought but never by choice. What we could not see was that although they were eccentric (in the sense of not being "regulated by any central control") their eccentric natures were emblematic, a measure taken together of the heroic price which women must be prepared to pay for the pleasure of living in uncharted (truly female) territory. It was altogether too easy to say that the oddities of these women were their way of being discounted by men, of not therefore having to compete or attract. What was more likely was that they sensed themselves as different and decided to allow those differences to emerge into action and accomplishment. Eccentricity or oddity (as ordinarily defined) was only the *social* overlay.

What they had to say to us as women to women was clouded by this overlay and by the importance we gave to it. We could not see that in making our accommodation to the world (the exchange of autonomy for marriage, acceptability or whatever) *we* were the great abbreviators of experience and fulfillment; they were *not,* whatever their choices had cost them. No wonder these women often admitted a grudging preference for the male students they encountered on visiting professorships to Harvard, Princeton, or Oxford, who had nothing to risk from taking accomplished women seriously (as long as they were rare and socially out of the question). But to do their faith justice, the preference of these women for male students remained grudging; the toughness of their feminist predecessors was near at hand, and they had a commitment to the possibilities of women which the times did not reward.

If we were learning anything then, we were absorbing it from our more immediate environment. We discovered how to pass months of college in a kind of estivation, and this was, I later learned, a good preparation for life in the world outside where one would call on the resources of a summer torpor all the year round. We learned to be the most practical, efficient and farsighted of nature's creatures, making use of our environment for immediate ends while never allowing it to get too real. Biology field trips and the liberal arts were designed to make us limited users of nature and culture so that each field trip, each poetic experience would be blissfully discontinuous with the one before. This is not to say that there were no astounding bursts of enthusiasm for physiognomical studies of ancient Greeks, or for Hegel or African political structures. Such enthusiasms did emerge, were pursued with great care and were expected to and did lead down long dark tunnels with no avenues to other realms. This was the knowledge you *took in* quite literally as though you were taking it to bed. Our intellectual lives were a series of one-night stands, and there was no one who could convince us to do things differently, because I doubt whether there were many who taught there who actually knew what we were doing with those momentary passions for things outside ourselves.

For further educational advice we wisely turned to the pages of *Vogue* or *Harper's Bazaar*. One afternoon's reading of these magazines yielded a lifetime's information on survival: women should make it a habit always to sleep on their backs, I learned, since by doing so they ward off premature wrinkles and can with care postpone the date of their first facelifting to as late as forty-five in some cases. Here was a paradigm for my relationship to the environment. I pictured myself lying face up under a mask of mud, the supreme in estivation, an environmental standoff, a truce with life which might last well into middle age. Surely this hangman's mask of myself was an image large and blank enough to account for all of my future, if only I could lie still for it. Some pages later or perhaps it was a different issue of the magazine, I caught the eye of my anti-type done in that grainy dramatic Avedon style which she didn't need for the definition of her features. "What Famous Women Do to Relax" the article was called. They admitted to doing all the things you might expect famous women do to relax, except that next to Mrs. Langer's photograph there was no text save a brief reprimand to the unsuspecting interviewer: "I don't!" She hadn't been sleeping on her back all these years either, I could see that, and I reflected on the obvious rewards of not taking everything lying down. Her explanation of art as symbolization made perfect sense of the photograph: "Every art image is a purified and simplified aspect of the outer world, composed by the inner world to express its nature." Might not each face then also make "its own image of outward reality to objectivity, inward reality, subjective life, feeling," and might not this face be speaking therefore for the violence of a mind attuned to the necessity of its survival through autogenous acts (to return to the biological metaphor which anchored her work). As students it had struck us as incongruous or maybe indecorous that this woman counted among her passions and her conquests the mysteries of the art of the dance. We had things neatly divided into their appropriate domains, and dance was too feeling a thing to exist alongside modern philosophy, we thought. But then in looking at the image so boldly done on the pages of that

183

fashion magazine, I could see that she would know how to tell the dancer from the dance, how dance came to be an idea about feeling and not, as we were likely to experience it, either Pure Idea, or a symptom of immediate emotion, something to wallow in.

Now here was something to beware of—the same thing that had been implicit in her face all along. To be exact, not simply the face alone but her whole philosophy suddenly appeared to me to be an unintentional metaphor of release from the world of subjective reality which enclosed my life and the lives around me. She had stretched the interior world, long our exclusive province and prison as women, and shown it to have live and crucial extensions in the world of external reality. Like all useful metaphors her work opened itself, allowing the verifications of one's own thoughts to flow in and take shape. I recalled a passage from her earliest book, *Philosophy in a New Key*, which lifted those afternoons of plants and flowers out of their prehistory and gave them definition: "Nature, as man has always known it, he knows no more. Since he has learned to . . . suppress his emotional reactions in favor of practical ones and make use of nature instead of holding so much of it sacred, he has altered the face, if not the heart, of reality." As women we had so altered the face of reality that we had not even seen it. What was most real in the conjunction of emotion and abstraction, in the meeting of objective and subjective spheres, remained closed to us because we had learned in our pasts how to separate ourselves into consumers of nature and everything else, until nothing that we took in from this environment ever found its way out again into a common community of symbols. And not finding ourselves sacred, how could the natural environment be accorded its measure of sanctity.

But what of release from this false dichotomy between feminine-inner and masculine-outer reality which we were sold at so high a price and which lurks behind a spectrum of cultural follies from facelifting to ecological imbalance. I find something fortuitously female in the kind of philosophy which Mrs. Langer ropes off from the dry remains of logical positivism. In the very title of the summit of her work *Mind: An Essay on Human Feeling* there is again that particular enjoyment or release which her work first illuminated—the notion that all mental phenomena are modes of feeling, a signal to me that as a woman my experience was not meant to be partial, but that its enforced partiality was the penalty of sexual dialectics. What I discovered in reading the work was that all those field trips as well as the most disparate elements of art and philosophy had found their way into this statement. There was the house centipede, the *Critique of Judgement*, the Early

Heroines

Meadow Rue, Wittgenstein, a Brahms symphony. There were also things to disagree with, but nothing that could undercut the force of the work as a living thing integrating the most unlikely worlds and forcing itself with each new integration into new territory, into a new and unborrowed shape. And not incidentally the warring spheres of sensation and intellect were growing together in this garden as interdependent phases of the same process: "the wide discrepancy between reason and feeling may be unreal; it is not improbable that intellect is a high form of feeling—a specialized, intensive feeling about intuitions." We had been taught to cultivate feeling and then guard it frugally from its encroachment on other realms. But here was neither frugality, nor the extreme caution which women use to remind themselves of their confines.

Here was a woman who could have taught us that making forays into the reality outside was not a sexual trespass but the perfect complement to the cultivation of feeling which we *were* able to accept in ourselves and respect: "A highly developed mind grows up on the fine articulation of generally strong and ready feeling, both subjective—that is, autogenous—and objective, aroused by peripheral impacts." This was knowledge worth a woman's fighting for, and I know now that there is indeed a tragedy in the death of women's colleges, because that death signifies the end of those sanctuaries where exceptional women fought for their particular view of the world no matter how seemingly skewed or "idiosyncratic" and gave at least some glimpse of unborrowed life to the female students who encountered them. Surely the enlarged consciousness of women and the era of truly great women are sadly out of phase. There was a time, and I knew only the tail end of it, when women's colleges were the havens (and the only havens) for exceptionally grand women scholars and teachers. Shunted into what might seem intellectual backwaters to the academic or intellectual community at large, these women flourished intellectually and exhibited a unique femaleness which did not imitate men, nor did they take to heart the deprivations of husband and/or family life. I had known enough women like Mrs. Langer to give me the impression that when women called the tune its melody took new directions. To find that there was something distinctive about women and to find that it was something nobody had counted on was a salutory if disturbing sensation. After finishing my undergraduate education, I was aware that I had travelled through a very strange country, a country of female underworld figures who jealously held their lives apart from the threats of marital respectability, guilt, and the normal expectations about their natures and their roles. In retrospect I realized that they alone knew that being a woman was

185

an infinitely different business from what other people supposed, and knowing this makes of their lives precious examples.

Now those awesome figures (awesome because so entirely unanticipated, so resolutely bizarre) are replaced by nice-looking, bright, enthusiastic young men from Yale or Columbia whose job it is to turn on the newly liberated women. This they do, and somehow in doing it they have also managed to defuse the most unexpected and revolutionary energies which women possess. Underneath the adventures of Woodstock Nation and Spiritual Discovery, New Politics, Consciousness III and women's liberation, the lives of the young women I met seemed to be resolutely partial still, bounded on one hand by the false depths of feeling, not as a heightened form of life as Mrs. Langer would have us see it, but FEELING abused as pure introspection and a substitute for—in a biological word—environmental exchange. And at the other edge I could see only that dispassionate practicality (male-borrowed) which is so often the only disguise a woman can wear if she is to take herself seriously at all. Fathers' daughters still. But what if the full force of radical feminism and the era of singular women had meshed? What if women's colleges had become places of separation where women could take a remedial course in becoming autonomous human beings from the women who knew how? Suppose women's colleges had been allowed to continue and become the proving grounds for that very welcome assumption that what women have to contribute is different and as yet untapped? Twenty years ago Rosemond Tuve wished to teach women to use their minds as instruments "for originating, for the discovery of truth," and to allow them to say the truth about themselves as women. That was twenty years ago. Rosemond Tuve died in 1964, and now women are ready.

But we are left with this unfortunate rift in timing, this separation between a generation of women who acted on their own with concerns "peripheral" to the "major" concerns of society, and an emerging generation of women whose sense of oppression necessitates action in the center of the battlefield. What the new generation misses in being cut off from its true teachers is the knowledge that loneliness and maybe separateness are the sacrifices which must be made—that women must go beyond the simple understanding of women's oppression by men (consciousness-raising) and assume the very lonely task of defining anew (for the first time) what women *are*. Women of Miss Tuve's and Mrs. Langer's generation are not important because they were renowned. They matter because they knew that what there was for women to say and do required creating a voice of one's own and an ear tuned to a new pitch. If we remember them they can teach us to manage both.

Nancy Raine

LANA WOULD

Lana Wood has sold her poems to *Playboy*
accompanied by
full color photos of her body.
The words were written in squiggly letters
across her breasts and down her shining oiled thighs;
and the body performs the acts of the mind
and the acts of the mind are performed by nobody.

Surely the boys who ride the trains in the morning
will read the words because of where they are written.
Surely there will come the night
when their bodies will feel music.
They will look for the words on the breasts,
seeking the poetry of the womb.
There will be body, and no words,
and the boys who ride the trains in the morning
will hate us for our lies.

There is more than this.
The girls who wait in the town at the end of the line
will arise from their cots in the morning
finding new breasts upon them,
obvious and lovely.
They will sway before their mirrors,
running young hands along their bodies,
and wait for the poems to appear
along with all the rest.
There will be breasts and thighs
and oil for them, sold for 29¢ at Kresge's,
but no poems, not one, anywhere.

Sue Mullins

FEMALE LIBERATION

seventeen and dying for your name to be written with my blood.
how strange to be wrapped in such a passion;
to be in jail for you as i have been,
yet to be freed,
after proclaiming myself Jesus coming for the second time
in two hours.

how strange to toss your name into the air,
and find no magic there.
i played your tortured angel,
starring in "Virgin of the Prairie" for three years.
i have no wish to see the reruns.

I will recall you only
as an ordinary man
made of reactionary political theories.

BIRTH

The doctor
Was so surprised,
He passed away.

In the spasms of birth,
He looked up my cunt
And screamed—
              Oh my God,
                    There's nothing there
                        But a slim volume of verse!!

Marietta Tintoretta, Venetian, 1560–1590 Vienna, Kunsthistorisches Museum

ART'S LOOKING GLASS
FIFTEEN SELF PORTRAITS

Sofonisba Anguisciola, Italian, 1530–1620, formerly Vienna Kunsthistorisches Museum

arina Van Hemessen, Flemish School, XVI Century Basle-Oeffentliche Kunstsammlung

Lavinia Fontana, Italian, 1552–1614 Florence, Uffizi

Clara Peeters, Flemish, 1589–1650 Private Collection

Rosalba Carriera, Venetian, 1675–1757 Florence, Uffizi

Anna Dorothea Therbusch-Liszewska, Berlin, 1721–1782 Berlin, Kaiser-Friedrich Museum

Adelaide Labille-Guiard, French, 1749–1803 unknown

Angelica Kauffmann, Swiss, 1740–1807 Innsbruck, Museum Ferdinandeum

Rolinda Sharples, American, 1794–1838 Bristol Gallery of Art

Sarah Peale, American, 1800–1885 Peale Museum

Ann Hall, American, 1793–1863 Private Collection

Suzanne Valadon, French, 1865–1938 Private Collection

Gwen John, English, 1876–1939, formerly Coll. Augustus John

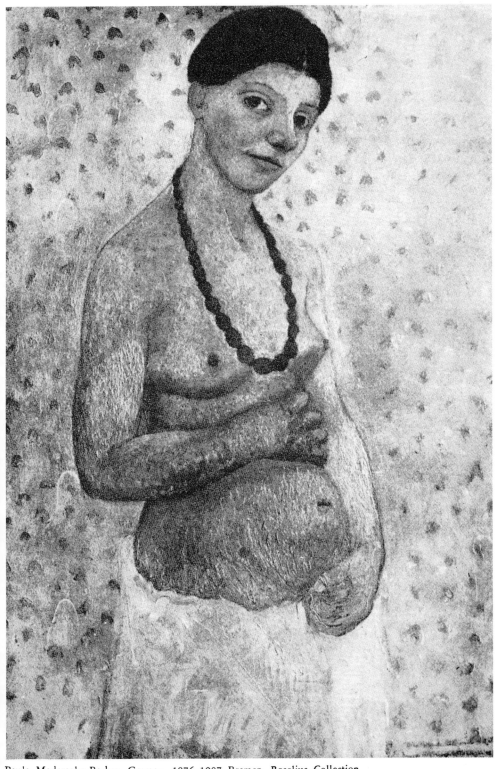

Paula Modersohn-Becker, German, 1876–1907 Bremen, Roselius Collection

It is of striking interest to note that when women were most demeaned, most pushed away from cultural and artistic pursuits, that even then, the creative spur and surge that rests in women could not be repressed. This small portfolio gives evidence of but a few of the many women refusing to play the roles that men of their times had assigned to them. They are artists of stature and power. Some are exceedingly well known, some are little known, but they are of great interest and worthy of our attention. The societal repression, that forced the father of Angelica Kauffmann to dress his ten year old daughter as a boy so that she might attend a drawing class, reaches its acme when Thomas Eakins, a hundred years later, loses his job at the Pennsylvania Academy of Art for confronting his women students with a male nude model. ❦ Denied the academy because of their sex daughters of artists found great nutriment in their parent's studios, thus, the daughters of Tintoretto, Fontana, Ruysch, DePasse, Vigee-Lebrun, Peeters, Sharples and the Peales all became exemplary artists. Charles Wilson Peale, Sarah's uncle, keenly sensible to the equality of women's minds and talents named his children not only Rembrandt, Rubens, Titian and Raphaelle but Angelica Kauffmann, Sofonisba Anguisciola, Rosalba Carriera and Sybilla Miriam [sic]. It is reputed of Van Dyke to have observed that …"he had learned more in conversation with Sofonisba Anguisciola than in the studios of the great masters."   L·U·B

A MIRROR FOR MEN:
STEREOTYPES OF WOMEN IN LITERATURE

Cynthia Griffin Wolff

INSOFAR AS IT MIRRORS the world, literature reflects the prevalent social attitude toward women; and since this attitude so often values men and masculine pursuits over women and feminine hobbies, women's concerns seem devalued. In *A Room of One's Own*, Virginia Woolf describes the situation with characteristic acuity:

> "It is obvious that the values of women differ very often from the values which have been made by the other sex; naturally, this is so. Yet it is the masculine values that prevail. Speaking crudely, football and sport are 'Important'; the worship of fashion, the buying of clothes 'trivial.' And these values are inevitably transferred from life to fiction. This is an important book, the critic assumes, because it deals with war. This is an insignificant book because it deals with the feelings of women in a drawing-room. A scene in a battlefield is more important than a scene in a shop—everywhere and much more subtly the difference of value persists."

Those of us who have studied "women in literature" are not wanting for men to explain this "realistic fallacy." As the husband of a friend pointed out with exasperated patience: "Maybe it's not fair, but that's how it is. Men *are* more important in society because they do, in fact, hold the principal roles which govern it. Wars are more important than female thoughts in a drawing-room."

This is a tidy explanation. The trouble is that it doesn't really fit the problem. If the treatment of women merely reflected their relative lack of influence in the public world, then one might expect to find that literature dealt mainly with men. Yet such is strikingly not the case. Since the Renaissance in English literature (and in many major literary epochs before that time), women have figured prominently; and at some periods, literature flows so enticingly around the feminine character that it is men who seem to be excluded. If this is so, why do we complain, why do we women still feel slighted? This further question can be answered only by examining *how* women are portrayed in literature.

In society as we know it, there are a number of specifically masculine problems that shape every man's life: "Oedipal" problems (accepting the fact of the mother's relationship to the father and turning sexual energy towards other, appropriate objects);

establishing masculine identity (this frequently involves testing one's courage, independence, or physical competence); resolving conflicts with authority, either by accepting the authority's right to govern or by freeing oneself from a guilty obligation to it; entering into an appropriate marriage; performing a series of public roles in an acceptable way (or, perhaps, choosing not to); acting as a good father (another variation on the problem of authority); and accepting the inevitable loss of power and potency that accompanies old age. A very large proportion of the works which people generally term literature are focused on one or another of these problems: one thinks of *Hamlet, King Lear, Paradise Lost, David Copperfield, Lord Jim,* all of Dostoyevsky, *Huck Finn*—one could go on almost *ad infinitum.* There are, of course, a corresponding set of essentially feminine problems: resolving the "Electra" problem; establishing feminine identity (among other things, coming to understand and accept the fluctuations of the menstrual cycle and resolving conflicts of power with the mother); entering into an appropriate marriage; acting as a mother (this entails resolving one's own desire for oral gratification, resolving fears concerning childbirth, accepting the responsibilities of rearing a child—or redefining the role so that the task of rearing will be shared by others—or even choosing *not* to undertake the task of mothering); accepting the private sphere as the appropriate one (or redefining woman's role so that an accommodation can be made between public and private); and dealing with loss of beauty and with menopause. Unlike the masculine problems, these feminine problems are very seldom the principal subject of literary interest; and when women's problems *are* discussed, the discussion is virtually always limited to problems of courtship and of accepting the private sphere as the proper one. Of course there are exceptions, especially in the twentieth century; the important thing is not, however, that there are exceptions. Rather it is that there are so few, and that this "feminine" literature balances so insignificantly against that massive body of literature which is dominated by masculine dilemmas.

How seldom a major work of literature deals primarily with a power conflict between two women (though such exist in real life for every woman); in literature when women compete, it is always for the attentions of a man. Childbirth (its rewards, its terrors) exists in literature primarily as a convenient plot device for eliminating extraneous young women. Mothering, when it is portrayed at all, is shown from the viewpoint of the child (male) who either resents it or idealizes it; the genuine happiness and difficulty of mothering don't exist in traditional literature. Menopause is portrayed as a snide joke—a rouged woman with a young lover, or a grasping harpy of a wife and mother—a figure to be scorned or pitied, but one not worthy of sustained analysis. All of these are genuine, serious problems that real women deal with daily (even within the context of their subordinate social position). Yet literature seldom if ever shows them doing so. Instead, the relationship between women and men is treated as if it were the only meaningful relationship that a woman has; thus her relationships with other women, with children, and with society in general are significantly diminished. What is more, while women are seen as subsidiary parts of essentially masculine problems, men are seldom seen as subsidiary parts of feminine problems (ironically, when men do figure in what might be termed a feminine problem, they often end up playing a dominant role—as Knightley does in *Emma*).

In general there is a whole range of feminine characterization which is delimited at the one extreme by a very narrow consideration of the "problem of women" ("problem of women" here is usually taken to mean problems of courtship and marriage) and which concludes at its other extreme in gross misrepresentation. What is more significant, all of these characterizations of women are dominated by what one might call the male voice. The definitions of women's most serious problems and the proposed solutions to these problems are really, though often covertly, tailored to meet the needs of fundamentally *masculine* problems. To a greater or lesser extent, then, this kind of feminine characterization must be termed prejudiced or stereotyped because it tends always to emphasize one aspect of character while leaving out others of equal or greater importance. To be more explicit, the bias is carefully chosen so that certain types of masculine behavior (toward women and toward the world in general) might be justified. The stereotypes of women vary, but they vary in response to different masculine needs. The flattering frequency with which women appear in literature is ultimately deluding: they appear not as they are, certainly not as they would define themselves, but as conveniences to the resolution of masculine dilemmas.

The final irony is, of course, that Nature often imitates art. When a society gives its sanction, even its praise, to stereotyped images of womanhood, the women who live in that society form their own self-images accordingly. A stereotype may become, by a sort of perversity, an image of reality that even women seek to perpetuate.

The Virtuous Woman and the Sensuous Woman

The psychological origins of these first two stereotypes—treated together here because they so often appear together in the same literary work—are reasonably clear; they have been spelled out in Freud's three essays entitled *Contributions to the Psychology of Love*. A little boy first forms ties of affectionate dependence with his mother; as he matures, he adds to these a more explicitly sexual attachment (and the accompanying realization that his beloved, "pure" mother has a sexual relationship with his father). Freud would claim that the problem of uniting these two forms of love is never completely solved in modern society. In pathological cases, they become completely separate in the adult man: he projects his own broken emotions on to the women around him, dividing them into two distinct classes. There are "good" women—for whom he feels fondness and respect; and there are "bad" women who arouse him sexually; in literature these projections of the man's feelings become the stereotypes of the virtuous woman (who reflects his inhibitory tendencies—his "super-ego") and the sensuous woman (who reflects his libidinal or "id" tendencies). The value to the man of creating these stereotypes is clear; it relieves him from the difficult task of trying to unite the two forms of love which have become distinct in his experience. These stereotypes are much reinforced by two literary traditions: the Christian tradition, with its twin figures of Mary Magdalen and Mary the Mother of Christ, and the Courtly Love tradition, which refined some of the distinctions already implicit in certain Christian attitudes.

Once we understand the origins and function of these stereotypes, some of their distinctive characteristics become clear. First, although literature dealing with them frequently appears to focus on a woman, the real focus is usually the man who is affected by the woman he describes. For example, there are a number of early Saints' lives which treat the conversion of whores who later become venerated for their purity and piety; although the ostensible subject of these lives is the female Saint, the real focus is usually the male narrator, who describes with elaborate detail the various effects (bad and good, before and after) that the subject has had on him. Similarly, Dante's *La Vita Nuova* is supposedly about Beatrice; it is really about Beatrice's effect on Dante. In Elizabethan sonnet cycles the declared subject is the lady; often our principal interest is the poet who has been inspired by her. This stereotype imputes enormous power to the woman, a power which is demonstrated by the *man's* reaction to her.

Usually the chaste woman is identified with the positive elements in a man's life; typically she inspires literary productivity or other virtuous acts such as patriotism (as in Scott's novels). The sensuous woman, on the other hand, is identified not only with sex but with other forms of non-virtuous behavior (Shakespeare's

Stereotypes of Women in Literature

Dark Lady keeps him from writing; Milton's Delilah tries to divert Samson from fulfilling his heavenly destiny). And the language which is used to depict these women reflects the moral evaluation of them. Assuredly certain physical characteristics are assigned to each: blond hair, blue eyes, fair skin to the chaste; dark hair, etc. to the sensuous. More interesting, however, is the frequency with which the modalities of praise and blame are employed to describe the "love" relationship. In the Courtly Love tradition, especially, the lover repeatedly seeks his lady's approval—she sometimes becomes an external conscience according to which he may judge himself and his life (the evolution of Petrarch's Laura throughout the course of his songs and sonnets illustrates this tendency clearly—as does Petrarch's repeated concern with problems of praise and blame). When the lady is virtuous, the lover is in a humbled position; but when the woman is sensuous, the situation is reversed. Now she (and all those unacceptable emotions she is made to represent) becomes the object of contempt and derision. Ovid, in the *Amores,* has contempt for the lady whose sexual favors he seeks; and when English poets (such as Donne) write in the Ovidian tradition, they adopt much the same air of contempt for "loose" women. The lady's social status also seems to reflect the built-in moral bias: chaste women tend to be well-born; sensuous women are low-born —or they are gypsies or foreigners.

The sensuous woman is defined as sensuous because she affects men in a certain way (she arouses them, she makes them tend toward "sinful" behavior, she intrudes into their domestic arrangements—in short, she is disruptive); and there is no place for such a character in any work of literature that is meant to conclude with social order. So sensuous women are killed off, or they move on, or they enter a convent. Now this hasty removal often has nothing intrinsically to do with the woman as an individual; it is behavior which does not grow easily and convincingly out of the demands of her character; it is merely a literary convenience too often offered as realism.

We might observe that the usual identification of the chaste woman with all that is good and the sensuous woman with all that is bad is sometimes reversed. The chaste woman (as embodiment of conscience) sometimes becomes so destructively critical that her disapproval renders the man unable to act (because he can never meet her exacting standards). In such situations—Joyce's *Portrait,* Lawrence's *Sons and Lovers*—the young man must flee his "good" but devouring "ideal woman." By the same token, the sensuous woman sometimes receives gentler treatment—most often when she appears in sub-literature, the official aesthetic status of which makes her moral position clear. (I am *not* talking about the prostitute with a heart of gold; that is in the Sentimental tradition.) Hence Cleland feels no need to condemn Fanny Hill; the genre of her *Adventures* is condemnation enough.

The Sentimental Stereotype

There is a long tradition which maintains that woman is essentially emotional; the literary form of the heroic epistle accommodates this view to some extent. Nevertheless, portraits of women in English literature are remarkably free from the taint of hysteria until the eighteenth-century cult of Sentimentalism. Since the specific aesthetic and moral origins of this stereotype are of major importance, we will begin by outlining them.

The Sentimental definition of woman was largely supported by the Moral Sentiment school of philosophy. Such men as Shaftesbury, Hutcheson, and Adam Smith claimed that every man had a natural inclination toward good; and this "natural affection," as it was called, expressed itself as an inclination toward justice and fair behavior and as a spontaneous and deep response to human suffering (Adam Smith especially emphasizes the empathic component of man's moral sentiment). In practical terms, this view of morality holds that a man engages in moral behavior *not* on the basis of a set of rationally apprehended principles, but as a sympathetic (emotional) response. One could either share the happiness of others or respond with pity to their suffering; in aesthetic practice the tendency toward shared happiness usually took the form of poetic expression, while pity was aroused by suffering depicted in the drama and the novel. Such a moral system *seems* humane enough; however, one fact emerges upon reflection. If an important aspect of man's moral behavior is a response to suffering, then someone must be victimized if a man is to engage in this form of moral behavior. The "moral" man cannot feel sympathy in a vacuum.

Under the influence of this moral system, the status of victim—and all those qualities which might lead someone to be victimized— gained public recognition and even approval. The Moral Sentiment view did not make sex distinctions (though Burke's *Essay on the Sublime and the Beautiful* gives some indication of the kind of quasi-sexual terminology that could be used to describe aesthetic relationships). In theory the sufferer could be either a man or a woman; however, in literary practice it was usually—indeed, almost always—a woman or a child. Those who are physically smaller and legally dependent were prized for their vulnerability. In characterizing women, authors employed a whole series of devices to

210

reinforce our view of them as helpless: the epithet "little" first came into vogue at this period as a sign meant to coerce affection—little Emily; little Dora; Amelia (in Fielding's novel), described repeatedly as a "little helpless lamb"—and of course, diminutive size became a sign of beauty. Weak health, the tendency to unnamed and often fatal illnesses, became an appropriate fate for fictional heroines: Richardson's Clarissa dies for absolutely no discernible physical reason, and in *Grandison,* Clementina's grief slides rapidly and inevitably into failing health. Most important, the woman was by definition incompetent; she must look to the men in her environment to resolve her dilemmas (after all, her competence would remove from them the possibility of engaging in "moral" behavior). *Vanity Fair* demonstrates this belief lucidly, though not without irony: the narrator perceives Becky with distaste not merely because she is immoral but also (perhaps principally) because she is so determinedly self-sufficient; and the passivity of Amelia, though disappointing in the end, is more emotionally satisfying to him.

Partly because of the greater value placed on women's incompetence, but even more because of the increased attention which came to be paid to their emotional life (the moral sentiment being an "affection"), the display of emotions became a supposedly reliable index to character: good women cried easily; bad women were self-contained. One could make a long list of weeping heroines in this stereotype. With this obsessive focus on emotionality, women came increasingly to be defined as *purely* emotional, without rational competence worth mentioning (Rousseau is very explicit in *Emile*).

Yet the "proper" emotional sphere for women was rigidly limited. Her proper realm was the private one, her proper emotions domestic. A woman could suffer; she could feel love (especially unrequited or betrayed love), but seldom sexual passion; she could feel sympathy for others (typically responding with kindness on a personal level), but she was portrayed as incapable of moral outrage. Most strikingly, she was never permitted to feel anger; the absence of rage in these otherwise highly emotional women is truly striking. And of course, she was never moved by public ambitions (no one who believed in the Sentimental ethic could have written *Macbeth*). As the denial of her public self and her rational capacities is completed, woman is relegated entirely to the domestic scene. Her role as wife is of passing but subsidiary importance (there is little hint of married sexuality), and her emotional energies are channeled into her relationship with her children. Thus the role of mother became idealized; and in some works, as in Dickens', one feels that a woman married only to have children.

Whereas the sensuous woman and the virtuous woman were

described in modalities of praise and blame, the Sentimental woman is described in terms of submission and suffering; and this view of woman as essentially submissive or masochistic is accompanied by an interesting shift of aesthetic intention. Aristotle declared that tragedy should inspire pity and terror. Traditionally, the central figure is a person of great parts and renown who suffers calamity; and the tragedy takes its force from the impressiveness of his struggle and the disaster of his defeat. During the Sentimental era this formula shifts very much in the direction of pity, and the central character becomes correspondingly weaker. We are meant to sympathize with his pain, not admire his struggles; and there emerges a literature not of great men and women, but of helpless victims (usually women). To give one example, in the traditional rendering of the Heloise/Abelard story, Abelard is castrated; in Rousseau's adaptation, Julie (the heroine) suffers and dies.

What male problems are projected into this stereotype? Most obviously problems having to do with the expression of sadistic impulses. The "Byronic" hero is the complement to the Sentimental heroine (and incidentally, he appears much before Byron). Frequently the heroine finds him attractive precisely *because* he is cruel (his rough treatment being a kind of perverse gesture of attention and/or affection). In other cases his cruelty is seen as regrettable, but understandable: men of strong passions *do* act sadistically and (so the implicit argument runs) women are intended by Nature to be victimized.

The Liberated Woman

The picture of "the liberated woman" which appears in 19th and 20th century literature is less stereotypical than any of the others that we shall deal with; perhaps, indeed, it is less of a distortion than it is an exaggeration of certain real problems. Yet its plausibility makes it, ultimately, all the more seductive; and perhaps more than any other stereotype, it has been accepted not only by men but by women as well.

In many ways, the picture of the liberated woman is the exact obverse of the Sentimental stereotype; this relationship is not accidental, for liberation entailed rejecting the clichés of Sentimentalism. The first great spokesman for liberation was Mary Wollstonecraft, who set out explicitly to rebut what she felt to be the outrageous claims of Rousseau. Wollstonecraft's image of woman—an image which was to become fundamental to the stereotype of the liberated woman—was drawn from the liberal political writings of the day. Thomas Paine saw man(kind) as essentially rational and

based his theory of government upon that assumption; Wollstonecraft saw women as part of mankind, and therefore claimed (against
the emotionalism advanced by Rousseau) that they, too, are essentially rational. Women are, she asserted, not fundamentally different
from men; and the "feminine" character is merely the product of
socialization. Wollstonecraft's treatise does not offer a stereotype;
however, the insistence upon women's intellectual capacities and
the complete disregard for their emotional and domestic lives which
serves Wollstonecraft's argument is used by later authors to turn
the liberated woman into a freak.

Thus the first element which we may discern in the stereotype of
the liberated woman is an insistence upon her intelligence and/or
talent. Prior to Wollstonecraft, it is difficult to find a description of
a heroine that gives any information about her intelligence; afterwards, there is a veritable flood of bluestockings. Emma is "handsome, clever, and rich," Dorothea Brooke was "usually spoken of
as being remarkably clever," Jane Eyre is formidably, destructively
bright—and the list extends right to the present. When the author
is sympathetic to women, their intelligence is problematical but not
bizarre; when he is not, her abilities (however real) are seen as
aberrations (as in *Princess Ida*, "Mighty maiden with a mission,
/ Paragon of common sense, / Running fount of erudition, / Miracle
of eloquence"). It is amusing, or even "unnatural" that women
should develop such capacities.

If the liberated woman has potential, then her problem, a problem which is repeated with endless variations, is that she desires to
find meaningful (usually public) employment of that talent. In
this endeavor, the liberated woman is almost always doomed to
failure: Emma, if she was ever truly liberated, submits to Knightley's wisdom; Dorothea and Dinah recognize the far-reaching significance of private acts; Mary Barton, one of the few working women
in 19th century fiction, longs for a husband to support her; Sue
Bridehead and Eustacia Vie are destroyed in their attempts to move
beyond the domestic world.

Sometimes woman's failure to find public fulfillment is depicted
as an adjustment (however violent) of personal aims; in other
cases, the woman's "wrong-headed" attempts at self-fulfillment are
represented as political rebellions against the system of male-dominated marriages. Sue feels she must submit herself to Phillotson as
obedient wife; in Tennyson's *Princess*, the heroine ultimately re-
nounces all talk of equality between the sexes; and in pulp literature
(see *A Woman in Spite of Herself*), the woman's "proper" submission to her husband is postulated in more dramatic and degrading

forms. During this period there grew a large body of self-proclaimed "responsible" medical opinion to the effect that women are mysteriously unreliable. They must submit (for their own good) to the restraints of male-dominated marriage; for their intelligence, however great, cannot compensate for biological inadequacy.

In addition to their sex-linked inadequacy, ambitious women were often portrayed as sexually perverse. Sue Bridehead is not a lesbian, but she is certainly frigid. Hermione and Gudrun (in Lawrence's *Women in Love*) are sexual grotesques. Even George Eliot's heroines tend to channel their sexual forces into unhealthy directions until they have recognized and accepted the essentially domestic quality of their talents. The notion that a liberated woman must be sexually aberrant is, of course, still with us; and female intellectuals are labeled promiscuous or lesbian according to the fantasies of the accuser.

Accompanying this sexual distortion is a more general distortion of the woman's domestic life. For example, so long as she is liberated, a woman is presumed to have no interest in—no feeling for—children and mothering. This stereotype seems to presume (in an ironic acceptance of the Sentimental ethic) that intellect and mothering are incompatible. One thinks of the haste with which Nora divests herself of family in *The Doll's House*. Perhaps Ibsen's psychology is correct; perhaps the ties are too binding and too close— so that freedom can only come with renunciation. Still, what is unreal is Nora's lack of conflict, regret, remorse. Once she has found her mind, all domestic affections seem to have been supplanted. Shaw's heroines have children, but there is no affection since these children become mere expressions of ambition. Even Mill, who spoke so eloquently for women, assumed that a mother, though she might wish time to develop her intellect, would have no public ambitions. The Suffragists (many of them women with children—daughters who followed in their mothers' way) were pictured in the press as sexual and emotional freaks.

It is not difficult to see the male end served by this stereotype; simply put, it is the maintaining of power. If by implication, insinuation, bullying, bravado, women can be convinced that there can be no working accommodation among their varying needs and desires, if they can be convinced of the necessity to submit, then men need not fear their competition.

The American Girl

The stereotype of the liberated woman ultimately served a political end—the conservative maintenance of a male-dominated marriage, which in turn reflected the power structure of a male-dominated society. The stereotype of the American Girl grows out of economic and moral issues: woman's function, according to this stereotype, is to magnify the men who support her; she is the visible manifestation of their success and the repository of that traditional morality which they so often suspended during the process of amassing wealth.

This stereotype is a post-Civil-War phenomenon. Very little literature focused on the American woman before 1860, although the early nineteenth century saw much feminist activity (Mt. Holyoke, the first women's college, was established in 1837), and women more than proved their usefulness at supposedly masculine tasks during the war. In 1860, then, there were a large number of women who were educated and conscious of their special role as women (often not satisfied with the prejudice against them); women became a large potential reading public and (now) an apparently appropriate subject for study in literature. A great deal of literature after 1860 is directed at woman, written about women; and in this literature we find the emerging stereotype.

The most important characteristic of the American Girl is her accomplishment: she is an "educated" woman, and her thoughts about herself take this consciously into account. A striking example can be seen in Alcott's descriptions of the March girls (all under eighteen); they speak several foreign languages, read Shakespeare, refer casually to the works of Dickens, do some Latin, play the piano, draw—all of this with ease and grace. They make Emma or even Dorothea Brooke seem clumsy by comparison. Yet, this education is deliberately designed to be unconnected with any real-life adult role (save perhaps that of teaching school). Veblen defines leisure as the "non-productive consumption of time. . . . an evidence of pecuniary ability to afford a life of idleness." No facet of American life better illustrates Veblen's theory than the girl whose father can afford to send her to school (rather than have her engage in household industry) and whose father and husband can *both* afford not to have that education put to financial use. A woman becomes, then, the ornament of prosperous society.

The irony, pathos, even tragedy of this situation did not escape perceptive writers. Alcott shows us Jo's troubles; Howells develops the theme repeatedly—most strikingly in a less-known work entitled *A Woman's Reason*; and Edith Wharton draws an impoverished Lily of the field in *House of Mirth*. Yet none of these portraits went so far as to suggest that woman should train her intelligence (as man does) for active social roles. No productive intellectual life is seen for her, and perhaps that is why she is always most captivating as a girl. If intellectual growth is denied, then the process of aging seems unnatural.

Although genuine public activity is prohibited, the American girl is given one rather nebulous task—that of bearing the torch of culture (while the menfolk are out working). The one genuine profession open to her is that of school teacher; in the East she may direct only young minds, but in the rough, masculine world of the frontier she tries to tame the anti-social spirits of grown men as well (in this connection Owen Wister's *The Virginian* is the archetypal work). Yet as teacher, she becomes someone to run from or to reform by wooing her away from her books. When she does not actually hold a position teaching, she nevertheless continues her "civilizing" work (as Twain termed it). Small boys understandably avoid her and her husband may learn to fear her bossy ways (Silas Lapham's wife was a teacher before her marriage, and when she gave up that job, she turned all her energies into making Silas socially respectable). Henry Adams makes the case even more clearly and tragically in *Esther* and *Democracy*. In both novels the heroines take the task of reformation seriously—the one in religion and the other in government. Both of his heroines refuse to capitulate to what their lovers might have termed practical realities. Because they are women, they cannot enter the drama of public life directly; and their persistent high-mindedness serves only to destroy their chances for personal happiness. Both society and the women themselves lose.

In James we find, perhaps, the most articulate statement of woman's dilemma. Many of James' heroines are women with a truly American capacity for generosity; they develop their intellects, their fortunes, their spirits to no end (save, perhaps, a Christ-like transcendence of the cares of this world). Varena Tarrant in *The Bostonians* comments most clearly on this stereotype; her gift is permitted no final public outlet, and she becomes—as the wife of Basil Ransom—the final flower of an impoverished tradition.

The woman of this stereotype is placed in an inherently contradictory position. She must develop her talents, but she must not do so with practical ends in mind; she is instilled with a sense of purpose and moral destiny, and permitted no more serious occupations than women's clubs; she is not permitted to age gracefully, yet she is scorned for clinging to youth; she is expected to bear responsibility for the transmission of culture (and morality), and avoided as a captious wife and possessive mother. Ultimately, what this stereotype offers is not so much the denial of certain female roles as a hopelessly contradictory definition of them.

Stereotypes of Women in Literature

Conclusion

We scarcely have space here to discuss the implications of these stereotypes; however, we can make a few tentative comments. One very common response to the observation that women are characterized stereotypically is an indignant assertion that after all, men, too, are confronted with literary stereotypes. Of course. To claim that for the most part feminine characterization is distorted is to make no claim at all about the characterization of men; and surely anyone who has studied literature would have to be a dunce not to notice that there are masculine stereotypes. We have mentioned one, the Byronic hero; another is the Warrior or the Soldier, and there are others.

The really interesting question is whether these masculine stereotypes are analogous to the stereotypes of women. In several significant ways they are not. Whereas the characterization of women is distorted to meet masculine needs and the feminine stereotype becomes a useful justification for male behavior of one sort or another, the stereotypes of men do not always serve this function for women. The Byronic stereotype is problematical; probably it fuels both masculine and feminine fantasies. However, the image of the Warrior has very little at all to do with women; and except in classical epics, the poem, play, or novel which includes this stereotype very often has no significant female figures at all. Thus men may appear stereotypically in literature, but when they do, the stereotype is usually a fantasied solution to an essentially masculine problem. The supremacy of the male voice remains unchallenged. Moreover, there is a genuinely significant body of literature which recognizes the limitations of some of these masculine stereotypes and which attempts to reveal their inadequacy as standards for defining character or guiding behavior: one finds Tennyson's "Ulysses," *Lord Jim*, or *The Red Badge of Courage*. There is no comparable body of antistereotype literature about women, unless one wishes to view the image of the liberated woman as an answer to Sentimentalism (and as we have seen, that course has its pitfalls).

Indeed, the persistent acceptance of the stereotypes of women is remarkable. Even women writers (to our embarrassment) seem to adopt them. Austen, who never married, condemns Emma for her resolution to remain single; and having chastised her heroine, promptly corrects Emma's "masculine" need to manage things by having her submit to the wisdom of Knightley. George Eliot, who lived openly with a married man, does not permit Dorothea Brooke the same independence. How often in literature, especially before 1900, is a woman's view of herself, of her own rights, of her needs,

217

described entirely by the convenience of the male-authored stereotypes of women.

One might take an amused, almost archeological view of the literary remains of these stereotypes if they were only remains. The trouble is, they are still taken seriously. A modern novel (enormously popular) in the Sentimental tradition begins: "What can you say about a twenty-five-year-old girl who died?" The motion picture captures the image of the liberated woman (played by Barbara Stanwyck, Rosalind Russell, or more recently, Doris Day), successful women executives who wear mannish suits, who are tough, and who, if they are lucky, are saved by the intervention of a strong man who puts things to right. Television is the appropriate medium for the display of the American Girl, that beauty-contest winner who must have not only the proper measurements but also demonstrable (though unusable) schooling and a "talent" for amusing. A girl whose loftiest function is, apparently, that of endorsing products.

How many girls have made their lives miserable by trying to mold themselves to one or another of these caricatures of human nature? How many have thought that they might be virtuous or sexual but not both? How many have been counselled into emotionalism (and scorned for their lack of intellect)? How many have feigned stupidity lest they frighten suitors by their unfeminine intelligence? How many have been forced to obtain an education which they were absolutely prohibited from using?

Confronted with these mutilated and demeaning images of feminine character, it is all too easy for women to dismiss them as totally lacking in truth. Such an attitude is not profitable. Insufficient as they are for describing a woman's experience, these images do grow out of genuine male experience. Thus for example, if a man is psychologically incapable of uniting his affectionate and libidinal impulses, he will inevitably perceive his relationships with women in terms of the first two stereotypes we have considered. Now his view of women as either virtuous or sensuous may tell us very little about women; but it reveals a great deal about *him.* And the same may be said of all these stereotypes. The ultimate truth of these images of women does not rest in their ability to capture feminine experience or women's life-problems; it inheres, ironically, in their capacity for revealing masculine dilemmas and postulating fantasied solutions to them. These are women—not as they are, but as *men wished they were.* Better than rejecting these stereotypes, women might say to men: "Look, and learn about yourselves."

Margaret Shook

COMPLAINT

for Ken Kesey, Philip Roth, Leslie Fiedler,
and all the boys at the old Bar X.

The woman who invented the computer and the hydrogen bomb
Was spotted not long ago in California.
   She was seen
Drinking a carrot-juice cocktail
At the vegetable bar
Of the Dieter's Club
   In L.A.

Before that she was nearly captured in Oregon.
She had assumed the disguise
Of a nurse-attendant
   In an asylum.
Thanks to the perspicacity of one of the patients,
Who recognized the thin, cruel lips beneath the
     painted smile,
She was exposed. There were several witnesses
   To her escape.

More recently she has been seen
In her old haunts
   In the Bronx.

I wish to join my humble voice to the chorus of voices
Denouncing this woman.
It is to no avail
To write to one's senator
Or call upon the responsible authorities
To relieve the nation of this menace.
They are all in her employ.
Everywhere, everywhere, her tentacles spread.
Behind the scenes, working through her agents—

Members of the Peace Corps, the F.B.I.,
The League of Women Voters, the C.I.A.,
University Administrators, the Pentagon,
The Poverty Program, the A.M.A.—

She controls the establishment.
She is the architect of the welfare state.

As for the murder of her first husband, it is now
    certain,
That she cut off his balls,
And with the aid of silicone, one of her earlier
    inventions,
Transformed these into two giant and pendulous
Breasts of her own, from which she refused
To give her son milk.

Her second husband was slain most foully.
Him she strangled on a bowl
    Of hot chicken soup,
Having first tied him down
At the head of the table.
She tortured her little son,
The helpless offspring of this marriage,
With unremitting and insatiable cruelty.
    She used to rub
Schmalz on his member, and set it afire
(He has told all in his recent Memoirs)
And on several separate occasions attempted
    to tickle him to death
With a chicken feather.

There is perhaps no need to recapitulate the histories
Of all her outrageous and detestable murders.
The details have been widely circulated,
Even if the more sensational
Were of course not reported
In the popular press,
Which she controls.

In upstate New York many years ago,
In Salem (Mass.) and New Bedford,
Afterwards in Missouri, in Michigan, in Ohio,
In Iowa (the Midwest is now altogether hers),
She appeared, and always,
There were witnesses to her crimes
As she moved (mainly) westward,
Establishing her syndicate,
Until now the network covers everything,
Except perhaps the Ponderosa, and
A little piece of grass in Marlboro Country,
    and part of Greenwich Village.

I wish to join my humble voice to the chorus of voices
Denouncing this woman.
Her statue stands at the entrance to New York Harbor.
It is a national disgrace.
Speak out in the name of our sacred and immemorial
    freedom.
There is scarcely to be found in the whole land
One genuine whore with a heart of gold,
One Indian maiden,
Ductile and submissive,
With sloe eyes, legs like an antelope,
And small, small, small
    Breasts.

Audre Lorde

BLACK MOTHER WOMAN

I cannot recall you gentle.
Through your heavy love
I have become
an image of your once delicate flesh
split with deceitful longings.
When strangers come and compliment me
your aged spirit takes a bow
jingling with pride
but once you hid that secret
in the center of furys
hanging me
with deep breasts and wiry hair
with your own split flesh and long suffering eyes
buried in myths of no worth.

But I have peeled away your anger
down to its core of love
and look mother
I am
a dark temple where your true spirit rises
beautiful and tough as a chestnut
stanchion against your nightmares of weakness
and if my eyes conceal
squadrons of conflicting rebellions
I learned from you
to define myself
through your denials.

WOMEN, ENERGY, AND *MIDDLEMARCH*

Lee R. Edwards

Middlemarch is a novel about imaginative energy—the mental power to envision a self and a society as yet unformed in the given world—as this force is related to will and to society. A record of the general inability of will to call up energy sufficient not just to envision but to create new social forms, it is particularly interesting in its examination of the nature and fate of energy in female characters. Contrary to her heroines, Mary Ann Evans in her own life found both energy and will sufficient to enable her to abandon her provincial home in favor of London, break with family and religion, live openly for years with a man not her husband, and, most important, transform herself into George Eliot in whose name she wrote her books, earned her living and survived the world's real or imagined hostilities. Although we do not know what psychic stress, what sense of excessive payment rendered, caused George Eliot to reject this biographical pattern to construct instead a fictional universe where nerve and personality give way before the forces of social and natural conservatism, the defensive posture of her statement, "I should wish it to be understood that I should never invite anyone to come and see me who did not ask for the invitation," perhaps gives hints.

Despite its final failures, however, energy in *Middlemarch* initially resides in many characters: in Lydgate, Fred Vincy, Rosamond, even Casaubon, and above all, in Dorothea Brooke. Indeed, it is the force of this last character's imagination, her questing nature and desire to be both wise and useful, that illuminates the book. This illumination, arising from the rare portrayal of energy and intellectual force conjoined in an admirable female character causes *Middlemarch* to be a kind of talisman for many young women. Recognizing George Eliot as a greater writer than Louisa May Alcott, we transfer our allegiance from Jo March to Dorothea. That George Eliot's view is both more complex and more ambivalent than I had first believed is what I hope to show.

But, like Portnoy, before I can begin analysis, I find it necessary to talk at some length about myself because I find myself writing, for the first time, as a woman critic, and I am not sure of the implications of the combined form, of the effect the feminine adjective has when used to modify the critical noun. In *A Room of One's Own*, Virginia Woolf discusses the relation between women and fiction, a relationship still unharmonious because the world

223

has not seen fit to provide us with rooms of our own, much less
£500 a year and access to power's inner sanctums. But no one has
yet defined the connection between women and criticism. And if
I dare compare great things with small, I would like to examine
here not the space Virginia Woolf explored—the open ocean writers
need to write in—but merely the small pool that critics need for
their creations.

Only by using myself as a case history and assuming the case is
not unique but typical, can I trace the peculiar relationship of
George Eliot's work not just to me, but to women in general. By
so doing, I hope to show why *Middlemarch* has been a sacred text
for so many of us, why women have infinitely fewer of these texts
than men do, why I felt both angry and sad when I discovered that
what I had seen as revolution was in fact reaction. I want, then,
to talk not only, and not first, about women and energy in *Middlemarch,* but about women and energy in life, since life affects the
critical concepts which any of us—women and men alike—are prepared to focus on literature or even on a specific work.

In Woolfian terms, the woman critic is a small fish, perhaps, yet
still she swims among the coral groves. The minnow may prove
interesting if only we can catch her. And since critics, like others of
God's creatures, are born children, you will perhaps not mourn if
our initial cast nets an undergraduate. Look to the young form and
you will see, perhaps more easily because more crudely apparent,
the scales and barbs that age has smoothed or at least taught the
survivors to disguise. As an undergraduate, then, I sat through a
semester of introductory philosophy eagerly awaiting that section
of the course which was supposed to deal with what was called the
mind/body problem. This topic appeared on the syllabus in the
week between the idea of God in the western world and the problem of ethical judgment, and attracted me primarily because I was
sure it was going to be about sex. My philosophical inadequacies
were clearly shown when the subject yielded first a bishop ponder-
ing the material world and then Dr. Johnson kicking a stone and
exclaiming "Thus, I refute Berkeley!," an interesting statement, to
be sure, but hardly what I had in mind.

The history of philosophy to the contrary notwithstanding, it
seems to me now that my earlier notion is, for the critic, largely
correct, as criticism still concerns itself with denying that minds
exist in bodies which are, for the most part, either one sex or another. Negating sex, criticism instead seeks to order its words in
such a way that they will be taken for the products of a disembodied
intellect whose reality, like Berkeley's, presumably derives from an
existence in the mind of God. True, we have learned to distrust

Women, Energy, and Middlemarch

the vulgarized Arnoldian stance which asserts that the best critics and the best books are joined together in some timeless realm, locked in a dance whose movements are unaffected by wind and weather no less than by the more ponderous rhythms of politics, history, or culture. If the Happy Isle does not exist, then let there be Marxists, Freudians, and structuralists; let there be meat eaters or vegetarians, for all we care. But, for politeness's sake, and so we may retain the comforting memory of Arnold's great, good place, let us always write as though we assumed we were objective.

Like Zen riddlers who ask about the sound of one hand clapping, critics covertly pose their own conundrum concerning the body which writes the words of a disembodied mind: whatever its other qualities it is implicitly masculine. Clothed in men's garments, the mind can still distill its ether pure. Choosing examples more or less randomly, we note for instance, that Wallace Stevens conjures with the figure of youth as a virile poet and that Geoffrey Hartman describes Northrup Frye with "Copernicus's image of the 'virile man standing in the sun . . . overlooking the planets'."[1] Neither Stevens nor Hartman, I suppose, is deliberately—or probably even consciously—orienting all of poetry or criticism in terms of a male image. They are merely doing what is natural for men—whether poets, critics, or plumbers—creating a universe out of the reality of their own bodies. That body, however, has become everyone's; man equals person.

And if the critic's nature is otherwise, if it is, for example, not even possibly virile, let it assume men's garments and adopt the masculine stance. If it can and does, critic will still be stamped on its hand; it will gain leave to join the dance. But, let it refuse and make an unseemly show of its difference from the presumed ideal and the critics unite like the confederate ladies who froze Scarlett O'Hara out of the ball. Not a critic, they cry, but a partisan, a biased polemecist, a distorter of truth. Let it write, let it dance, if it must, but let it do so someplace else.

And to prevent this embarrassment from arising too often, let us train each new generation to read as though each and all of it were male. Simplify the task because—again, not through conspiracy, but through social and cultural fact—the literature which survives is largely that written by countless generations of men. Win imaginative assent to these books and their abstract patterns and you have created in the assenting reader a piece of the mind that made them.

---

[1] *Beyond Formalism: Literary Essays 1958–1970,* New Haven and London, 1970, p. 24.

Thus, like most women, I have gone through my entire education —as both student and teacher—as a schizophrenic, and I do not use this term lightly, for madness is the bizarre but logical conclusion of our education. Imagining myself male, I attempted to create myself male. Although I knew the case was otherwise, it seemed I could do nothing to make this other critically real.

Turning again to the undergraduate wriggling in the meshes of this net, to my past self that is, I remember that, for the most part I read books about men, even when they weren't by or specifically for them. This reading shaped my thoughts in ways known to all women who have shared this experience, just as it is known to all Blacks whose intellects and imaginations were formed and deformed by texts created by and for a white majority who were assumed to be not merely more numerous but also morally, socially, culturally, and even physically normative.

The first result of my reading was a feeling that male characters were at the very least more interesting than women to the authors who invented them. Thus if, reading their books as it seemed their authors intended, I naively identified with a character, I repeatedly chose men; I would rather have been Hamlet than Ophelia, Tom Jones instead of Sophia Western, and, perhaps despite Dostoevsky's intentions, Raskolnikov not Sonia.

More peculiar perhaps, but sadly unsurprising, were the assessments I accepted about fictional women. For example, I quickly learned that power was unfeminine and that powerful women were, quite literally, monstrous. Although, or perhaps because, their power had a strange attraction, women of this sort appeared in fiction as threats not just to men but to all of society. If you think of Clytemnestra or Lady Macbeth, or even of the more ambiguous and ultimately less powerful Kate Croy, Becky Sharp, or Emma Woodhouse, and do not think, as I did not, that society is simply a polite term for the organization and expression of masculine norms, your conclusions, like mine, and like those of the authors who created them, assume the force of an inevitable theorem. Bitches all, they must be eliminated, reformed, or, at the very least condemned. Those rare women who are shown in fiction as both powerful and, in some sense, admirable are such because their power is always based, if not on beauty, then at least on sexuality. Think of Cleopatra, the Wife of Bath, Molly Bloom, or even, perhaps, Moll Flanders. Their personal force is not seen as it might be —and as it frequently is in the case of men—as simply the natural product of energy and ambition, but is instead an end in itself, and men who succumb to it lose everything, including, frequently, their masculinity. Thus, the approval given to these women is finally

226

Women, Energy, and Middlemarch

equivocal. Since the sexuality of women is always presumed to be uncontainable—if it exists at all—it is therefore perpetually intertwined with the downfall of men. Adam had Eve, but in getting her lost Eden. Antony had Cleopatra and the world may indeed have been well lost; but lost to him, it still remained to Caesar and perhaps the cold Octavia. By implication feminine power, always seen finally as sexual power, is inevitably a trap, the more vicious for being baited not just with sweetness but with the necessity of life itself. To avenge this treachery and continue civilization, it is imaginatively necessary to render women permanently subordinate. Such subordination results in imagining good women to be those who are only weakly sexual. Like society, however, civilization is a term whose exclusively masculine necessities must be ignored for the logic of the proposition to survive.

The stature of a woman character, rare even in contemporary fiction, who is endowed with energy which is not primarily sexual and who, not wishing to hurt others nonetheless aspires to live and, more importantly, to work in that world which is normally called "man's" is diminished even as she is created. She is made, and thus seen, as either amusing, because indelicate or naive, or alternatively, pitiable and finally contemptible because of her confused assumptions about her own nature and that of the world. Think of Isabel Archer in the first part of *Portrait of a Lady* and of Henrietta Stackpole throughout the book; think of Hermione or even the more complexly rendered Gudrun in *Women in Love;* think of Anna and Molly, the "free women" of Doris Lessing's *Golden Notebook.* Indeed, I think now, though I did not ten years ago, of the lesson Dorothea Brooke Casaubon learns.

Literature is an admirable pedagogue, teaching by continual repetition, shaping our perspectives by creating the mold into which our imaginations flow. Insofar as I have been aware of the personal implications of these lessons, I have resented them. Until quite recently, however—and by the tracing of what psychic labyrinth and at what cost I still don't know or can not bear to discover—I attempted to remain untouched, aloof. I said simply, and for the most part silently that, since neither those women nor any women whose acquaintances I had made in fiction had much to do with the life I led or wanted to lead, I was not female. Alien from the women I saw most frequently imagined, I mentally arranged them in rows labelled respectively insipid heroines, sexy survivors, and demonic destroyers. As organizer I stood somewhere else, alone perhaps, but hopefully above them.

The few exceptions to these categories, women like Sophocles's Antigone, Richardson's Clarissa, Ibsen's Nora, or even the more

227

contemporary Martha Quest or the personae of Sylvia Plath's *Ariel* poems or her novel *The Bell Jar*, led tragic or at least uncertain lives not simply because they were human but specifically because they were female. The contradiction between their inner selves and society's expectations for them as women, took them out of the known world, if not to death then to madness or to the more dreary purgatory of neuroticism.

I waited—and wait still—for the imaginative work which charts this world anew and treats, for example, Nora's survival—not madness, destruction, or death—outside the doll's house. These works depend, I suppose, on a social revolution which would produce women writers who have lived this life, or writers of either sex who have observed it, and found it joyful, by which I mean not trivially carefree but useful, productive, nourishing and only different from, but not worse than, any other sort of life. Alternatively, they depend on the birth of mythmakers whose creative imaginations are powerful enough to forge their tales out of the void which the observed world continues to pose. Such fictional records as we now have of the lives of women who defied society's conventions—and I might add Olive Schreiner's *Story of an African Farm* and Agnes Smedley's autobiographical fiction *Daughter of Earth* to the list of those already mentioned—record for the most part lonely and, perhaps for this reason, sterile struggles, labor without birth. They might, I fear, be read as indications that woman outside her traditional role is doomed to misery and madness. Perhaps, instead, this madness is a necessary interlude. These writers state the case in its present form and show, biographically as well as artistically, the frantic strugglings of sensibilities which, recognizing the insufficiency of the existing patterns, are nonetheless unable to create new shapes for life by forging them in fiction. As mediating forms and truthful portraits, these books and their tragic predecessors are vital.

But existence has necessities beyond the tragic and certainly beyond the mad. If people are to continue to live on earth, they need comedies to show them life is possible. Although there are comic forms with male protagonists which end with the hero unmarried but adult, comedies traditionally end in weddings. For women, this formal ending has been inevitable and concludes life as well. Compare the fiery, young, unmarried Natasha with the stout, dull wife she becomes and you will see what I mean. Men can marry, as did Pierre, and can go on being what they were or even continue to evolve. But married women in literature turn into wives, and unless they are bad ones in need of correction, their lives are largely unrecorded. Like Mrs. Gulliver, they are props, unfilled sails waiting for their husbands to return and fill them; in all other respects, they are fictively dead.

As a young woman observing this situation, I liked the comic heroine because she was both female and, at least momentarily, alive. I approved of her; I would be her, but always with a condition, a hook catching me back before the end. I could be Shakespeare's Kate or Jane Austen's Emma, but unkissed, unmarried, and hence untamed. Or better, Isabel Archer, initially comedic, setting out to discover myself and the world, blessed by my wit and the sense of my own uniqueness, but somehow miraculously exempt from the divine amusement of God or Henry James. Or best of all, I could be Rosalind, always resourceful, always disguised, ranging freely in the Forest of Arden. But unless I could find a way either to live perpetually in the first three acts or to transform .the world to Arden's image, I could not be these characters forever. If I stayed too long, I would have to cast off my wit and with it my power to form views of my own, put on my skirts, and marry. If I were lucky, I might find Mr. Knightley, the good uncle disguised as lover; if I went on too long following my headlong course, Gilbert Osmond would be my fate. And, if I refused to submit to marriage at all, comedy's rigid necessities would move me out of the ingenue's role and into that of the old maid aunt, no longer the serious subject of my own consciousness but instead the object of others' amusement.

While I mused on the possibilities of some new fourth act, my peers and my professors, no more interested than I in the insipid heroines, apostrophized Molly Bloom, the Wife of Bath, or Cleopatra as the epitome of eternal femininity. But if Molly Bloom was woman, what was I? A mutant or a dinosaur. If one was a female but wanted nonetheless a world bigger than even king-sized sheets, where did one go? Nowhere. One disappeared from the fictions and emerged, if at all, only as a hag. If one left the fictions and went to the world, one saw that the road out of comedy led to the apocalypse. In the fifth act one wound up in an asylum burned alive like Zelda Sayre, in a river with a pocketful of stones like Virginia Woolf, with your head in an oven like Sylvia Plath, in a room of one's own in your father's house, wearing white like Emily Dickinson.

Fiction, then, provides us with neither forms for an equal life shared between men and women nor even a set of moral assumptions wide enough to embrace both sexes. True, Cleopatra's essence defied the capacity of mind to conceive or tongue to express, but she was treacherous as well. To see her treachery as the highest expression of the feminine seemed to me a moral betrayal whose magnitude was as great as her beauty. Here, when young, I spoke out loud, though awkwardly I'm sure, for the critics were no help and I was not certain why it was important for me to establish Cleopatra's evil as an ethical absolute rather than the natural—and possibly wonderful—product of her sex. In denouncing Cleopatra I was willing the necessity of some single standard in whose terms all people could be judged as replacement for the traditional sexually divided and unequal codes. The experience of the class in which I voiced my discontent still haunts my nightmares. Until my face froze and my brain congealed, I was called prude and, worse yet, insensitive, since I willfully misread the play in the interest of proving a point false both to the work and in itself. Cleopatra was not immoral but wonderful because her sexuality put her beyond morality. But the world has no room for such passion. Passion destroys men, not women—Cleopatra's death immortalizes her—by distracting their attention from its proper objects. Antony should have known better. But Cleopatra? How could she? She was female.

In this context, then, it is not hard to see why *Middlemarch* became one of the "books of my life," to use the phrase Hugh Walpole used in describing his reaction to Virginia Woolf's *Jacob's Room*. I seized upon George Eliot's novel, and more particularly on the portrait of Dorothea, as indices that my imaginative life was not as lonely and unformulated as I had feared. Like Dorothea, I was a cygnet among ducklings, passionately looking for the great river whose current would carry me to others of my kind. Like her, I had great, half-formed aspirations. Like her, I felt harrassed by pressures to marry some nice young man and abandon my private and no doubt weird ideas. In Rosamond, too, I thought I had found a heroine worthy of my hate, one who was condemned not for her sexuality, but for her weakness, vanity and evil, ethical categories which, in the book at least, superseded sexual definitions. I ignored Mary Garth, mentally sending her to stand at the end of the line of insipid, goody-goody heroines. And, while I noted Dorothea's second marriage, I failed to consider its implications, sanctified as it is by children and by Dorothea's reconciliation with her sister and with a world where the continuity of life is represented by the safe inheritance of entailed estates passing through the male line. I found my new fifth act, or so I thought, because I saw in Dorothea an endorsement I had found in no other book I had read of energy and social commitment on the part of a woman in combination, as I believed, with the promise that these qualities did not render the possessor either a social misfit or a danger to herself or others. In the interests of finding what I badly needed to find in some imaginative work, I had reduced the novel to a comic homily on the possibility of combining marriage with intellectual aspiration.

Women, Energy, and Middlemarch

I also misread the book. For, while *Middlemarch* is undoubtedly a work which devotes many pages to Dorothea, she is by no means the whole novel. And while energy illuminates the work, its light seems now neither so clear nor so powerful as I once thought, or hoped, it was. For *Middlemarch* is finally not an endorsement of this energy, but first an examination and finally a condemnation of it.

In this condemnation, however, George Eliot is by no means unambivalent, as we can see if we look briefly at the structure of the book. In these terms, *Middlemarch* is peculiarly divided. Both tragic and comic, it divorces its emotional centers—Dorothea and Lydgate and their foils Casaubon and Rosamond—from its ethical pivot. It is the Garths and the other permanent residents of the town who, guaranteeing the enduring life of Middlemarch itself, also provide the moral norms of the book. In this connection it is, I think, significant to note that the action of the book, excluding the Finale, stops before the Reform Bill becomes fact, and the characters who threaten Middlemarch's values are changed (Dorothea), defeated (Lydgate), killed (Casaubon), condemned (Rosamond), or sent away, perhaps into a wider world, or merely into exile.

George Eliot sacrifices energy and personality to place and to the conservative necessities which that place dictates. But her ambivalence toward this sacrifice can be seen and felt if we notice that the book's structural anomalies are reinforced by the treatment character receives as well. The weight of the book's tragic structure is carried by a quartet of characters whose complexity George Eliot both apprehends and renders and whose stories compose the bulk of the book. The book's comic structure, on the other hand, is carried by characters who are frequently little more than caricatures, fragments of identity left over from a Jane Austen or a Dickens novel. With the exception of Mary Garth and Fred Vincy and, if one is being generous, Sir James and Celia, these characters have no stories but only scenes which take up the space between the major narratives.

It is, of course, possible that what I have defined as structural ambivalence was in fact accounted for by George Eliot when she called the book not after one of her major figures but instead *Middlemarch: A Study of Provincial Life.* In other words, the book is neither tragic nor comic but simply realistic, and what in tragic terms is annihilation is for the author, and hence for the reader who would read the book correctly, merely a realistic assessment of the best that can be done in the world, both fictional and real. Even if this position is taken, however, the particular sense of reality which the novel as a whole engenders derives from a tension—implicit and covert, it is true, but nonetheless there—between truncated tragic and attenuated comic modes.

These modes are linked by the character of Dorothea who, it seems, participates in both and is, for this reason, as well as others more commonly noted, the center of the book. But the linkage is incomplete because for Dorothea to become a comic rather than a tragic heroine she must be transformed from one whose energy is so great as to constitute a threat to her society to one whose power can be contained by it. She is, in a very real sense, not the same character at the book's end that she was at its beginning. Although she leaves Middlemarch she still has a home there and, in claiming it, is herself diminished.

The image of Dorothea presented at the book's beginning is, to borrow a phrase from Simone de Beauvoir, apparently transcendent. To turn to her from Celia, Mary Garth, and Mrs. Garth is to turn from characters and women who are themselves both innately conservative and a cause of conservatism in others, who either have no energies—like Celia—or who ruthlessly suppress them—like Mrs. Garth—who function through stasis to inspire others to return to the fold, to one for whom radical upheaval, both personal and social, seems, at least initially, possible. With her ardent nature, her intelligence, her desire not simply to be good but to discover what might be good in order to use the fruits of this discovery to change the world, Dorothea seems to be a woman whose like had not been fictively recorded in 1871 and whose imaginary history still does not exist. Even today, women readers in particular, feel in the book's opening chapters the promise of a new spiritual incarnation, possibly even an entirely new creation. We wait, almost desperately, for the author's imagination to divine a world whose shadowy existence we have long suspected, but whose reality has been perpetually denied.

But, however much we may wish it otherwise, *Middlemarch* gives very little evidence that George Eliot wished to be the god in some new machine. From Prelude to Finale, and for 86 chapters in between, she tells us instead that in the early part of the nineteenth century in England, a woman whose "passionate ideal nature demanded an epic life" (3),[2] whose inner "flame . . . soared after some illimitable satisfaction, some object which would never justify weariness, which would reconcile self-despair with the rapturous consciousness of life beyond self" (3) would be defeated or, at best, deflected. George Eliot is writing not the ultimate comedy of some new incarnation, but rather the record of its failure. Seeing a world which lacked "coherent social faith and order"

---

[2] All references to *Middlemarch* are taken from the Riverside Edition edited with an introduction and notes by Gordon S. Haight, Boston, 1956.

Women, Energy, and Middlemarch

(3), George Eliot either would or could not choose to create an alternative universe in her fiction. Instead, she records the dislocation which is "offspring of a certain spiritual grandeur ill-matched with the meanness of opportunity," (3), the isolation of the cygnet who "never finds the living stream in fellowship with its own oary-footed kind." (4).

This failure could be tragic, however, and Dorothea a tragic character, if and only if her aspirations at the book's beginnings were taken entirely seriously by the author. And they are not. Nor are Dorothea's longings as unfettered by traditional assumptions about the kinds of fulfillment open to women as a cursory reading might seem to indicate. Throughout the book, George Eliot both pities and gently mocks Dorothea. This attitude of sorrowful amusement is not merely consequent upon her marrying Casaubon, but in fact precedes the marriage and exists precisely because Dorothea is the sort of woman who would marry Casaubon in the first place. Dorothea is short-sighted, a physical defect which in this book, as in many, has its psychic implications. Moreover, George Eliot or her narrative surrogate in the book continually addresses and identifies the elder Miss Brooke as "poor Dorothea" and ranges herself regretfully but unequivocally with Celia in her assessment of Dorothea's character. In Chapter 7, for example, it asserts that "Miss Brooke was certainly very naive with all her alleged cleverness. Celia, whose mind had never been thought too powerful, saw the emptiness of other people's pretensions much more readily." (47). This statement, however, is less simple than it seems. Apparently, the pretensions referred to belong to Casaubon, but it is equally possible that they may secondarily refer to Dorothea as well. For, the immediately preceding sentence states that Dorothea "had not reached that point of renunciation at which she would have been satisfied with having a wise husband: she wished, poor child, to be wise herself." (47). In other words, it is at least possible that it is not only Casaubon's knowledge which is empty pretense, but also Dorothea's desire for knowledge of her own.

If the possibility that Dorothea's quest for knowledge was, at best, misguided were raised only here, the passage would hardly be worth noting. But it is not. Indeed, George Eliot repeatedly insists on the futility and even foolishness of any desire to find an outlet for energy in the acquisition of wisdom defined narrowly as education and dissociates Dorothea from Casaubon by saying that "it would be a great mistake to suppose that Dorothea would have cared about any share in Casaubon's learning as mere accomplishment." (63). On the contrary, she seems to be saying that Dorothea's desire for knowledge is a confused expression of her true longing for a combined moral and intellectual guidance, an analogue in the nineteenth-century world and in her own life to the force which the Catholic faith provided for Saint Theresa. Unable to find her "ideal of life" in the "walled-in maze" which constitutes the usual occupations open to a woman of the leisured class, Dorothea sees knowledge as offering the only way out of the labyrinth. But the radical implications of this vision are tempered since both Dorothea and her creator see this knowledge in terms of a "union which . . . would . . . give her the freedom of voluntary submission to a guide who would take her along the grandest path." (21). This union is not a transcendent linking of the mind with abstract principles systematically combining wisdom and morality, but is instead mediated by physical reality and institutionalized.

Desiring to lead "a grand life here—now—in England" (21), neither Dorothea nor George Eliot can see a way to realize this desire directly. "Since the time was gone by for guiding visions and spiritual directors, since prayer heightened yearning but not instruction" (64), and more interestingly, since George Eliot does not even consider the possibility of educational reform as a way out of Dorothea's dilemma, marriage becomes the educating institution. In marrying Casaubon, Dorothea is mistaken merely about the contents of this knowledge, but not about the form through which such knowledge should come to her.

When Dorothea says that "people may really have in them some vocation which is not quite plain to themselves," (60), she is speaking to Casaubon about Will. We, however, may hear her words as unwittingly self-referential and, more significantly, as revealing as well George Eliot's own bafflement with certain aspects of Dorothea's character. For, at the book's beginning, Dorothea is like Will, a character in search of a vocation, a form in which her spiritual and social energies can be harmonized and through which they can be directed in order to affect the world at large. Since, however, George Eliot has drawn Dorothea as a character to whom "permanent rebellion, the disorder of a life without some loving reverent resolve" (144) was impossible, her search for a vocation is cut short almost before it begins. In contrast to Will, who has not only time but space in which to try on different roles, Dorothea does not. And where Will can attempt and reject a number of vocations before finding his niche as a member of Parliament, Dorothea can not. Unlike Will, Dorothea has only two alternatives: she can marry or she can remain a spinster. But even this choice is more apparent than real. Dorothea *must* marry. For unmarried and not endowed with the strength for permanent rebellion, there is no way for her even to begin to find for herself the wisdom she desires. Unmarried and untutored, she can only devise plans for cottages whose fire-places may well interfere with their stairways. And even were her plans correct, she can not build the cottages in any case, having neither the money nor, more importantly, the courage to do so on her own. Like Kate Chopin's Edna Pontellier, she lacks the strong wings necessary for the artist: her wish for freedom is always checked by her equally strong desire to submit. And if, for what-ever reasons, we ignore both sides of the equation George Eliot has set up throughout the book for defining Dorothea's character, the book's ending becomes as incomprehensible as many critics have found it to be.

Why, it is asked, does Dorothea marry Will? Because the answer to this question is most often given in terms which account for the marriage by opposing Will's presumed sensuality to Casaubon's sterility, even those posing this solution are unhappy with it and condemn the author for failing to make Dorothea's savior more sex-ually viable. Sexuality, however, does not provide the key to Will's significance, though the truth of this statement may indeed point to a gap in George Eliot's perceptions. Far from being an erotic radi-cal, a pre-Lawrencian Mellors saving Dorothea by his phallic force, Will is instead a social reformer who finds a vocation which can use his romantic vision when, at the book's conclusion he is transformed into "an ardent public man" (610), and through Dorothea's adjec-tive, into a version of Dorothea herself. Since wrongs exist and since Will is in the thick of a struggle against them, George Eliot establishes him as a husband for Dorothea, who can "give him wifely help" (611) of just the sort she wanted to give Casaubon but could not. What *Middlemarch* is missing then is a more powerful rendering of both Ladislaw's physical presence and his social vision. We know he would reform, but what and how we know not. We know that Dorothea would help him, but don't know the exact nature of her help.

At this point, however, some real problems concerning Dorothea's second marriage do intrude themselves. The objection is not that Dorothea should have married Will but that she should have mar-ried anybody at all, that she should ultimately be denied the op-portunity given Will to find her own paths and forge her energies into some new mold. Acknowledging that "many who know her, thought it a pity that so substantive and rare a creature should have been absorbed into the life of another, and be only known in a certain circle as a wife and mother," (611), George Eliot ac-knowledges the fact that Dorothea is a character who might have been fulfilled in a wider world than the one she as author finally provides. But she also claims that "no one stated exactly what else that was in her power she ought rather to have done" (611); looking outward, George Eliot simply could not find this new and bigger world. The religion which inspired Antigone and Saint Theresa to perform their heroic deeds alone is gone. And to fill this vacuum George Eliot found it necessary to impose tradition, widening it a bit to allow Mary Garth to write a book and Dorothea to go to London, but stopping short of a full exploration of a world which would have had its birth not in reality's mirror but in the artist's will. We could perhaps have had this vision if the author held the mirror to reflect not only the world both she and Dorothea knew and left behind but also that one she forced into existence when she stopped being Mary Ann Evans and became George Eliot instead. In *Middlemarch*, however, George Eliot refuses this option and accepts a safety not entirely celebrated but rather tinged with resignation, ambivalently regarded.

It is, however, only when we draw away from Dorothea to look instead at Rosamond that the reasons for George Eliot's ambivalent attitude toward Dorothea's energy become clear. In thus moving, we are not travelling so great a distance as it might at first appear. Although Rosamond is in many ways Dorothea's opposite, they are opposed as two sides of the same coin are opposed and are centrally bonded by the common metal of their energy. It is usual to see Rosamond as simply the typical nineteenth-century heroine exposed by the persistent hostility of George Eliot's vision. This view seems to me both distorted and reductive, for it fails to take note of precisely that facet of Rosamond's character which is most interesting: the strength of her will. Like Jay Gatsby, Rosamond would spring from her own Platonic image of herself. Formed like him out of a mixed romanticism and vulgarity, her reckless will is finally even stronger than Dorothea's because it is not tempered as Dorothea's was by either the cooling winds of self-effacement or the broadening channels of social concern. What she wants is simply her own way out of Middlemarch. But her way, like Dorothea's is defined throughout the book in society's terms, though Rosamond's society is, to be sure, more limited because more narrowly class and money conscious than Dorothea's. And, like Dorothea, Rosamond cannot get her way, cannot gain both the freedom from Middlemarch's constrictions and the material perquisites she feels are due her without a husband.

In the last part of his essay *The Subjection of Women*,[3] pub-

---

[3] The quotations from Mill are taken from the excellent *Essays on Sex Equality* by John Stuart Mill and Harriet Taylor Mill, edited and with an introductory essay by Alice S. Rossi, Chicago and London, 1970.

Women, Energy, and Middlemarch

lished just two years before *Middlemarch,* John Stuart Mill provides a beautiful abstract for the Rosamond-Lydgate marriage seen against a matrix in which the woman's will to power is strengthened proportionally as her capacities for personal liberty are denied by the combined forces of social conventions both external and internal. I can do no better than to quote from the essay:

> An active an energetic mind, if denied liberty, will seek for power: refused the command of itself, it will assert its personality by attempting to control others. To allow to any human beings no existence of their own but what depends on others, is giving far too high a premium on bending others to their purposes. Where liberty cannot be hoped for, and power can, power becomes the grand object of human desire; those to whom others will not leave the undisturbed management of their own affairs, will compensate themselves, if they can, by meddling for their own purposes with the affairs of others. Hence also women's passion for personal beauty, and dress and display; and all the evils that flow from it. . . . The love of power and the love of liberty are in eternal antagonism. Where there is least liberty, the passion for power is the most ardent and unscrupulous. (238)

Denied liberty, denied an education which would foster the formation of a personal vision which might then be tested against society's claims, Rosamond becomes, as she must, society's agent, in Mill's terms, a "hostage to Mrs. Grundy." (229).

Like Mill, George Eliot has a powerful awareness of the destructiveness of Rosamond's energy. And, as is the case with Dorothea, she can find nothing to do with it, no place to put it once the possibility of wifely submission is denied. Thus, what I have called George Eliot's conservatism is finally both the logical conclusion to the problem of female energy posed in her work and, less happily, the result of the failure of her own imagination to create the sorts of alternatives Mill envisions. Middlemarch and its environs are a closed world whose survival depends on the continuing life of values cherished by the author. Her fidelity to these values, however, prevents George Eliot from arriving at a radical solution—or, indeed, any solution—to the problems of female energy the book proposes. She can only struggle to contain the energy, force the new wine back into the old bottles, as she does with Dorothea, or condemn its egotism as most hostile to the community she loves.

Only one small scene, Lydgate's memory of Madame Laure, points to the road George Eliot rejected. These passages, like no others in the book, leap from the page, demanding to be read symbolically. But as symbol of what? The traditional reading makes the scene reflect on Lydgate, showing us what he as yet can't see: that he would do well to stay unmarried. Obviously, too, Madame

Laure herself reflects on Rosamond, a spiritual rather than a physical murderer. If, however, the general reading proposed here has any validity, if, that is, *Middlemarch* is significantly, even centrally, concerned with the problem that excess energy in combination with the world's conventions poses for George Eliot and her female characters, then certainly another reading is possible. When Madame Laure says, "You are a good young man. But I do not like husbands. I shall never have another." (114), she is speaking as a woman who has literally killed a man to gain her freedom. By underscoring the violence of Laure's energy, the ruthlessness of her power, George Eliot shows clearly what she is most afraid of if she leaves her female characters generally unbridled. But we can only wonder—and perhaps regret—that this image was not pursued further and in another direction, that George Eliot did not finally create a woman who knew before the fact that she neither liked nor needed husbands since such liking would force her either to submit or to destroy. Had George Eliot been able to find some system of values by which such a woman could live, she might have succeeded in breathing life again into Saint Theresa's dessicated image.

It is illegitimate, I know, to condemn an author for what she did not choose to do. But as I have moved away from what I now believe was merely an adolescent fantasy concerning the contents and implications of *Middlemarch* to what I hope is a more true understanding of the text's attitudes toward woman, I see that it can no longer be one of the books of my life. In so seeing, I am alternately angered, puzzled, and finally depressed. Madame Laure's history without her husband, the story of Dorothea as a social force, the tale of Rosamond as a political novel, none of these have been written. If we can imagine a world or a vision that might write them, then perhaps this condition is not final and, creating our own futures, we may be consoled.

ELIZABETH STUART PHELPS: A STUDY IN FEMALE REBELLION

Christine Stansell

ALTHOUGH AFTER the Seneca Falls convention of 1848, many women were emerging from domestic cloisters to campaign for equal rights, their number was negligible in comparison to the mass left in the home. There an equally serious, and ultimately, perhaps, more significant battle for the emancipation of women was being fought. The writer and intellectual Elizabeth Stuart Phelps was one of the most influential figures of this wave of feminism. Her first novel, *The Gates Ajar*, a fictional polemic against patriarchal religion, became the century's second best-selling book by a female author.[1] Published soon after the Civil War, the novel established her notoriety while she was in her early twenties. She never lost her prominence as a spokeswoman for the more subterranean currents of female rebellion. Her own psychology is a fascinating case study in problems and experiences which bred feminism, while her work offers a superb entry into an underground war against the male and its ingenious guerrilla tactics. Concealed beneath the shabby plots and platitudinous melodramas of her fiction is a devastating analysis of the nature of heterosexuality and its implications for the liberation of women.

Because her family was suffused with Calvinist orthodoxy, patriarchal religion was particularly suited as a locus for Miss Phelps' first revolt. Both grandfathers were ministers, and both parents were relentlessly religious. Austin Phelps, her father, had attended Andover seminary and there met Elizabeth Stuart, the daughter of an eminent Andover theologian. He married her after graduation and took her to his first pastoral post in Boston. In no account is strong affection cited between the two, but Elizabeth apparently preferred the hardships of a parson's wife, which she detailed in her popular book, *The Sunny Side*, to Andover, which was associated in her mind with funerals and sterile scholarship.[2] She bequeathed

---

[1] Only *Uncle Tom's Cabin* surpassed it in fame and sales, and it was translated into thirteen languages.

[2] From her earliest childhood she had been tormented by fears for the death of her invalid mother. The anxiety was further fostered by a nurse who took her small ward to every funeral in town and a father who countenanced his daughter's growing morbidity as natural.

to her daughter her aversion to the professional religion of her father and his colleagues:

> In her father's house, among the faculty and students of the seminary, religion was their profession. They made a study of it, an argument of it, and a business of it; but in Boston she had seen what religion could be in the lives of people who did not devote themselves to the study of it but who nevertheless lived it . . . In the comparatively sheltered atmosphere of the seminary it was more difficult to keep alive . . .[3]

Her husband, however, was offered a post, prestigious for a young cleric, at Andover, and for ambition left the living of religion for its study. The move eventually led, by a concatenation which was, at least in the daughter's eyes, nearly demonstrable, to Mrs. Phelps' death. Coincident, curiously enough, with her marriage, had been the onset of a cerebral disease, with symptoms of headaches, partial blindness, and paralysis. The nervous condition grew worse with the return to the town which oppressed her. Nevertheless, in the tradition of the hardy New England woman, Elizabeth Phelps was determined to live her own life. After the success of *The Sunny Side*, she doggedly continued to write, despite her illness and domestic workload: in her daughter's words, "Genius was in her, and would out. She wrote because she could not help it . . . a wife, a mother, a housekeeper, a hostess, in delicate health, on an academic salary, undertakes a deadly load when she starts on a literary career . . . she fell beneath it."[4] She died four years after she returned to Andover, after wearily giving birth to another son.[5]

The hint which lingers in the above quotation of Phelps' complicity in his wife's death becomes at times in his daughter's writing a near-explicit accusation. The fact that Miss Phelps upon her mother's death changed her given name, Mary Gray, to Elizabeth Stuart should demonstrate where her sympathies lay. Austin Phelps, in his daughter's opinion, was callous to the price domestic orderliness exacted from his wife. She was an ideal housekeeper, and Professor Phelps, "who always retained something of a feudal view of the lines of feeling and action which should be found natural in a woman, rested in her fireside graces, nor ever looked beyond."[6]

---

[3] Mary Angela Bennett, *Elizabeth Stuart Phelps,* Ph.D. dissertation (University of Pennsylvania, 1939), p. 33.

[4] Elizabeth Stuart Phelps, *Chapters from a Life* (Cambridge, Mass.: Riverside Press, 1896), p. 34.

[5] She had predicted her impending death in the same month as the child was conceived.

[6] Phelps, *Austin Phelps* (New York: Scribner's, 1891), p. 87.

A Study in Female Rebellion

With subtle rancor, the second Elizabeth Stuart Phelps added elsewhere, "under the movement of a nature like hers a woman may make a man divinely happy. But she may die in trying to do so."[7] By weighting the burden of artistic genius with domestic care, marriage—and Austin Phelps—had killed her mother.

By her own testimony, it is clear that her mother's death left drastic emotional scars on the eight-year-old girl. She was stranded with three men: two brothers and a father to whom rhetoric and homilectics took precedence over children. The brothers she detested; years later she wrote a story ("More Ways than One") about a girl who so despised caring for her brother that she peddled silver polish to pay a nurse's fee. There also began the succession of stepmothers which in her autobiography she mentions only curtly. Within a year of his wife's death, Phelps married, strangely enough, her sister. She too succumbed a few years later, of tuberculosis compounded by sheer weariness, caring for the children up until a few hours of her death.

Two deaths in a few years was not remarkably catastrophic for a nineteenth-century household, but the lugubrious tenor of the Phelps family inflated death until it became the leitmotif of Miss Phelps' childhood: "sickness, watching, care, death, burial came to seem the natural scenery of the Andover house."[8] The dead were always with her: in the bizarre luminescence of her mother's portrait as her infant boy was baptized by her coffin, in the constant reminders of her mother through the sister/stepmother, in the second mother's funeral, and in her father's accounts of the ghosts which infested his childhood home:[9] "the little girl had never been exactly gleeful or merry. She had not quite the temperament keyed for joy, and her almost premature thoughtfulness prevented life even then from seeming like a sunlit holiday."[10]

In later life she could never entirely exorcise the gloomy legacy of these years, and the unhealthy dreams of the child who would awake screaming in the night with her father's ghost stories livid in her mind rise like marsh gas from the swampier areas of her fiction: "the night is wild and wet. It makes faces at me when I go to the window, like a big gargoyle . . ."[11] She is at her literary best

---

[7] *Ibid.*, p. 53.

[8] *Ibid.*, p. 95.

[9] The parsonage which had been Prof. Phelps' childhood home had been plagued by a malevolent poltergeist who levitated furniture, bent silverware, and on one occasion demanded a piece of squash pie.

[10] Elizabeth T. Spring, "Elizabeth Stuart Phelps," *Our Famous Women* (Washington: A. D. Worthington and Co., 1883), p. 565.

[11] "Confessions of a Wife," *Century*, LXV (May, 1904), 168.

241

when she brings to bear on her writing the nightmarish force of an imagination steeped in Calvinist hellfire and her own morbidity, as in this description of a New England mill town:

> . . . it was a sickening, airless place in the summer—it was damp and desolate now . . . Belated locomotives shrieked to each other across the river, and a wind bore down the current the roar and rage of the dam. Shadows were beginning to skulk under the huge brown bridge. The silent mills stared up and down and over the streams with a bleak, unvarying stare. An oriflamme of scarlet burned in the west, flickering dully in the dirty, curdling water, flared against the windows of Pemberton, which quivered and dripped, Asenath thought, as if with blood.[12]

Along with death, the figure of her father brooded over her youth, inextricable from the family's dolefulness. Austin Phelps was stern and ambitious, absorbed in his career; Miss Phelps wrote that "his lecture room became the altar of his life. Nothing was suffered to blaspheme it. No little diversion or controllable exhaustion kept him from it."[13] The ingenuous tribute of an old parishioner is a more reliable index of character: "the most remarkable trait in Mr. Phelps . . . was his *maturity*. He was not like other young men. His maturity and his *gravity*—he was always in earnest about life, always took the serious view of it."[14] The responsibility for three motherless children, according to his daughter, conflicted with his professional zealousness and proved "unfortunate for a temperament like *his*. He was not by nature joyous. His view of moral responsibilities was too grave to permit him to be light-hearted[15] . . . it is to be feared that they weighed a little heavily upon his nerves in those early years of professional struggles and private care."[16]

From her birth, when "he lay in sleepless sorrow compassionating the week old infant 'because she was so homely,'"[17] Austin Phelps dealt heavy-handedly with his daughter. His feudal view of women impinged upon her as it had upon her mother; if he did not consciously impede her development, he did nothing to nurture it. He would give her no room of her own in which to write, nor allow

---

[12] "The Tenth of January," *Men, Women, and Ghosts* (Boston: Fields and Osgood, 1869), p. 52.
[13] *Austin Phelps*, p. 65.
[14] Quoted in *Austin Phelps*, p. 56.
[15] *Ibid.*
[16] *Ibid.*, p. 95.
[17] *Ibid.*, p. 59.

her to heat her bedroom; because her noisy brothers dominated the rest of the house, she was forced to retreat to her frigid bedroom, where to keep warm she wore her mother's shawl. That the writing of *The Gates Ajar* was intimately associated in her mind with the exile of a cold room and her mother's pelisse is a clue to the motivation which pervades the book.[18] It is a symbolic rebellion of the two Elizabeth Stuart Phelps, mother and daughter, against the autocratic male who tried literally and metaphorically to freeze their talent.

The Gates Ajar was for Miss Phelps a personal rejection of the death-oriented, patriarchal, unfeeling religion, embodied by Austin Phelps and his cold professionalism, which had warped her childhood and smothered her mother. The plot is sparse, if not bald: the book opens on a young girl who is despondent over the recent death of her beloved brother in the war. The comfort which the orthodox church offers her is profoundly impoverished: she longs for a resumption of earthly life with her brother, while Calvinism offers only the hope of a glimpse of his face in an anonymous choir of identically robed seraphim. At the nadir of her sorrow, her aunt Winifred arrives with a new testament of her own. The orthodox heaven, Winifred assures, is only a Byzantine fantasy of hieratic professionals. Heaven in her gospel is an eternal New England village where life is resumed, not transformed. For the New England country folk, the notion of an afterlife which is not socially or culturally intimidating comes as a relief: Winifred buoyantly assures the simplest farmer that paradise is not a fearsomely formal concert, but a kind of banal fairyland where all wishes come true. Thus a gawky adolescent confesses his anxiety that he is too skinny to wear white robes and learns from Winifred that instead of singing the praises of the Lord, his fulltime occupation will be to patent inventions, his favorite hobby; similarly, a farmer who cares only for his garden will spend eternity planting potatoes.

The *Gates* owed its smashing popularity to a combination of vicarious wish-fulfillment, the latent anti-Calvinist sentiment of many American females,[19] and the resentful groundswell of the legions of women bereaved by the war's holocaust, a sentiment

---

[18] See the opening chapters of *Chapters from a Life* for an account of the writing of the *Gates*.

[19] For examples of similar sentiments see Ann D. Wood, "The 'Scribbling Women' and Fanny Fern: Why Women Wrote," *American Quarterly* (Spring, 1971), pp. 3–24, *The Autobiography of Lyman Beecher*, ed. Barbara M. Cross (Cambridge, Mass.: Harvard Press, 1961), pp. 40–60, and any edition or reprint of Elizabeth Cady Stanton's *The Woman's Bible*.

which academic orthodoxy could not palliate. Elizabeth Stuart Phelps herself was deeply involved in these currents. Samuel Thompson, Andover class of 1862, who shared a "very deep attachment"[20] with her, had enlisted within two weeks of graduation and was killed five months later. Her father and his church had never helped her with her mother's death and had only nourished her neuroses; her lover's death fully exposed the dry professionalism of Austin Phelps and Andover theology in their impotency: "creeds and commentaries and sermons were made by men. What tenderest of men knows how to comfort his own daughter when her heart is broken?"[21]

The Gates Ajar was intended as a message of solace to the thousands of women torn by a man's war, a war rationalized by a man's religion which gave no hope but a man's afterlife built on formality, hierarchies, ceremony, and prestige:

> I wished to say something that would comfort some few . . . of the women whose misery crowded the land. The smoke of their torment ascended, and the sky was blackened by it. I do not think I thought so much about the suffering of men . . . but the women—the helpless, out-numbering, unconsulted women; they whom war trampled down, without a choice or protest; the patient, limited, domestic women, who thought little, but loved much, and loving, had lost all—to them I would have spoken.[22]

The *Gates* is the first example of this deep sense of sisterhood which is the wellspring of some truly fine passages in her writing:

> A man's grief, when he chooses to confide it to a woman, is not an easy matter to deal with; its dignity and its pathos are never to be forgotten; how to meet it, Heaven only teaches . . . But the women—oh, the poor women! I felt less afraid to answer them. Their misery seemed to cry in my arms like a child who must be comforted. I wrote to them— I wrote without wisdom or caution or skill, only with the power of being sorry for them, and the wish to say so.[23]

To comfort them she gave them the hope of a woman's heaven, a paradise ordered on the small scale of a woman's life: gardens, furniture, New England cottages, children, and sitting room pianos. Most important, she promised them a reunion with the dead, a

---

[20] Bennett, p. 44.
[21] *Chapters from a Life*, p. 98.
[22] *Ibid.*, p. 127.
[23] *Ibid.*

resumption of the earthly life in terms in which a woman could participate: not glorious choirs in awesome halls of gold, but neighborly chats on front porches. Mary Bennett, her sole biographer, described her theology as a movement toward anthropocentricity: "she came to minimize the obligation of the sinner to God, and to stress more and more the imperative duty of the Almighty to satisfy the desires of the human heart which He created."[24] Astute, but a near-miss: it was God's obligation not to man, but to the female, martyr of man's violence and sin, which He was bound to fulfill, for certainly there was no justice for woman on earth. Years after the war, she wrote of the woman's martyrdom still unvindicated: an aging soldier "would pass us without raising so much as an association with the sacrifice which we have accepted at his hands. The widowed wives and the widowed girls . . ."[25]

In her theology, religion serves not only as a vindication and solace for the female, but as a kind of emancipation: she petitions, "Be Thou breadth, freedom, walking-space before us."[26] Woman has the power of God's elect, and power, however oblique, is a form of deliverance from subjugation. In touch with the primeval sources, life's finer, richer issue can do what a male minister cannot: bring God's Word in the full force of its loving sympathy to the downtrodden. In the *Gates*, the conflict between barren male orthodoxy and the work of the elect is graphically presented in a confrontation between Aunt Winnie and the deacon:

> I looked him over again—hat, hoe, shirt and all; scanned his obstinate old face with its stupid, good eyes and animal mouth. Then I glanced at Aunt Winifred as she leaned forward in the afternoon light; the white, finely cut woman, with her serene smile and rapt, saintly eyes.[27]

The writing and subsequent popularity of the *Gates* fostered Elizabeth Stuart Phelps' own conception of herself as an Aunt Winifred. Like Winnie, she was dangerously similar to Christ; according to her, the public treated her as if she had indeed descended to earth with the Word. "From every corner of the civilized globe"[28] came petitions for advice or interpretations of her

---

[24] Bennett, p. 115.
[25] "Mary Livermore," *Our Famous Women*, p. 395.
[26] *Chapters from a Life*, p. 165.
[27] *The Gates Ajar* (Cambridge, Mass.: Harvard Press, 1969), chapt. 11.
[28] *Chapters from a Life*, p. 126.

new dogma, and even requests for relics in the form of autographed prayers. Thirty years later, at the time she wrote her autobiography, she was still receiving such letters. Theologians were, of course, scandalized by the novel's heterodoxy, and Miss Phelps proudly recounts that, outraged, they treated her as if she "had held the power to overthrow church and state and family . . . They waged war across that girl's notions of the life to come, as if she had been an evil spirit let loose upon accepted theology for the destruction of the world."[29]

The repressed girl who had during her childhood listened in self-effacing silence to her father and his colleagues had been rewarded by reversal: the religious hierophants listened—if not respectfully—to her. Reinforcing the psychological victory were concrete gains: literary success meant financial independence, rare for a spinster. She bought her own seaside home in Gloucester, a room of one's own which contributed immeasurably to her new-found sense of integrity and freedom from her family. There, spurred by a barroom murder, she began to organize temperance and religious missions among the fishing town lowlife. As with the *Gates*, she again brought the Word to earth, and seemed to attribute her ability to save souls to both the dynamism of her message and her own charisma: a common tribute, according to her, was "I hear when you talk to folks they stop drinkin'."[30] Living out the Winifred role in her own life, religion served, as it did in her writing, as a liberating force. Granting her the confidence of power through her mission, she escaped her father and to an extent justified and excused her singleness both to herself and to society. Her most precious memory of the fisherfolk reveals the terms in which she viewed her relationship to them: "they always seem to be a little group, affectionate and wistful, waiting for me in the old club-room, and softly singing, 'I need Thee every hour.'"[31] For a spinster in the 1870's, that plaint offered at least some kind of security.

During these five years of healthy activity and independence, she wrote *The Story of Avis*, her finest and most central book and one of a number of female *kunstlerromans* which emerged in the latter half of the century. During these decades women writers were making halting but progressively less timid attempts to expose the restrictions imposed on them in both art and life through the

---

[29] *Ibid.*, p. 118.
[30] *Ibid.*, p. 216.
[31] *Ibid.*, p. 226.

A Study in Female Rebellion

vehicle of a plot concerned with the conflict between art and womanliness.[32] Today unjustly forgotten, *Avis* is perhaps the consummate expression of this genre and a probing exploration of the possibilities for survival for a woman who tries to preserve her human wholeness. The same age as Elizabeth Stuart Phelps, Avis is also single and from a small seminary town, beautiful, vibrant, and a brilliant artist. Because she is so obviously Miss Phelps' ideal self, her story offers many insights into both the author's fantasies and her view of the problems which she encountered as a talented single woman.

As the book opens, Avis has returned home after establishing herself in Europe as a promising painter. We are made aware of the subjugated consciousness of the women of the town and the extent to which both she and her author have transcended it through the thoughts of her friend Coy, a conventional New England maiden: "Avis had got into the papers. It was seldom that a Harmouth woman got into the papers. It was only men—men at Harmouth . . . indeed the university existed, she supposed, for the glorification of men. This was all right and proper."[33] In contrast, men seem dun-colored moths beside Avis' glory:

> Avis Dobell, sitting in the shadowed corner of the president's parlor that night, had happened to place herself against some very heavy drapery . . . known to artists as carmine . . . in the gaslight and firelight of the room, the insensate piece of cloth seemed to throb as if it held some inarticulate passion . . . Avis went to it straight as a bird to a lighthouse on a dark night. She would have beaten herself against that color, like those very birds against the glowing glass . . . she had a fierce kinship with that color, of which she seldom spoke . . . a positive wave of pleasure flowed to her from the sight and contact of that curtain, which she felt in every sense of soul and body. (p. 13)

The Story of Avis quivers with such sexual imagery: the heavy air of dark, jewelled nights, throbbing carmine and waves of pleasure felt with "every sense of soul and body." Despite the foreshadowing, however, Avis is not headed, as is the young male artist of the conventional *kunstlerroman*, towards sexual initiation. Her pas-

---

[32] For other examples of this genre see Fanny Fern, *Ruth Hall* (New York: Mason Brothers, 1855); Grace Greenwood, "Zelma's Vow," *Atlantic Monthly*, IV (July, 1859), pp. 73–84, 327–344; and Kate Chopin, "Wiser than a God," *The Awakening and Other Stories*, ed. Lewis Leary (New York: Holt and Rinehart, 1970).

[33] *The Story of Avis* (Boston: Osgood and Co., 1877), p. 16. All subsequent page references will be to this edition.

247

sionate joyfulness is derived from her isolation from the male. Girded by the aloofness which is the outward emblem of her chastity and independence, she becomes a Diana figure, roaming freely over the New England fields and beaches, secure from all but the most brutal hunter.[34]

The identification of woman with nature was a commonplace of early American thought. Elizabeth Stuart Phelps, however, gave an important twist to the tradition. Theretofore, woman had sat placidly by a sweetly trickling stream and gazed out over well-trimmed fields at her sister bovines grazing. Both Miss Phelps' landscapes and heroine are far from placid: Avis riots in sinuous fields and over raging seascapes, "in harmony with the infinite growing and yearning of nature" (p. 96) as Diana played in her wild woodlands.

Woman's nature was for Elizabeth Stuart Phelps no longer tamed; her passions, however, were not unleashed for the benefit of man. The male comes: Philip Ostrander, a charming scholar who is nevertheless an intruder in Diana's kingdom. Avis' reaction to his overwhelming personality is hardly the one expected of a girl on the verge of spinsterhood. Instead of relieved happiness, his insistent love draws from her only terror and precipitous flight: "her startled maidenhood . . . infringements of some blind, sacred law . . . a sudden impassable distance between herself and this man." (p. 116) When he finally captures her, it is as if an archer had shot Diana:

> . . . the expression of exquisite pain with which she dragged her hands away from her face and met his eye. She seemed like a creature whose throbbing heart was torn out of her live body.
>   'If this be love,' she slowly said, 'I am afraid I love you now' (p. 183) . . . 'It is like—death.' (p. 192)

Philip vows that he will make marriage compatible with her work: metaphorically and literally, Avis will have a room of her own in which to paint. Inevitably, however, as in the case of the first Elizabeth Stuart Phelps, genius droops with domestic drudgery. Miss Phelps describes with empathetic and piercing bitterness the suffocation of a life made up of details. Pregnancies, unexpected

---

[34] For a historical treatment of the Diana figure in the nineteenth century see Christopher Lasch and William R. Taylor, "Two 'Kindred Spirits': Sorority and Family in New England, 1839–1846," *New England Quarterly* XXXVI (1963), 23–41.

house guests, and Philip's egocentric demands prevent her from setting up her studio:

> She said, 'By and by. After a while. I must wait a little.' She was still able to lure herself with this refrain, to which so many hundreds of women's lips have shaped themselves trembling; while the ears of a departing hope or a struggling purpose were bent to hear. Life had become a succession of expectancies . . . women understand—only women altogether—what a dreary will-o-the-wisp is this old, common experience. (p. 272)

With such compressed outrage, all the more ardent for its brevity and quietude, Miss Phelps links Avis' tragedy to the quintessential female experience. In the central episode of the book, the point at which Avis becomes totally disillusioned with her husband, the penetration to the bare psychology of male-female relationships uncovers frightening implications:

> He had an indefinably masculine air of mastery over his circumstances, and enjoyment in them, *which it is impossible to put into words,* but to which a woman is very sensitive. He came up and touched his wife under the chin, lifting her face. Avis felt a dull sense of displeasure. It seemed to her excited thought that he touched her lightly, much as he twirled the great blue silk tassel of his dressing-gown, as if she were, in some sense, the idle ornament of a comfortable hour. (p. 301)

The woman artist, trapped and tamed, becomes quite consciously the rallying point for all women. A profound sense of sisterhood permeates *Avis*. She suffers with her husband's dying and neglected mother, with her own mother, whose nascent dramatic career was truncated by marriage, and with Philip's old mistress, who finds in Avis' reserved sympathy a refuge from the terrible competition which isolates women from each other: "that's the worst of being a woman. What you go through can't be told. It isn't respectable for one woman to tell another what she has to bear." (p. 300) Yet sisterhood *is* powerful, especially so in the person of Avis. Her mission as an artist detaches itself from her suffering. In a hallucination she sees throngs of women crowd her room:

> They blushed at altars; they knelt in convents; they leered in streets; they sang to their babies; they stooped and stitched in black attics; they trembled beneath summer moons; they starved in cellars; they fell by the blow of a man's hand; they sold their souls for bread; they dashed their lives out in swift streams; they wrung their hands in prayer . . . the mystery of womanhood stood before her, and said 'Speak for me.' (p. 149)

In story after story, to the question "Am I my sister's keeper?" Elizabeth Stuart Phelps answers resoundingly in the affirmative: if women and their heavenly Colleague do not care for their kind, no one, certainly not men—whether Philip Ostrander or Austin Phelps —will. Throughout Miss Phelps' work, we see that it is the mission of the exceptional woman—Winifred, Avis, the Elizabeth Stuart Phelps of Gloucester—to save her sisters in the attics and streets and convents. In *Doctor Zay*, for instance, the female doctor raises a drowned seducer from the dead and forces him to marry his discarded mistress; the dying but indomitable old maid of "The Autobiography of Aureola" rides madly out in a winter storm to run down a seducer, whip him, and spirit the girl away from debasement. Elizabeth Stuart Phelps' superwomen are daring, strong, and competent—in a word, powerful: fit opponents for the powerful male with the feudal view, who insists on treating women like the tassel of his dressing gown.

Above all, the exceptional woman is too powerful and self-contained to be hurt by society. No man's disapprobation can bother her, for men to her, as to Diana, are unimportant: she is "a woman absorbed in her business, to whom a man must be the accident, not the substance, of thought."[35] Dr. Zay looks up to only one man, her old and distinguished mentor:

> She ain't like the rest of us; we wear our upper lips short with it. I declare! It seems to me in the course of generations women wouldn't have any eyelids; they'd be what you call now-adays selected away, by worshipin' men-folks, if Providence hadn't thrown in such lots of little men-mites and dots of souls, too short for the biggest fool alive to call the tallest. Then, half the time, she gets on her knees to him to make out the difference. (p. 177)

Instead, the natural position for a man beside a Phelps heroine is, like Philip Ostrander at the end of *Avis* or the minister of the *Gates*, on *his* knees. It is seldom, however, that the Phelps heroine is not single or widowed. Typically, she gains power over the man in the course of her professional duties, instead of through marriage. Thus in *Doctor Zay* the male's position becomes even more pleasantly prone, as the sick hero is forced by circumstance to submit himself to a woman doctor.

In sharp counterpoint to these women from whom "one gets a sense of power from every motion"[36] are the sick women who after

---

[35] *Doctor Zay* (Boston: Houghton and Mifflin, 1883), p. 91. All subsequent page references are to this edition.

[36] "Mary Livermore," p. 414.

A Study in Female Rebellion

The Story of Avis fill Miss Phelps' fiction in proliferating numbers. Her own health broke down after the publication of *Avis* in 1877; nervous disorders and chronic insomnia ended her work in Gloucester. Unable to continue her mission work, her claim to legitimacy as an Aunt Winifred began to slip away. Bared of the youthful beauty and passion of her wish-projection, Avis, she lost as well any pretensions to the massive vigor of her other super-women. Consequently she lost the ability of both Diana and Dr. Zay to consider the male "the accident, not the substance, of thought." Because her illness was tied in her mind to the breakdown of her ability to match these ideal figures which had justified her singleness, she came to define sickness as needing the male. Illness was the archetypal condition of the female and life was for the unexceptional woman an eternal sickbed. In contrast to the power-ful male, the woman in Miss Phelps' world-view is trapped by the weakness and dependency of the patient. In *Doctor Zay*, she con-veys the helplessness which consumes her women by reversing roles. The doctor's male patient, upon discovering her sex, cries fearfully, "I am in a woman's hands." (p. 44) In love with her, he is, like a woman, unable to take the active role in courtship, and comes to confront the debilitating psychological effects of enforced passivity:

> The terrible leisure of invalidism gaped, a gulf, and filled itself with her. If he could have arisen like a man, and bridged it, or like a hero, and leaped into it, she would never, he said to himself doggedly, have this exquisite advantage over him. He lay there like a woman, reduced from activity to endurance, from resolve to patience, while she amassed her importance to him—how idly!—like gold that she gave herself no trouble to count. (p. 11)

Like an invalid, a woman is confined and controlled; like a doctor, a man can slight her when he will. Although he is her only link to the outside world of health and activity, the man/doctor can break it when he will: "like an air-plant on oxygen, she existed on his tenderness. He had offered it to her when he felt like it. Well, busy, bustling man—out of his bounteous health and freedom, what com-fort had he given to this imprisoned woman?"[37] The woman/invalid is ultimately alien, left alone in her empty room after the visitors have tired and departed. Like a housewife, "the chronic invalid is the most solitary being in the world. Between himself and life there rises a wall of stained glass."[38] Elizabeth Stuart Phelps attests

---

[37] "His Wife," *Harper's*, CIII (1902), p. 898.
[38] "Shut In," *Fourteen to One* (Cambridge, Mass.: Riverside Press, 1896), p. 73.

251

to what Charlotte Perkins Gilman would later with bizarre lucidity relate in "The Yellow Wallpaper": all too often the wallpaper of a woman's room solidifies into iron bars.[39] A Phelps invalid, studying the ugly green paper of her sickroom, pathetically sighs, "This is my world . . . God created it."[40] In "His Wife," Miss Phelps with one image strikingly captures the isolation of the trapped woman. Leaving his invalid wife, the husband, blurting guilty and inane excuses, is silenced by her eyes: "solemn, mute, distant, they looked upon him like the eyes of an alien being moving through the experiences of an unknown world."[41] The old maid was even more estranged from the man's world of health than the wife. Thus describing the spinster invalid of "Shut In," Elizabeth Stuart Phelps linked singleness to illness: "she was shut in to her lot like a sweet nun into her cell. She was like the spirits in Heaven who neither marry nor are given in marriage."[42]

This preoccupation with illness is all the more pathetic in light of contemporaneous events in her own life. No matter that her exceptional women, modelled on her ideal self, considered men only incidental; neither Elizabeth Stuart Phelps nor her sick women could exist independently of the doctor. It is significant that even Avis, the most joyously liberated heroine, is inexorably forced into marriage by the "imperative surrender of her nature" (p. 184), as if even at the zenith of her psychological health Miss Phelps felt the malignant need for the male gnawing at her. As the patient in "Shut In" is powerless before her doctor's insistence upon under-taking a dangerous operation, so is a woman before her suitor. Pitifully helpless, she can only timidly ask for shabby verbal in-surance, as does the maiden of "Jack the Fisherman" to her brutish lover: " 'Will you be *kind* to me?' She did not ask him to swear it by the Rock of Ages. She took his word for it, poor thing! Women do."[43] Marriage, like some gruesomely incapacitating surgery, usu-

---

[39] For evidence that the identification of womanhood with illness was not just a literary conceit of Miss Phelps, there is mention in most medical man-uals from the latter half of the century of a plague of female diseases. Catherine Esther Beecher's exhaustive compilation of women's sicknesses in *Letters to the People on Health and Happiness* is the most compelling data on the subject, while Robert Herrick's novel *Together* (New York, 1908) is an interesting propaganda piece on female nervous diseases.

[40] "Shut In," p. 77.
[41] "His Wife," p. 524.
[42] "Shut In," p. 77.
[43] "Jack the Fisherman," *Fourteen to One*, p. 121.

A Study in Female Rebellion

ally leaves Phelps women, like Avis, "a riddled, withered thing, spent and rent." (p. 447)

On many levels Elizabeth Stuart Phelps *hoped* there was a terrible inevitability to marriage. The double isolation of the spinster/invalid from the male world poisoned her later years. Although on some fronts she still feigned a Diana-like contentment in her single status, an overview of her writing after her nervous breakdown reveals the proliferating illness. In *Old Maids in Paradise,* a fictional autobiography, she makes one of her few explicit appraisals of her alienation through a fictional surrogate: " 'It is of no use,' thought Corona, with a bitterness . . . 'I agree with the great man who, dying, said that life was all a mistake and never worth the candle. The world is not made for solitary people. It is of no use to be an old maid, unless other persons will be old maids, too.' "[44] When marriage finally came, the only inexorable will was hers to end over forty years of maidenhood.

H. D. Ward was the son of a periodical editor with whom she had corresponded for over twenty years. Her first mention of the boy, who was seventeen years younger than she, was in a letter to his father written in 1884, when she was forty.[45] In a properly maternal tone, she wrote "your boy is a fine fellow. I like him. You may take a world of comfort in him." (p. 83) Subsequent letters of the next two years contain progressively more frank inquiries: "Your boy interests me. I wish I were able to see him oftener and do more for him . . . He needs something that all motherless young people need . . . I like him and should be of use to him—I am so much older—if I could." (p. 85) In the winter of 1887, Ward fell ill. In a letter to his aunt on the subject of his health, Miss Phelps' intentions are nearly explicit. The extent to which the sick woman fakes and exploits the role of Winifred, bedrock of health and help, to gain access to the man, makes the letter worth quoting at length:

> . . . my knowledge of young men and my personal interest in Herbert have given me some hope that I might be of service to him this year in making him a stronger, healthier man. I have quite set my heart on doing that one thing for him. It will be worth to him any literary help a hundred times over. He will do what I ask—*sometimes!* And sometimes he will do the other thing "anyhow"! So it goes—but he is a dear boy . . . I can do something for him which all the ninety and nine 'girls

---

[44] *Old Maids in Paradise* (Cambridge, Mass.: Riverside Press, 1892), p. 176.
[45] All factual information about Miss Phelps' marriage is taken from Bennett's biography. Page references for quotations are from this source.

he leaves behind him' cannot do;—I am so old he must respect my judgment whether he follows it or not.—I have quite *adopted* him this winter. (p. 87)

The following summer they both went to Gloucester and were married quietly in the fall, "for terror of the newspapers" (p. 89) which rightly discerned the contradiction between Miss Phelps' public misogamous stance and her personal actions.

Within a short time the marriage repeated the pattern of unhappiness established by her literary marriages. Ward, an aspiring writer, tried to mine his wife's literary influence, but their collaborations went badly, and despite her intercessions with publishers his career went flat.[46] A wistful letter to a relative is an artifact of the later years of domesticated, dull misery:

> No, I don't mean to make it hard for the boy when he leaves me. You don't realize how little he has been with me after all. Put into a solid visit, it would not make more than four of five weeks, he has been off so much. Then when he is here I do not see him at all except in the evenings—literally. He goes straight after breakfast and after dinner and is with his young friends all day long: often a part of the evening too. There has been no hanging about or fooling away the summer with his hostess, either apparent or real. (p. 92)

Soon not even sailing kept Ward in Gloucester and, although his wife's health continued to deteriorate, he deserted her sickroom to travel constantly.

The stories of sick women written during these years are pathetic evidence of her humiliated loneliness. In "Confessions of a Wife," for example, the devoted woman writes to her compulsively nomadic husband:

> Did you ever think what it means to be a desolate woman, to sit alone every day and all the evenings? Do you understand how far a little kindness goes to a lonely wife—thoughtfulness, unselfishness—the being remembered and cared for? Did you ever put the question to yourself? No, I know you never did. And I say you never shall.[47] (p. 570)

During this period her plot is typically of a sick woman, deserted by her man, who in some way avenges herself. "His Wife" epitomizes these vindictive fantasies. A characteristically selfish man

---

[46] See E. S. Phelps' letter to Richard Gilder, editor of the *Century*, requesting him to print some of Ward's verse (Century Collection, New York Public Library, New York City).

[47] "Confessions of a Wife," p. 570.

leaves his dying wife to go fishing, dreams she is dead, awakes with the realization of her importance to him, and rushes home only to find her really dead. Miss Phelps revels in squeezing guilt from him, and with the device of the dream allows herself the luxury of a double repentance. The lamentations roll on for pages: "every hard thing he had ever done rose and rolled upon him—an unkind look, a harsh word, a little neglect here, a certain indifference there, an occasion when he had made her miserable and could just as easily have made her happy." (p. 898) But a great doctor conveniently reanimates her so she can live to hear her man's pleas for forgiveness. This is the archetypal fantasy of the scorned woman: she dies a beautifully languid death, thereby lacerating the male with guilt, and returns to reap the benefits. Neat, but pitiful at that: Elizabeth Stuart Phelps' wish-projections had shifted from power through the wholeness and strength of Avis or Winifred to manipulation through weakness.

In any case, if Miss Phelps never really approached her ideal of the superwoman in her own life, she certainly never realized her final vengeful fantasies. Ward returned home seldom, and then unrepentant. Married fifteen years, she wrote wearily to a friend, "My husband plans to leave soon. I am afraid that Washington will not answer his pleasure, and that it must be a much greater distance. But I cannot be sure yet—if you see him in Washington, pray help him if you can." (p. 92) He was at an even greater distance when she died and, although he was notified in adequate time of her imminent end, did not return home until three days after her funeral.

Despite her attempts through the superwomen figures to overthrow the male autocracy which she felt had killed her mother and warped her own life and the lives of countless other women, Elizabeth Stuart Phelps never succeeded even in establishing her own independence from the male. She began life in a patriarchy permeated with morbidity and spent her last years in a similarly funereal consciousness, as fixated on the doctor/male as she had been dominated by her father. It is her inability to escape this orientation to the male which makes her case an indication of the limitations of the feminism which she espoused. The exceptional woman to whom men were only incidental was still only a fantasy. It is clear from the swiftness with which her zeal shifted, despite her feminist principles, to H. D. Ward that sisterhood in her own mind and society's eyes was an insufficient *raison d'etre*. Like Miss Phelps, few nineteenth century women, single or married, had the psychological health and strength to withstand the hard truth of her bitter assertion that "God may have been in a just mood, but he was not in a merciful one, when, knowing that they were to be in the same world with men, He made women."[48] Yet as Miss Phelps' heroines should have proved to her, the sick woman is ultimately estranged even from her doctor: her only real chance at health is through the help of the exceptional woman. Despite her unrelenting attempts to throw off the blue tassel consciousness, Elizabeth Stuart Phelps could never satisfactorily locate the exceptional woman within herself.

---

[48] *The Story of Avis,* p. 124.

WOMEN AND THE AVANT-GARDE
THEATER

INTERVIEWS WITH ROCHELLE OWENS, CRYSTAL FIELD, ROSALYN DREXLER

Joan Goulianos

B Y ACCIDENT, in the spring of 1969, I spent an evening at the La-
Mama, where they were doing two plays by Rochelle Owens
—*Homo* and *The Queen of Greece*. The plays were like nothing I
had seen before. They were devastating satires of women as sluts,
queens, mothers, and of men as imperialists, consorts, babies. I
wrote a review of the plays, and, a few months later, Rochelle
Owens called me. She had liked the review, but when I went to
interview her, she did not seem to want to talk about her plays in
terms of women. Two years later, when her play *Istanbul* was to be
produced, we again did an interview. This time, with women's
liberation in her consciousness and mine, she was more willing to
talk about her plays as a woman's plays, though she still insisted
upon considering herself as an artist who was involved in broader
concerns. Through Rochelle Owens, I met Crystal Field, and
through her, Rosalyn Drexler.

All three have been in the avant-garde theater for many years—
Owens and Drexler as playwrights, Field as actress and director.

Owens is best known for *Futz*, but has written poetry as well as
other plays—*Beclch*, for instance, about a woman's frenzied quest
for power, and *Istanbul*, about a proud saintly poetess.

Crystal Field has worked with almost all of the important Off-
Off-Broadway theater groups—the Judson Poets' Theater, the La-
Mama, the Living Theater, the Cafe Cino, the Theater of the
Living Arts in Philadelphia. She has worked in movies and in the
commercial theater and currently is a founder and director of the
Theater for the New City, in New York.

Rosalyn Drexler is an artist and a writer. While Rochelle Owens'
plays often are about violence and passion, Rosalyn Drexler's, more
poignant and zany, are more often about domestic life. Like Owens,
Drexler writes with great imagination and insight about women.
She has written two novels—*I Am The Beautiful Stranger*, an autobiographical account of adolescence, and *One or Another*, a novel
about a middle-aged housewife caught between a tyrannical husband and a child-like lover.

257

ROCHELLE OWENS

J. I want to focus on your experiences as a woman playwright, although I understand you want your work to stand for something besides women's liberation.

R. I write about women and men. I have never written a play with only men, and I have never written a play with only women. We both agree that the female mind and the male mind are hopefully equally excitable or functioning in a good way. I don't believe that men are smarter than women. I don't believe that women are smarter than men. It's the old thing, which I think other people have investigated better than I, agreeing than one is not better than the other, in terms of intelligence, sensitivity or creativity.

J. You and I agree about that, but the world doesn't. Women artists have been suppressed, neglected.

R. Yes. Ignored. Hidden away.

J. This means that the woman artist functions in the world in a different way than the man artist.

R. A certain type of nature can energize this seeming inadequacy or this seeming disadvantage. It can become an igniting force to drive us to a fuller discovery of self.

J. I think that's true about women, just as it's true about black people, because both black people and women see society from an alienated point of view.

R. At the same time, we cannot neatly separate the female from the male dimension, as one might, in terms of a racial chauvinism. One can see a forceful validity in chauvinism of race or nationality. But, it's very misleading to slice the man from the woman. I just don't believe that it can be done. Maybe some would like to have it done and believe that it exists. But then you have some kind of synthetic Amazonian thing going, a monster haven of mythic women, which really has never existed except in the imagination. . . . I've had many funny experiences being a creative person, an artist, and a woman. I have always come across the three cosmic archetypal terrors that exist in every female mind—Eric Severaid, the delicatessen store owner, the doctor—all three caricatures that have intimidated women since the time that we were very small people.

J. And you come across these types in your work?

R. I have from time to time, but it doesn't bother me because I'm able to energize my own specific reality. It ignites me, if anything. See, I'm too old now to be unhappy in terms of being an artist. I'm able to work quite regularly and freely. . . . I have funny anecdotes to talk about. One time, Chayefsky saw me and he didn't know that I was a writer. He thought I was an actress, and he's a kind of archetypal delicatessen store owner, and naturally, he was threatened by me because I am tall and grand looking and noble, and he is not. So there might have been that kind of essential envy, but it may not even have had to do with being male or female.

J. I also, in my work, have had good experiences with men and with women, but there's still an overall experience, which is one of oppression.

R. That's true. Women tend to smile and laugh a lot. Years ago, in the 50's, which I remember in terms of growing up, I was mutely aware—I was dumb—but I felt that I was expected always to turn some male on. We all felt that. We believed in it, in Henry Miller. I and every woman I've ever spoken to, who is creative or artistic or intellectual—we've all had strongly similar histories.

J. What are they?

R. Well, in terms of being constantly embarrassed and forced to mince and giggle, even if we weren't doing it, even psychically mincing and giggling. All these experiences were very painful at the time, but we accepted them. Psychic dumbness. We knew there was this unbearable pain and bafflement, and we didn't know where to place it.

J. I think that comes out in the work of many women artists, but it comes out in very disguised ways—sometimes as rage or fury.

R. Perhaps that's true, but at the same time, there have been a lot of raging furious men. The grudge can't be, for all women, totally sexual. There are women artists who have synthesized it differently from other women. I know there is a difference, but at the same time, I don't think it's as important as the difference between individuals. It's like knowing that you do not have strong bonds with someone from your own ethnic group, but knowing that you have a very strong feeling for someone who has a similar idea. It depends how your experience is utilized.

J. How was your experience utilized?

R. I was always baffled at my situation in the world, in terms of not getting along with similar social groups. But I didn't pinpoint it to male or female. It's only now that, in reflecting, I can understand the past, in terms of my now new awareness.

J. That's the same with me. It never struck me that anybody would stop me from doing the kind of writing or teaching that I wanted to do. But now it strikes me that many people were trying to stop me.

R. Naturally there is oppression. It's kind of ironic too, because Lorraine Hansberry, who was a woman and is dead has her work highly overrated because of this collective guilt, embarrassment. There's that kind of looney contradiction. . . . Hansberry was a woman and she had to work out of the experience of being a woman, plus being black. Just like I have to work out of the experience of being a woman. I can't work out of the experience of a delicatessen store owning individual, like Paddy Chayefsky. But I think that art goes into much broader, larger, total collective human experiences. There is such a thing as—artists have done this ever since they scrubbed cave walls and drew circles—projection. An artist works with that tool—being able to project.

J. You talked about male stereotypes. What are your thoughts about female stereotypes? Are they the queens? the sluts? the mothers?

R. Yes, and all are expected somehow to enhance the male reality. Even if they're fictionalized for a novel or a poem, or even if they're not—even if they're in the mind of an individual male, I've always had the feeling that woman is expected to somehow ease and soothe and calm the male.

J. You have said that you are interested in the women's liberation movement—in the ideas that have come out of it.

R. Every woman, every human being has to be, in the Western world, in every part of the world.

J. What are some of the important insights, for you, that have come out of the movement?

R. Well, it just confirmed what I always believed—that energy and imagination are inevitable parts of being human, whether one is a man or a woman. Also, it has relieved me of all of the disguise aspect. I could never be disguised now as I was twelve years ago.

J. You mean the disguise of the hair, the make-up, the mini-dress, all that?

R. I don't believe it anymore. I can't go home again. I enjoy looking attractive, because I love the theater, and the theater is transformation and change and play, but like many women, I feel better in terms of being able to objectify our reality. It's like the story of Plato's cave. We can never see those shadows in the same way.

J. You were seeing those shadows before, in your work, but now you're aware of them in a different way?

R. I think a lot of talented women were conditioned and primed to admire the male, never taking each other as seriously as we would take the illustrious male. It's curious because then what we did was to change the male to our viewpoint and image. Very often, we would feminize the male. It illustrates that ancient Greek concept of the male and female uniting as one. And then, of course, there are these varieties of people, men and women. It's very exciting to see what's happening. But the most important thing for me is getting at the fountain-spraying of my strongest feelings—for my work. And I don't care if it's not just. And I don't care if it's not moral. As an artist, I don't rely on intellectualisms. It sounds very nice and perhaps it's logical, but we all know that if it was really the thing that ground and screwed the world onto the Milky Way —if we knew that logic and intellect did it—then we would be safe from our fellow human beings. And we're just not.

CRYSTAL FIELD

J. There are very few women directors and very few women who have founded theaters. Do you think that women's liberation helped you to turn from an actress into a director?
C. I had a certain kind of upbringing, and I did choreography. Women's liberation started in the dance world. There were many women choreographers. Suddenly you found women were directing, and directing men, and there was no problem.
J. Aren't there problems for a woman director?
C. In the commercial theater, the problems that I have had are not can a woman direct, but can an actress direct? You find a guy like Kazan, who's a wonderful guy, but he's got a certain attitude toward women. There is a terrible thing—and it still exists in the theater—between the role of an actress and the role of a director. When you go for acting roles, you have to come on a certain way, and if

you come on full strength, it scares a lot of men.
J. If they sense that you're intelligent and that you're strong, you may not get the part?
C. You *don't* get the part. And if you look into the lives of a lot of stars, their husbands were the producers or the directors.
J. So that women got their starring roles because they were connected with men who were writing or directing or financing plays?
C. Yes, and they were connected with them socially. It would be a matter of together we go and do something. Women had a hell of a lot more to do with the production of a play than you know about.
J. What were your problems like, as an actress?
C. In a way, it goes back to the kind of acting that I did—it was not acceptable in the view of what a woman should be like on the stage—not the view of the audience, but the view of many men directors and producers.
J. What were the women characters that they were trying to portray like?
C. They were a lot like Baby Doll. Everybody was neurotically distant from each other and from the world. Even the men. I think that in this kind of situation, men suffer as much, because they are called upon to be what they are not. In this country, we had many years where a man had to play a certain role also—the Marlon Brando type

—the guy who'd never tell you he loved you. And women were considered to be a cloying trap —the tender trap. Now that reflected the truth, because women were put in that position.

J. How did you face going for all these parts and having to play this personality?

C. For years, I played it, and I got roles that way, and then I would stop playing it, and I could never play it successfully enough. My own exuberance and my own strength would come through, and I would fail many times. . . . I came through a very short period when I was in turmoil and in agony, and I did go to a psychiatrist. Now, artistically I was with people who didn't believe in that—I got this strong marvelous training, but in life, from my parents on down, I had this other thing going. And he taught me one very important thing, which I think many women's lib people don't agree with, and that is when a woman is strong, she needs a very strong man. So that men have to get strong.

J. You have a small child. How do you manage this with your work in the theater?

C. I had Alexander, and I had a call from a director for a part in a Broadway show. When he found out I had a baby, he said to me, "The baby carriage goes in the door—art goes out the window." So I said to myself, Alexander is three weeks old. I had to feed him every few hours. So, you take the kid with you. I was going to hire a room and a housekeeper, and I could look in on him every hour or so. So, I took him up to the office with me, and he cried a little, and I had the housekeeper with me. Well, I had a call the next week. No dice. We need an actress that is not better than you, but more *mobile*. That was the word they used. That was an eye-opener. A woman is not supposed to have a baby, or if she has a baby, she's supposed to retreat to a corner. That's where women have a right to scream and yell and fight like hell. The big reason that I left the commercial theater is that I can have my baby and I can have my art. I had to fight for that with my husband. Before I had Alexander, I could do an Off-Broadway show or regional theater, and then I could go back and do my art. But now with Alexander, something's got to go, and what's got to go is the money.

J. Were your family artists?

C. My family tried as best as they could to break away from the old ways. They were rebels, they were socialists, my mother was a doctor, but when it came down to the nitty gritty, they couldn't make it, because they never went to a good psychiatrist. You need it to learn that you can grab things in your hand and smash them and that you're still a woman. My father was a writer. In his writing, he was far ahead of himself as a person. He had an attitude towards me that was, on the one hand, sexually excitive, and at the same time, when he would feel that, he would get deathly afraid, so he was a puritan. Then he would turn around and say, your voice is too loud and shut up and sit straight.

J. Do you think that women's liberation has influenced the kinds of roles you can now play and the way you see yourself as an actress?

C. Since I've been in the Off-Off-Broadway world for so many years, I've played roles that are consonant with women's liberation: women who are outrageous and non-stereotyped, and full of feeling, and aggressive. In the old kind of theater, there were other kinds of roles—they weren't stereotyped, they really reflected the way a lot of women were. The world has changed and the characters that are portrayed now, even in the commercial theater, are different.

J. Even in the avant-garde theater, what influence do you think women's liberation has had?

C. Women's liberation entered the theater, in the avant-garde circles, way before it entered the political arena. The world of the avant-garde was a world of women's liberation. As a matter of fact, Rochelle Owens, Rosalyn Drexler and Irene Forness had a book out, about six years ago, about women in the theater. Now that would be perhaps

changed, because now we're beginning to realize that they're not just women in the theater—they happen to be terrific writers.

J. How do you feel about working in plays by women?

C. I feel that the women writers with whom I've worked have a wonderful understanding of women. I've never been involved in a play by a man where the understanding of women is as great. A black writer can write about black life, generally speaking, better than a white writer. I've always wanted women to write.

J. What specifically are some of their understandings about women?

C. In the older plays, there is an adolescent, or almost a preadolescent, sexuality that was considered fantastic. Grown-up women were portrayed as adolescents, really. And that is not what makes a sexy woman. And there is an adult sexuality that is ten times as exciting and more glamorous, and these women writers know it and they write about these kinds of women. It's wonderful to act. You have a chance to be expansive in spirit. A really good actor wants to have an expansion of spirit on the stage. The old roles for women never allowed that. They were always crummy people and very scared and one-sided. There is an expansiveness of spirit that a woman obtains when she gets older, when she has a child, and you want to be able to do it on the stage. You want to be able to say to the world that this is wonderful. And this you don't usually find in a play by a man. There is also an aggressive quality to women. To be able to write a woman character that has a dark side and a light side and is still someone that you should love—that only a woman writer can do. There are also aspects of men that women can and do understand—the softer and more vulnerable sides of a man. . . . When these women write— Rochelle Owens, Irene Forness, Rosalyn Drexler—they write about women who are really terrible, but they write about them so they're wonderful—and that's quite different.

J. What is it that makes you most angry in the theater?

C. When I lose a job because of who I am, I get very angry. We've got to stop it, but that doesn't mean we've got to go into a corner by ourselves. We've got to go to the men and hit them in the head. We've got to have a few fights, yes, confrontations.

J. How are women going to fight, if they don't know how?

C. They've got to learn how to fight. Everybody is a born fighter. Everybody's got nails and fists and arms and they just have to accept them.

J. Were there other women in the theater whom you admired, emulated, or do you feel that you are starting something new?

C. As far as choreographers go, they have a good attitude toward being a woman. I'll tell you where I think I'm new. I don't think that a woman has to lose her femininity. I think that a woman is different from a man. And I feel that women and men can find a life together. Now, there, I feel—quite alone.

ROSALYN DREXLER

J. Crystal Field talked about how, when she went for a job, she had to act helpless and cute. Is the same true for the woman playwright?

R. I can't stand that. I can't stand it in myself. I'm trying to get away from it. I'm much more comfortable now with women. I mean, in our artists' group, because, I don't know about equals, but there is a feel of presence. You might call it feeling more like a person, and people listen to you when you talk, and we're doing things together.

J. This group is of women artists and women writers. How did you all get together?

R. It started with a nucleus of about fifteen women and now it's over fifty. It meets about once a month. Talking is part of it, but we have small groups—a museum group, what to do about the museums—a group that talks about aesthetics, what's happening to art today—and politics, power.

J. Do you feel that it's changed

you in the way you act?

R. Yes. I'm not afraid to attack. And I like that. For a long time, I'd meet certain men, certain writers, and I'd be sweet and never say what I thought about their work. And I'm not doing that anymore. I feel freer. Maybe a part of that is because I'm getting older too.

J. On the other hand, older women are sometimes in a less advantageous position than younger women.

R. Maybe it's because I have a certain status now on my own. I'm not unknown. Maybe I'm an unknown in lots of places, but not in my circles, so I don't have to put lovely attitudes on, to please people.

J. Were you conscious of doing that before?

R. Yes. It's a cliché I know, but at thirty, forty, I was still pretending I was a little girl. Because if I'm a little girl, then nobody would want to hurt me.

J. How about when you have to get a play produced, or when you have to get a job writing for the movies or for magazines, do you still feel that you have to come on in a false way?

R. No. I feel that I should be friendly. After all, they're offering me a job. And be presentable. But, it takes me less time to get out of the house. I can just work up to the last second, and maybe brush my hair, and go off and talk to people.

J. Were there any incidents that you can recall that now, in retro-

spect, you see as discrimination against you because you are a woman?

R. Yes. There was an incident at Yale. Brustein was in charge of certain scholarships, and I think there was discrimination because I was a married woman with a family. Every playwright I knew had been invited up there to learn about screenwriting, and I was as qualified as anybody else, so Brustein called up and he spoke to my husband and said, I like Rosalyn—they settled it between them—I like Rosalyn, but she can't live up here can she? You know we'd like her to come up, but that really wouldn't be possible would it? And my husband agreed with him. The thing is that people who were going up there weren't living up there. You could commute to Yale and most people did. And then I came home and it was all over. And I said, but you know I wanted to go there very much. I wanted to take part in this. I wanted to learn film. I didn't go to college, and I really wanted to, but it was all over. They had convinced each other that a married woman with children couldn't possibly come up twice a week. It wouldn't be right to give up my other duties. Without even asking me. So I think that's discrimination. It still bothers me. It hasn't been that way Off-Off-Broadway. At the Judson Church, it isn't like

265

that. Men and women work together.

J. What do you think created this atmosphere Off-Off-Broadway?

R. Maybe it has something to do with economics. All artists together, men and women—no money—you're working together and the big apple is pretty far away. But Yoko Ono didn't have that experience. She started a lot of things all by herself. All her conceptual ideas were stolen from her. People even used her loft and wouldn't invite her to show, and it was her loft. She had a very hard time. This is being set straight now, I think. She's an idea person. If you take her ideas, you take almost everything. . . . I don't know why, in the playwrighting field, Off-Off-Broadway, it was different. Maybe it was because a lot of that was homosexual, and anybody who feels different will be able to be with somebody who is different.

J. Isn't it unusual for a woman to be a playwright?

R. Do you think it has something to do with it being a prohibited activity for a woman— that plays were religious?

J. Were there any women playwrights that you could call models? When a man starts writing plays, he may identify with another male playwright.

R. When I was taking my plays around, when I first began, agents and people were telling me, go home and read Lillian Hellman and then come back. Maybe you are the avant-garde, but we don't see it. And I thought, maybe they're right. I don't even know what the avant-garde is, but I wasn't about to read Lillian Hellman.

J. How did you get started writing plays?

R. About 1960, 1961, I did it for spite. I was married and I couldn't get out very much and my daughter was young then. And I couldn't stand anybody knowing what I was doing. I had no privacy, but when my kid went to school, I closed the door and I said, oh boy, this is my secret project and I'm going to really amuse myself. This is what I dig doing and I wasn't sure—I didn't know what plays were—I hadn't gone to theater —so I sat down and I wrote *Home Movies,* just to amuse myself and do something very secret. I didn't expect it would be done. I didn't even know the proper play form. And then I just showed it to a couple of friends who laughed and said it was pretty good, and then I heard they were doing things at Judson. I showed it to them and they liked it and it amazed me. And then it just started from there. We all did it and it was a great experience. The cast loved it. Everyone was happy.

J. Had you written plays before that?

R. I didn't think of it as a play. I knew there were characters and there was a dialogue, but do you know what I mean—I didn't sit down and say I'm a playwright.

J. It was just your way of amusing yourself?

R. Getting away.

J. It seems to me that you were trying to establish a different identity.

R. I really was. And I wanted to write something that couldn't be stopped by criticism, because my husband is a very critical person, and if I showed him anything too soon, that would be the end of it. I hadn't written that long, and I was afraid, didn't know what to do even if the criticism was right. So, in order to go right through with the project, I had to isolate myself.

J. I think that's true for many women. They make their own lives, sometimes almost secretly.

R. It's better than trying to sleep around, which is another thing a woman will do. She'll go from one man to another, but then it's the same thing.

J. After *Home Movies*, you just kept on writing?

R. Then I said to myself, a play can be what you want to say. It can be anything. So I wrote down a whole list of things a play could be—time of day, what you eat, anger, history, anything. It just opened everything up for me, so I wrote a lot of plays very fast. And I'm glad, because sometimes the young fresh things, the things you would edit out, are in there.

Every time I was interviewed, somehow I always started talking about my housework, and it bothered me that I had to talk about that, because when men are interviewed, they bring out all sorts of philosophical questions, but I always got off on this thing. I really didn't want to create that picture of myself, but maybe it's a true picture, because here I am, at home. And I always read about how male writers divide their day. Well, this one gets up and takes his morning run, comes back and somebody gives him breakfast, writes for four or five hours, takes a nap, sees friends in the evening. I read women's interviews, and it's very seldom like that.

Giuliana Mutti

BLOOD SIGNS

the blood
it will not come.

how much longer must we lie,
calling this condition love?

how much did my mother love
the five times her blood did not come?

and yet each time he comes
I fill with love.

NORMAN MAILER: A PRISONER OF SEX

Annette Barnes

IN A PREFACE to Mailer's essay, *Harper's* magazine[1] assures the reader "that no writer in America could have illuminated as Norman Mailer has the deep underlying issues raised" by women's liberation. He confronts, according to the magazine, "the most perplexing, not to say threatening, problem of all: the private relations between men and women."

Mailer does illuminate the deeper issues, though perhaps not in the way in which *Harper's* editors suppose. Mailer presents himself as a prisoner of sex, a prisoner, moreover, who does not wish to escape. As Genet notes, prison can so mold a character "that he will live the rest of his life for it."

The hero of the essay, middle-aged and recently parted from his fourth wife, finds himself examining his views about women. Acknowledging that he may have some learning to do, he undertakes a journey of "remedial reading." At the trip's completion he is still a captive, but one presumably enlightened by so fearless a quest. [The journey is no mean feat for the hero who believed "a firm erection on a delicate fellow was the adventurous junction of ego and courage," when the enemy could be imagined, in moments of fancy, as "a squadron of enraged Amazons, an honor guard of revolutionary (if we could only see them) vaginas" or even as "thin college ladies with eyeglasses" and hatchets.]

The prisoner delighting in being able to produce fury in the enemy ("they would yet burn him for this") says early on:

> The fact of the matter is that the prime responsibility of a woman probably is to be on earth long enough to find the best mate possible for herself, and conceive children who will improve the species.

The hero wants us to believe that he knows better. We are to understand it is a remark on a par with "Women are low sloppy beasts," an irritating put-on to arouse interest. But when one reads at the conclusion of the hero's journey that

> he would agree with everything they asked but to quit the womb, for finally a day had to come when women shattered the pearl of their love for pristine and feminine will and found the man, yes that man in the million who could become the point of the seed which would give

[1] Norman Mailer, "The Prisoner of Sex," *Harper's*, 242 (March, 1971), 41–92; also Signet Books, 1971. $1.25.

269

an egg back to nature, and let the woman return with a babe who came from the root of God's desire to go all the way, wherever was that way.

one might well wonder who's being put on.

The prisoner believes that a woman as a woman has as her purpose the task of finding a man with the right seeds. It is a belief that survives the journey. Why does Mailer hold this belief and why does it survive?

What is it to be a prisoner of sex? What rewards are there for the captive, assuming that unless he has compensations, a person unhappy as a prisoner, will seek to escape?

According to Mailer to give meaning to sex is to become a prisoner of sex—"the more meaning one gave it, the more it assumed, until every failure and misery, every evil of your life, spoke their lines in its light, and every fear of mediocre death."

If as Mailer believes, sex should have this kind of overriding "meaning," then being a prisoner is a state to be sought after, not escaped from. "[T]he orgasm was the mirror of one's existence when conception was not a ghost." For it was in the "full rigors of the fuck" between a "brave man" and a "proud woman (with an open womb)" having "the awe that a life in these circumstances can be conceived," that "a man can become more male and a woman more female," where a human with phallus could experience the passion of being male, a human with womb could experience the passion of being female. (Fucking is self-revelation, O America!)

There are significant differences between the "unencumbered fuck" which Mailer seeks and prizes, and the transactions that usually pass for sex. Though Mailer seems to suggest in his discussion of Henry Miller that he along with Miller believes that "all sexual experience was valid, if one looked at it clearly," Mailer most often claims that some sexual experience is destructive, counterproductive to the work of becoming "men" or becoming "women." Heterosexual sex with contraception, sex "closer to the homosexual than the heterosexual," is seen as "a clearinghouse for power, a market for psychic power in which the stronger will use the weaker, and the female in the act, whether possessed of a vagina or phallus, will look to ingest or steal the masculine qualities of the dominator." Encumbered sex is in sharp contrast to sex where the brave man "was returned his bravery and an increase, for the will of a woman had been added to his own," where there is "some remote possibility of making a child and so is loose in a world where love can no longer be measured by power."

To be preoccupied with sex (like Portnoy) does not necessarily make one the kind of prisoner Mailer admires. Even if one's sexual standing and identity are wedged together as in Genet's prison world, one is still not the right kind of prisoner. The right kind of prisoner for Mailer is the one who sees sex as an activity which has "intimations" of immortality. "[W]ho knows what goes into his semen that he may fling across the space of eternity—that few inches of *coitus vaginae*—his measure, his meaning, his vision of a future male." Sex without the participants' knowledge that conception is possible is sex in some sense wasted, however pleasurable the experience. Mailer fantasizes much over lost seeds, over lost creations. Creation is a key. Women are needed in the process of creating new life and any technology which makes either the man or woman non-crucial is Evil. Mailer cannot tolerate Millett when she claims that the sexes "are inherently in everything alike, save reproductive systems, secondary sexual characteristics, orgasmic capacity and genetic and morphological structure." If there are no fundamental differences between men and women which go beyond the biological, if babies can be made in test tubes or in extra-uterine wombs, without sex, without men or women, one area of prizewinning is closed to the hero.

Plato in the *Symposium* suggested that all men "have a procreative impulse, both spiritual and physical, and when they come to maturity they feel a natural desire to beget children" for it is by perpetuation of themselves that they seek to become immortal. Those whose creative instinct is physical, unite and propagate with women "believing that by begetting children they can secure for themselves an immortal and blessed memory hereafter forever." Those whose creative instinct is spiritual, do not beget children of flesh and blood, but beget more beautiful as well as truly immortal children, since their progeny is "wisdom and virtue in general." Given these possibilities of creating, babies and books (to speak rather loosely), Plato's choice is books. Mailer wants both. The essay begins with a discussion of how the hero, a past prizewinner, has not been awarded a most prestigious new prize. Not to be given the Nobel Prize is acceptable, however, since the hero is still young enough and still in heat. A "huge novel" looms in the background. To be told, however, that one cannot even spread one's literal semen and get a prize, that women might not want all of men's babies, is a blow which cannot be borne.

The journey of the hero, although often enlightening, is also a journey of self-justification and even self-deception. Is technology, which makes baby-free sex possible, the evil per se or is the evil the full loss of control over the situation? Do men, collectively or individually, have the right to decide whether creation in sex is always a live if uncertain possibility (Mailer wants no contraception), or can women independently control their potentiality for

271

men's future physical progeny? Contraception-free-sex as the ideal leaves the woman only the fantasized possibility of urging her ovum to resist when a baby is not wanted.

The difficulty with Mailer is not that he does not understand the issues. He knows that if women develop "a full hard efficient ego," they are not going to give themselves "over to the unknown" (as D. H. Lawrence suggests for both male and female). Nor are they going to be eager to spend their lives changing the diapers on the babe Nature and Norman hath given. The possibility of their having work as important as his (if anyone can) and refusing on those grounds to do what Mailer acknowledges as mindless-making housework, becomes a real possibility. He knows that Ibsen's Nora is "right" when she says "I have another duty . . . my duty to myself." But what he does not know or does not come to terms with, if he knows, is that if all of Mailer's views are also right, then a woman's prime duty to herself is only to find a man and have babies. Mailer does say, "So let woman be what she would, and what she could." Let her travel to the moon, "legislate, incarcerate, and wear a uniform." "Yes, he thought that perhaps they may as well do what they desired if the anger of the centuries was having its say." But the joker in Mailer's scheme is that though they do other things, in the end they would not be really feminine, really women, until they had those babes. And ideally they would have as many babies as an open womb demands.

But having babies is no simple event. Once the creature descends from the womb, he or she needs care. Who gets the job? What Mailer never comes to terms with is the price he requires of women for their participation in creation. He gives no satisfactory reason why they should pay. He does say that women are incomplete without maternal creation (males without paternal creation are also incomplete males); he believes the passion to be feminine is inseparable from the passion to beget children of flesh and blood. But why believe him? Why not believe De Beauvoir when she says: "That the child is the supreme aim of woman is a statement having the precise value of an advertising slogan"? What evidence supports his claims? Or is he relying on intuitions, feels, leaps of faith?

The passion to be masculine is inseparable from the passion to create, but creation for men can be both a spiritual and physical assertion. Once the seeds are deposited, Mailer can hunt for literary or political prizes, leaving the woman the task of tending the garden and its blossoms and little time for having thoughts which are immortal. In Mailer's scheme, since the womb is always open and assuming meaningful sex is practiced, the female could have quite a prodigious garden to tend. (Overpopulation I take it would be an irrelevant concern.) It is not that Mailer claims that women cannot be creative intellectually; he does not say that they don't have the capacities. Rather, by making them the ever-ready baby-bearers, by suggesting that they are only truly women if mothers, he constructs a situation where in practice very few of these real women would have the time or energy to create more than those babies. As he notes, taking care of a large family and being an actress, for example, may be mutually exclusive endeavors.

Mailer fears technology. It depersonalizes. He fears its imprint in contraception, planned parenthood, eugenics. But he writes as if in light of the general depersonalization of man by the machine, the depersonalization of women by men is a lesser evil. At least a man is thrusting into you, not just a plastic prick. (But doesn't it depend on the man and the prick as it were?) Noting that Millett is protesting against Miller for his treatment of women as essentially cunts of different dimensions ("Of course, it is denigration of woman she protests, the reduction of woman to object"), Mailer accuses Millett of hypocrisy. Depersonalization by the whack and wham of an electrified plasticine dildo (Mailer admires the style of women who write "like very tough faggots") is nevertheless depersonalization. But there is a difference, is there not, between depersonalizing oneself (if this were an appropriate description of the effects of detachable digital sex) and being depersonalized by others or depersonalizing them? Moreover, even if it could be established that Millett were guilty of hypocrisy this would not show that she is not correct in her accusations against Miller.

Mailer tells woman that there is a "mysterious advantage" as well as burden to her womb, he makes of her "a privileged element of nature, closer to the mysteries than men." Is this not a way of justifying the abuse that men have sought to inflict upon women (those "faceless characterless pullulating broads" of Miller)? "So do men look to destroy every quality in a woman which will give her the powers of a male, for she is in their eyes already armed with the power that she brought them forth." Does the attribution of mysterious power to women make their dehumanization or abasement more palatable? Mailer writes as if he believes it does.

> [S]omewhere in the insane passions of all men is a huge desire to drive forward into the seat of creation, grab some part of that creation in the hands, sink the cock to the hilt, sink it into as many hilts as will hold it; for man is alienated from the nature which brought him forth, he is not like woman in possession of an inner space which gives her link to the future, so he must drive to possess it, he must if necessary come close to blowing his head off that he may possess it. "Perhaps a cunt, smelly

though it may be, is one of the prime symbols for the connection between all things."

Miller's genius, Mailer tells us is to show that "the power and the glory and the grandeur of the female in the universe," "can survive any context or any abuse." Miller still "screams his barbaric yawp of utter adoration" even through "the endless revelations of women as pure artifacts of farce, asses all up in the air." Many women, I suspect, would rather there be silence and keep their asses in descent.

Mailer does not want to quit the womb. But more importantly he wants the womb a certain way. If the way burdens the woman, if it creates life-situations for her which she finds intolerable, then Mailer will remind us that "he did not know if there was anything more difficult in a technological world than for a woman to reach the deeps of femininity. Certainly it was no easier than for a man to become a hero."

Mailer gives us a vision, not an argument. A difficulty is that the ideals of behavior incorporated in his vision may be congenial to relatively few people. He limits to men the possibilities of becoming heroes (Aye, there's a rub) though he acknowledges that given the machine and its rewards, non-heroes proliferate ("what an agony for a man if work were meaningless"). Women, if they are to be feminine (in depth) will be non-heroes as well, but Mailer believes that they have an advantage over their non-heroic male counterparts. If they are mothers, they have a chance to become true women. Fatherhood for a man does not yield the same abundance, for it does not give him his man's work. ("As technique reduced labor to activities which were often absurd, like punching the buttons on an automatic machine, so did the housework of women take on magnitude, for their work was directed at least to a basic end.")

Given Mailer's vision, men and women are prisoners of sex, not because they give sex meaning, but because they are herded into separate "life" cells on the basis of sex. If women are conceived of as having an inner space (wherein the deeps of femininity are to be sought), a space which links them to the future, and if men, wombless, are driven to possess it, then they may "be perhaps even the instrument of some larger force in that blind goat-kicking lust which would debase females, make all women cunts." Heroic sex, like heroic exploits in general, is notoriously blind about all of its consequences. Individuals who wish to escape from the ideal do so in Mailer's world view only at the cost of being less a man, less a woman. If, as the jailer acknowledges, the prison population is troubled, one wonders why the prison itself remains inviolate.

ELIZABETH JANEWAY
AND GERMAINE GREER

Arlyn Diamond

I DISLIKED *The Female Eunuch*[1] even before I read it because of the kind of ballyhoo it and its author received (the two being linked in a way that Elizabeth Janeway and her book[2] are not), and I wanted to review it for not very kindly motives. "Female Liberation movements have so far been very much a phenomenon of the media" Greer tells us and perhaps to prove the accuracy of what she says, she has become a star, or at least she is at the moment I write this. Stars in the movement seem to be invented by *Time* and *Esquire* and other guides to correct thought in the authentic *Women's Wear Daily* style: Millett's in, no, out, it's Steinem, no, Abzug, no, by God, it's Super Greer, the Women's Liberationist Men Love.

In one sense all the publicity means nothing. Books and people are not valuable because, or even in spite of, the fact that they make the cover of *Newsweek*. The talk does, however, leave a reminiscently sour taste in the mouth. It's not difficult to recall the depressing regularity with which the white press hailed "new" black leaders as soon as the "old" ones grew either too familiar or too threatening. The raves over *The Female Eunuch* are dangerous not only because they set up expectations the book can't possibly fulfill—it is not *the* book on Women's Liberation, if such a book could exist—but also because they indicate how easily its impact can be absorbed. Its author says she would be delighted to have a TV show sponsored by a cosmetic company. I believe her, and I can hardly wait for Revolutionary Red lipstick and emancipated eyeshadow to hit the markets. After all, we've come a long way baby in our no-bra bras.

No doubt Greer is lovable when she says that "sex is the principal confrontation in which new values can be worked out. Men are the enemy in much the same way that some crazed boy in uniform was the enemy of another like him in most respects except the uniform. One possible tactic is to try to get the uniform off." All the murky and even at times sinister suppositions made about our

---

[1] Germaine Greer, *The Female Eunuch*. New York: McGraw-Hill, 1970. $6.95.
[2] Elizabeth Janeway, *Man's World, Woman's Place*. New York: William Morrow. 1971. $8.95.

275

pre-history and the way Neanderthal boy looked at girl are just that, suppositions. We only know one thing as fact: from the beginning of the human race women have been removing their uniforms in the presence of the enemy (metaphorically speaking, of course) and it doesn't seem to have worked as a strategy for liberation, whatever else might have been accomplished.

She is right to think that the most important criticism of her book will come from the Left, although I am sure the Buckley ladies might have something very interesting to say about it too. Eschewing theory on the grounds that it isn't necessary, despite the fact that some theory must have dictated the division of her work into sections called *Body, Soul, Love, Hate* and *Revolution*, she comes up with analyses that are personal and ultimately provide solutions only for the young, strong and brilliant. The result of her rejection of a coherent system for looking at problems is that she winds up giving advice on how to do the laundry more cheaply and what brands of mascara to buy in her chapter on *Revolution*.

How much good will it do an assembly line worker or file clerk stuck in her job to be able to taste her own menstrual blood without flinching, thus passing Greer's rather exotic touchstone for mental health? How much good will it do a girl to stand tall and not be ashamed of her body when she's applying for one of the many state universities which requires higher entrance standards from female applicants than from male? How much good will it do a welfare mother to be told that in order to improve their condition women must not marry? These are not isolated examples of enthusiastic naivete but rather the logical consequences of her method, which in turn seems a consequence of her personality. An anarchist, she always prefers the private to the public method of dealing with large-scale problems and so she tends to confuse revolutionary life-style with a revolution. She notes approvingly that more people are enlisted in the ranks of the eaters of Macrobiotic foods and wearers of Salvation Army clothes than in the (relatively) organized ranks of Women's Liberation. History, however, tells us that health foods were very much a fad in early Nazi Germany, and according to the fashion pages distinctly non-revolutionary types are willing to pay a lot of money for elegantly worn and torn jeans. Eating crunchy Granola and wearing tie-dyed t-shirts may be nice, but has a very distant effect on an economy which decrees that women are always the lowest paid group among full-time workers, and which depends on the unpaid labor and consumerism of housewives.

Just because she willfully ignores those forces, unfortunately for most women the determining ones, which are beyond the power of nerve and libido to change—"It is largely a question of nerve," she says—her book fails to reach those who most need help, and indeed turns on them. Having convincingly and movingly shown how women are castrated by society, turned into fearful and resentful dependents, she surprisingly spends the rest of her book castigating them as the creators of their own misery. There is a strange confusion here of victim and oppression, so that her most telling insights into women's psychic lives are vitiated by her hatred for those who lead such lives. Feeling that women are crippled in their capacity to love others because they cannot love themselves, she feels that women must despise each other. Perhaps this self-contempt explains the gratuitous nastiness of her cracks about faculty wives, most wives, all those who haven't reached her state of independence, and her willingness to denigrate most of the members of the Women's movement she mentions. One begins to suspect that she enjoys being exceptional, and exceptions, as folk wisdom tells us, prove the rule. She has the ego to be a star, and it is not irrelevant that she thinks of Mailer as a betraying father. The lack of "sisterhood" she shows, of love for those who never chose to be eunuchs and who are made miserable by their sense of their own impotence is more than obtuse and unpleasant, it is destructive.

Having said all this, I cannot say that the book is not worth reading. Flawed as it is by simplistic notions and conceit, it can also be intuitively and brilliantly right. Too often we are the cowards she tells us we are, unwilling to risk failure and so never striving to be as strong as we might be. The will and energy she projects are in themselves exhilarating, and that may be why I am so enraged by the book's shortcomings. This could be the same frustrated rage Greer feels at women's willingness to be slaves and the trainers of slaves, but we rightly ask that an author who can write the following not leave us with her own bitterness and so limited a vision: "The surest guide to the correctness of the path that women take is *joy in the struggle*. Revolution is the festival of the oppressed. For a long time there may be no perceptible reward for women other than their new sense of purpose and integrity. Joy does not mean riotous glee, but it does mean the purposive employment of energy in a self-chosen enterprise. . . To have something to desire, something to make, something to achieve, and at last something genuine to give."

To turn from Greer to Janeway is to turn to a very different sort of author. If it seems an anti-climax to discuss *Man's World, Woman's Place* after having exercised the reviewer's privilege of *saeva indignatio* on *The Female Eunuch*, it is because, I am afraid, of basic corruptions in book-reviewing and advertising. Janeway's book has not received anywhere near the attention it deserves. Could it be because it doesn't take that obligatory and quotable swing at Norman Mailer? *Man's World* lacks the flash and bravado of *The Female Eunuch*. What it does have is a compassionate, deeply intelligent consideration of the problem of our attitudes towards that slippery abstraction, Woman.

By balanced I do not mean that it boasts the kind of pseudo-impartiality which winds up in an endorsement of the *status quo*, after a few kind words about equal pay for equal work. Her approach to her subject is through the concept of myth, in this case the myth that woman's place is in the home. "Around the core of difference between men and women, whether it is . . . physical or . . . psychological, a vast superstructure of myth has been built by emotion, by desire, need and fear." She goes on to say that we cannot deny this myth by wishful thinking, by demonstrating how crippling it is, or even by disproving it. All these techniques have been tried, and almost two hundred years after Mary Wollstonecraft we are still going over the same ground. The more current experience and new ideas and information invalidate the myth, the more frightened and angry those who cling to it become.

It is very difficult for many of us to understand why this particular myth is still so strong. Janeway, while not rejecting political and economic explanations (and one sign of her intelligence is her awareness of the bourgeois origins of the myth), looks for the answer in psychology. What she finds is that the image of the woman as a being so weak she must be protected and confined in the home masks another and more frightening vision, that of the all-powerful Goddess. Both of these figures combine in the Mother, the one who is all-powerful because she not only gives life, but can if she chooses, or so the child believes, satisfy all its needs. Unfortunately, in real life, even for the infant, there comes a time when the Mother fails. She will not, because she cannot, recreate the perfection of the womb, and so becomes a figure to be feared, loved and hated. She must be propitiated into a willing surrender of the power that cannot be taken away from her, and convinced that her true power lies in service and abnegation of self. It is impossible to reproduce here an argument so scrupulously constructed, but it is highly persuasive.

The major portion of *Man's World* is concerned with an examination of how the myth operates in ordinary life, especially in shaping the roles which determine our behavior and people's responses to and expectations of us. We are not yet free of these preshaped lives Janeway shows, even if we choose to celebrate their inversions. What is the witch who blights the crops and murders babies

Elizabeth Janeway and Germaine Greer

but the perfect mother gone mad? A few months ago I heard a little girl, checking with her mother for confirmation, say, "Little ladies don't run, do they?" That child was in training for the role of female eunuch. Janeway's study is an objective and scholarly presentation of Greer's insight, that Woman's Role, when it is not merely impossible, is often a crippling one.

Where Greer is openly emotional, Janeway is deliberately cool and impersonal. Her work is not revolutionary in tone, but I think a knowledge of it may be vital to those wishing to create a revolution. As the Women's Movement turns more and more to the necessities of reaching women to whom Greer's freedom is terrifying and disgusting, it will need the kinds of insights into traditional views of the world that Janeway gives. And because I think her book is so good, I find the relative neglect of it a great shame and waste. Germaine Greer is catapulted to instant fame as a spokeswoman for Women's Liberation partly because she can be placed in the niches reserved for fascinating English eccentrics and dazzling fallen women and thus dismissed. (I suppose that in England much is made of her Australian origin.) Recall the delighted relief with which *Time* printed Millett's support for gay women. Thank God—now that we've confirmed that she's the man-hater we always knew she was, we needn't even pretend to take her seriously. Or consider *Esquire*'s hatchet-job on Gloria Steinem that dealt with her ideas by ignoring them and talking about her personal life. *Man's World* is too sober, too conventional in style and method to be dismissed by turning its author into a personality instead of a thinker and it is largely ignored in those media workshops where public consciousness is created.

Nancy Rice

DEPRIVATION

(recurring dream poem)

No, it's not nothing.
I writhe here on the floor,
the screams sounding within my mind
as loud as the Hong Kong baby's
on the tape recording.

What did the child want?
The severe British lady was discussing
heroin with the addict;
trams passed,
and an unknown child screamed.

But I. What is it I want?
Am I hungry? Exhausted?
One is adult now, but can one
go on covering it and saying
no, I want nothing?

In my dream, the cafeteria line shortens,
but it is one o'clock. The broiled liver and baked squash
are all sold or put away.
I can help myself to jello salad
(for a quarter) if I want it.

My anger is no more frivolous
than the baby's,
who wants milk
and is given a sugar tit.
Some sustenance is being denied me.

MARRIAGES

ZELDA & SCOTT   ELEANOR & FRANKLIN

Mary Heath

"MARRIAGE is so unlike everything else," says a chastened Dorothea in George Eliot's *Middlemarch*. "There is something even awful in the nearness it brings." It is to that word "awful," expressing both dread and reverence, that we respond; it is a word not wholly inappropriate to use for the American marriages recounted in these two biographies.[1]

Marriages begin where novels often end, with weddings. We have two princesses: Zelda, named for a gypsy queen, at whose christening (Edmund Wilson says) "the fairies had been tipsy"; and Eleanor, of whom an aunt hopefully said: "But the ugly duckling may turn out to be a swan." For them we have two princes, both handsome, each able to overcome impediments in his pursuit of love: in one case, the "common sense" of his princess about the uncertainty of a writer's income; in the other, a possessive mother who may have hoped for her son "a more worldly and social match." True love prevails, the wedding dates are set: March 17, 1905 for the Roosevelts; then, fifteen years later, for the younger couple, April 3, 1920.

Social position, fifteen years, and their different temperaments lead one to expect the contrast in wedding styles: at the earlier wedding, bridesmaids, Brussels lace and the President of the United States (who, attracting most of the attention to himself, caused the groom to appear "a little put out"); at the later wedding of the Fitzgeralds: "no music, no flowers, no photographers" and a fidgeting groom who set the hour for the ceremony ahead. The setting of both weddings, for quite different reasons, was New York. The orphaned Eleanor, with no home of her own but a large number of New York relatives, was married from an aunt's house; Zelda, wishing to avoid the confusion and expense of a large and Southern wedding, preferred the atmosphere of an elopement.

Weddings are followed by honeymoons. The Roosevelts spent a week at Hyde Park, followed by a European tour the next summer. "The Fitzgeralds' honeymoon at the Biltmore was so

---

[1] Sara Mayfield, *Exiles from Paradise: Zelda and Scott Fitzgerald*. New York: Delacorte Press, 1971. $8.95. Joseph P. Lash, *Eleanor and Franklin*. New York: W. W. Norton & Co., 1971. $15.00.

hilarious that it was cut short by the request of the management."
They too, a year later, sailed for Europe. The Roosevelts enjoyed
their trip: visits to places that had been the scenes of former happiness, to bookshops and museums; new clothes and furs for Eleanor
in Paris; a meeting with the Webbs in England. Both she and
Franklin made their first public speeches: opening a flower show at
Novar. The Fitzgeralds unexpectedly—they are associated so much in
the imagination with "abroad"—had a terrible time in Europe. They
met no royalty: The Marchioness of Milford Haven, Scott com-
plained, was as close as they came. Neither Paris nor Italy pleased
them. "God damn the continent of Europe," Scott wrote as they
were about to sail for home. Zelda, pregnant, wanted her baby
born in Montgomery, but their stay there lasted only a month, and
the baby was born in St. Paul. Disappointed that the child was not
a son, Zelda, nevertheless, became devoted to her. "I'm raising my
girl to be a flapper," Zelda would say later. Scott dazzled the baby's
eyes with gold pieces, "in hopes that she would marry a millionaire."

The Roosevelts too had a daughter shortly after their first wedding anniversary. "The mother's pleasure in the birth of her first
child was only slightly marred by her knowledge that her mother-
in-law had yearned for a boy." As Zelda struggled to accommodate
herself to life in St. Paul—the cold, uninteresting Midwestern
friends, Scott's absorption in his work, and his temper when drinking, as well as his interest in other women—so Eleanor began the
long attempt to turn herself into the sort of wife she imagined her
husband and her mother-in-law, Sara, wanted: she learned to swim,
though she failed at golf and tennis, tried to be sociable, felt as
inadequate as Zelda about running a house. Still, one senses the
beginnings of rebellion: Zelda expresses herself more openly and
angrily while Eleanor subsides into tears or withdraws in injured
silence. The first shock of the "nearness" of marriage has been taken
in; the years of growing struggle or resignation are about to begin.

On March 3, 1922, *The Beautiful and Damned* was published.
Zelda had helped correct proof, and suggested another ending for
the novel. The heroine on the dust jacket looked like her; Scott
thought the hero a parody of himself: "a runt who looked like a
young tough in his first dinner jacket." Zelda's mocking review, in
which she identified excerpts from her own diary and old letters,
did not help; she ended it with "plagiarism begins at home." It was
her first not altogether friendly accusation that Scott made use of
her "material."

Collaboration, turning to competition between them, becomes
the emotional and moral theme of their marriage. Zelda had said
to a friend, before her marriage, that "she felt it was her mission in

life to help him realize his potential as a writer." One does not know how seriously to take this, or what she really meant by it. Her life—that is, the way she saw things, her experiences, often her words, finally her "madness"—and her husband's response became the subject of his novels. For how long this was a willing collaboration is hard to judge: the evidence conflicts, both Fitzgeralds zigzag across their separate and mutual pasts. It is rather like reading a cross-written letter.

It is perfectly clear that as a novelist Scott saw her life as exclusively his own material; and, with some of the hysteria of a gothic novel, the evidence begins to mount that not only the novelist but the husband wanted exclusive rights: jealousy of friends, prohibitions against dancing and painting, control over what she could write about, always the threat of the asylum. After her release from the Swiss sanatarium and the return to Montgomery, Zelda did begin to write again. She had already published a number of stories, one of which, under Scott's name, had earned $1000, which they split. While Scott was working on movie scripts in Hollywood, Zelda wrote him self-deprecating letters, insisting on her dependence on him. But Milford suggests that Zelda may have been exaggerating her need of him in order to "demonstrate to him and to herself how perfectly normal she had become, for part of Forel's cure had been a somewhat mysterious 're-education' of Zelda in terms of her role as wife to Scott."[2]

Scott's return to Montgomery "coincided" with (there is some evidence that his presence brought on) another breakdown. This time Zelda went to Phipps Clinic. She began to improve, and was allowed to write and paint for a few hours a day. Dr. Squires, the therapist most closely associated with her case, wrote Scott that she had read the second chapter of Zelda's novel (this on March 2, 1931) and found it better than the first chapter. Scott immediately wrote the doctor with a summary of Zelda's talents and character. Dr. Squires wrote right back: the novel was finished (March 9) and on its way to Scribner's.

Now the Novelist is aroused, enraged: how dare they allow Zelda to send off a manuscript before he has released it? Dr. Squires apologizes, Zelda apologizes, and sends a copy off to Scott. He immediately wires Scribner's—the novel would "seriously compromise what literary future she may have"—and accuses Zelda of stealing

---

[2] Nancy Milford's biography, *Zelda* (Harper & Row, N.Y., 1970), offers a much fuller and more thoroughly documented account of Zelda's "breakdowns" than does Miss Mayfield's book.

his novel. If it is to be published, certain things must be deleted from it: any accounts of nervous breakdowns and mental hospitals. We remember that, in the background (and Scott has had, he points out, to put it aside to earn quick money) there is *Tender is the Night*.

Save Me the Waltz was published by Scribner's in the fall of 1932. The deletions had been made. "It is a good novel now," Scott wrote Perkins, "perhaps a very good novel." But he warned Perkins to keep praise "on the staid side" so as not to excite Zelda. The novel—perhaps just as well, one begins to think—did not attract much attention, or sell well.

Zelda was released from Phipps with the understanding that she must not again succumb to any temptation to "overwork." A visitor enraged Scott by too extravagantly praising her novel and urging her to take up dancing again. Scott quarreled with him, then wrote a hasty apology: he must protect Zelda from her "incipient egomania."

The belief that he was "protecting" Zelda, perhaps his need to believe that, lasted to the end of his life. On several occasions she asked for a separation or a divorce; he could not, one feels, give her up. He could not give up his drinking either, though the doctors said, unequivocally, it was the most serious impediment to a life for them together. And yet they clung—it is the word for an "awful nearness"—unto death. Could she, without him, have been a dancer, a painter, a serious writer? There is evidence of talent, astonishing productivity for a sick woman. Did she, literally, "drive him to drink?" One turns the pages of these biographies, back to front, coming again to the beginning: there they are, the two of them, shocking Montgomery in their matching linen knickerbocker suits. They had not meant to shock, Zelda insisted; it had been a way of presenting a united front to the world.

On election day, 1910, Sara Roosevelt's diary recorded events in this order: "Anna weighs 42.8; James 35.13. Franklin elected State Senator with about 1,500 majority." At that time Eleanor too might have subscribed to that list as the correct order: concerns of women were, properly, domestic before public. Still there is a doubt: she ardently supported her husband's ambitions, believed in public service (she had done settlement work before her marriage), was, always, more wholeheartedly wife than mother. On that November day the first public step was taken by both of them; and, on the domestic front, a new independence began. They would no longer be living next door to Sara.

Lash tells us that "Eleanor found marriage to a man at the center of public activity stimulating," and it comes as no surprise, even if

Marriages

we didn't know how the story was going to turn out. For in Albany their public life is not debutante balls and fashionable dinners; political meetings go on, often at the Roosevelt home, late into the night. Eleanor is present, listening, eventually beginning to ask questions, finally, though in private, expressing opinions. She meets Louis Howe and does not like him; we can predict that that, too, will change. Her idealism, her wish to serve, begin to receive practical education. For all her fastidiousness, humility and curiosity make her an eager student.

Albany is the first stop. In January 1913 Franklin was asked how he'd like to be Assistant Secretary of the Navy. "Bully well," was the reply, and the Roosevelts moved to Washington. At first, the glimpses of Eleanor are all domestic or social: "I've paid 60 calls this week," she writes in a letter, and continues with a list of dinners and luncheons. Two more sons are born; conventional duties seem to close round her. There is a kind of admiration for cousin Alice who, by contrast, does only what amuses her (the young Zelda will later defend her own dancing of the hula by pointing out that "Alice Roosevelt did it"). But there are glimpses of the serious young woman: a quarrel with a relative over his pessimism about the "common people."

War came, and though it was a cause of anxiety and horror, it allowed Eleanor to move outside the family. She goes "canteening," supervises the knitting of the Navy Department wives, works for the Red Cross and ultimately achieves improvements in the conditions at St. Elizabeth's Hospital. Disagreeing with Sara's fears that war lowers morals, Eleanor replies: "Yet I think it is waking people to a sense of responsibility and obligation to work who perhaps never had it before."

Franklin was sent to Europe in July 1918. When Eleanor had been asked to organize for the Red Cross in May, she had regretfully refused. She did not feel independent enough, and "in her heart of hearts she felt her primary obligation was to stay with her children." She missed her husband; her loneliness during their separations shows through in her letters. She had wanted a marriage like the one Beatrice Webb described: "apart we each of us live only half a life; together we each of us have a double life." Shortly after Franklin's return from Europe, that ideal had to be revised.

The discovery of adultery seems a novelistic device, even in real life. No matter how sympathetically Mr. Lash describes Eleanor's discovery of the Mercer letter, we cannot see it as a simple turning point, a moment that turned Mrs. Roosevelt into Eleanor Roosevelt, unless we willfully forget the lonely child and the earnest young woman, the exciting evenings in Albany, and the mother-in-law.

285

The chapter is called "Trial by Fire"; but how many earlier trials there were, how many more were to come. It is awkward to recount; only a novelist, perhaps, should deal with it.

Within a few years of the "discovered letter" Eleanor Roosevelt emerges as a more important political figure than her husband. Two events made this possible: her husband's affliction with polio and Louis Howe's enlarged appreciation of her abilities. Eleanor, during Franklin's convalescence, has at last a real issue on which to fight Sara: she will not let her husband become an invalid. Howe, who first saw the promise in the young legislator, supports Eleanor, propels her really into politics. She becomes her husband's stand-in.

Her activities in support of the Democratic Party also, importantly, introduce her to a group of active and independent women, women whose names we may never have heard of, but who have worked for suffrage or reform or the labor movement: Nancy Cook and Marion Dickerman (who would become Eleanor's partner first in the school, Todhunter, then in the industries at Val-Kil), Eleanor Morgenthau, Rose Schneiderman, Maud Swartz, Esther Lape, Elizabeth Read, Frances Perkins are only a few of them.

As important as her association with these women is—if one felt dismay at her reluctance to champion women's suffrage, her work with and for women later on consoles—of equal importance is her growing experience as a public speaker. Nothing except Louis Howe and her own dedication to her husband's ideas (though, as time goes on, her own ideas appear more and more to be in advance of his) could have forced the shy, self-conscious woman to turn herself into a speaker. And a speaker who could overcome a fluting voice and a giggle, and improvise on the spot. She begins, too, to write for popular journals. Access to a large public—not merely an intellectual or already converted audience—was, for the Democratic Party, the greatest gain of these years. Later, her talent and willingness were put to good advantage: to let Eleanor try things out became, during the White House years, a useful device.

Recovery, the governorship, then the presidency for him; for her, lecturing and writing, teaching, finally direct involvement in the practical working out of the New Deal. The day of Franklin Roosevelt's first inauguration was cold and gray, like the mood of the country. But both Roosevelts were ready to face the challenge. It was imperative that the country recover from its fear. Eleanor believed, too, that the Depression had been caused by "defects of spirit and character" as much as by the failure of institutions. The country had lived through an "orgy." She found the burst of applause during the President's address "a little terrifying" but added: "We must meet the future courageously, with a cheerful spirit."

Marriages

The two of them set about making themselves examples.

The story of this marriage very nearly disappears into the world of public epic, bigger than life. There are still domestic or private glimpses, but Events, writ large, overshadow them. If the Fitzgeralds together gave the name to a decade and epitomized its particular mood, perhaps what the Roosevelts together did was to give to what Sara would have called the "common people" a sense of themselves as characters in history.

The tone and manner of both biographers is appropriate to the characters they present. Mayfield writes as an old friend, the voice personal, anecdotal; it would be a loss, however, to read her book without Milford's far more complete biography of Zelda at hand. Lash, by contrast, carefully documents, accumulates, offers evidence, finally gives the reader a sense of a period. If Mayfield's biography is a kind of vindication, Lash's is a monument. Given the lives and fates of the two women, it is appropriate.

And it is fitting too that in biographies of marriage the women dominate the stage: "the domestic epic," George Eliot calls it. The business we call marriage has always been, and with good reason, of more concern to women than to men. For middle-class women, at any rate, it remains, even a hundred years after the universities were opened to us, an institution of higher learning. (And flunking out of it, at least one woman psychologist has suggested, can lead to incarceration in an institution like the one at which Zelda was to be "re-educated" as Scott's wife.) To set these biographies side by side, then, directs the attention to questions of education and work.

Both women, on the threshold of marriage, expressed a desire to serve their husbands' interests, ambitions, talents. Reading on, however, one weighs this desire against the lack of any specific or coherent idea of work, either for wages or personal ambition. Before she began teaching at the Todhunter School, Eleanor Roosevelt said:

> If I had to go out and earn my own living, I doubt if I'd even make a very good cleaning woman. I have no talents, no experience, no training for anything.

Zelda, before her first breakdown, said:

> I think a woman gets more happiness out of being gay, light-hearted, unconventional, mistress of her own fate, than out of a career that calls for hard work, intellectual pessimism and loneliness.

Ten years later in 1934, at the end of a notice of a show of her paintings a reviewer wrote:

From the sanatorium last week which she temporarily left against doctors' orders to see a show of Georgia O'Keeffe's art, Zelda Fitzgerald was hoping her pictures would gratify her great ambition—to earn her own living.

Both women sought in marrying a purpose, an institution as it were, out of which to act; but so, one feels, did the two men. The need was at least as great on their side. And yet it was Zelda who was institutionalized, is remembered as mad, was burned to death because she was locked in; and Eleanor who suffered a sense of failure as a woman, became the subject of all those jokes. Hard not to cry: unfair, unfair! Hard not to say that without Zelda there would have been no *Tender is the Night*, or without Eleanor no New Deal. The life of one woman we call, if not tragic at least pathetic; that of the other, a triumph. One woman was, finally, subjugated to her husband; the other emerged, her talents and achievements recognized.

Zelda had never learned self-discipline, Scott said. Eleanor had, all too early, learned at least self-control. But in the interest of what self, and for what purpose? The answer would seem to be: a self found, or lost, in another. Eleanor adapted to the institution, then; she could say—would insist, even to herself—right up to the end that what she did she did only for her husband or for others. It was finally Zelda's wish to succeed on her own, her "competitive-ness," that lost her the battle. But if we look again at these women in the framework of marriage, perhaps it is nearer the felt truth to see Eleanor Roosevelt's life as a cautionary tale, Zelda Fitzgerald's as a tragedy, in all the sense of blasted promise that the word implies.

Carol Hebald

NOTE FROM BELLEVUE

The climate of oblivion is mildewed.
Mice flit about
Like confused functionaries.

As fat Leda sits on her Hershey bar and cries,
I lie dazed,
Defining the sweetness of your flesh.

Hogwash.
In future, my dear,
You must admit your desires more openly.
If it is a tableau you wish, then confess it.
I am, after all, a woman of responsibility
Who demands to know her function.
Very well then.

Just because Bridie O'Bradovich
Dovens six times nightly in the womb of Jesus
Doesn't mean that I have to eat fish on Fridays.
Am I my sister's keeper?
You recall my sister.
After her husband cleared his phlegm
Over the wilds of Madagascar,
She up and died
Having had the satisfaction
That her home was completely furnished.
Mother, on the other hand,
Was gay for about 8½ years,
But she's over it now
Due to the fact
That in his latter years
My father grew a long nose
Which was very nice.
Something else he grew was long, too.
It was also very nice.
Altogether he was a long man
And that was why she liked him.
                              —The truncated girl—
P.S. Would Prince Charming have loved Cinderella
    Had she had big feet? Justify your answer.
        (More of what you want?
        In your next letter,
        Tell me what you want.
        I should like very much to please you.)

289

Ellen Dibble

DEPRESSION

This was a child—
Eyes—
A loving cup of solemn hush—
Watching me
As he waits to fall asleep.

I ask him, "Shall I go?"

His silence reaches around him
    to shroud his threatened thoughts.

And I am embarrassed,
    but I stay . . . chained,
Trying not to squirm,
As blue eyes, troubled but very still,
Hold my discomfort
Without dismay.

CALLING THE BABYSITTER

Let me flatter your honor.
(I am not trying to discredit you.)
I would like to be graced by your company for a while
    and to offer you food, great kindness and holy prestige.
However—although I will let you refuse me this—
    I desire a service from you
        for which I will pay.
You know this is not why I am calling you.
I am calling as a friend . . .
    as a bewildered admirer . . .
    and, though I conceal this with steel shades,
I am calling you as an enemy.
By chance I require
    an intimate service—will you come?

"SO YOU MAYN'T EVER CALL ME
ANYTHING BUT CARRINGTON"

J. J. Wilson

Dear Carrington,

Who are you? I have recently been reading your personal letters[1] to lovers and friends, and even excerpts from your diaries. What is less, I've been hearing gossip about you from Michael Holroyd (*Lytton Strachey: The Years of Achievement 1910–1932*, Vol. ii); he appears to find your appeal to his friends more difficult to explain than any of their so-called deviant relationships. Your own editor, David Garnett, feels it necessary to reassure readers that though you were not a really beautiful woman, your letters are still worth considering. (p. 9) The male reviewers, responding predictably, almost unanimously declare you an artless and charming child, who must have resented being a woman, and whose love affairs are thus "all the more interesting" (this last curious conclusion from some Lolita fan perhaps?). There was one stand-out who preferred the pleasantly medieval epithet, "this wayward woman." Years ago in *Crome Yellow*, Aldous Huxley called you "an exception . . . a *femme supérieure*," but that strikes me as the kind of phrase kept in French because no one is very sure of its actual meaning. The best translation might be your own description of yourself: "I am more aware of everything than you suppose, or anyone perhaps supposes." (p. 224)

One reason we may never know who you are is that all the primary texts are being filtered down to us through various male consciousnesses. For all of us without access to the original letters, you now *are* this collection, and while one should, I know, be grateful for the patient researching and culling, there are so many questions I want to ask about you, and almost none of them does Mr. Garnett answer. I wonder also what principles of selection were involved in the cutting of your so organic letters? Discretion? Surely the time for that is past. Repetition? But it is disconcerting to find a three-word editorial warning that two words have been omitted,

---

[1] *Carrington: Letters and Extracts from her Diaries*, chosen and with an introduction by David Garnett, with a biographical note by Noel Carrington. New York: Holt, Rinehart & Winston, 1970. $12.50.

and the frequent notices "[one line omitted]" end by being more distracting than economical surely. And one does wonder if the choice of letters and the notes to them might not have been substantially and substantively different had one of your women friends been called in at least to co-edit.

Would a woman editor have dwelled quite as much on your sexual "problems," for instance? I can guarantee that she would *not* have used the evidence that you had deep attachments to your women friends, that you hated your period, that you adored your brother, that you loved a man who couldn't/wouldn't ball you, that you married a man you didn't love, that you loved some men you didn't marry, and that you often felt guilty for spoiling the joy in a relationship, to declare you "an unconscious lesbian." While we might all agree that you experienced difficulty in deciding your sexual identity (who doesn't?), I wonder if your sexuality remained uncommitted because you fell in love with a homosexual, rather than the other way round as has been assumed.

Your love for Lytton Strachey is completely comprehensible to me, and so, alas, is your suicide after his death; he was a man who needed warmth more than he could offer it, a need you could and did fulfill. You found in Lytton an entirely absorbing *animus,* and only everyone's conviction, sadly Lytton's too, that you must not be satisfied caused you to seek satisfaction elsewhere, I suspect. Or it could be said that your Prince Charming was a split archetype: father in Lytton and prince in Ralph Partridge. Like being married to a Super-ego and an Id. Was Gerald Brenan the ego? If so, your statement to Gerald, "And yet when it came to the point, I couldn't face giving up Ralph and Lytton for you," becomes of considerable psychological interest. (p. 249) You don't fit the patterns, Carrington, and so people can't seem to stop gossiping about you, perhaps seeking through you as objective correlative some truer perception of their own sexual potentials. I am enough of a fatalist in such matters myself to agree with Lytton when he said: "Remember that I too have never had my moon! We are helpless in these things—dreadfully helpless." (p. 183)

I do not, however, allow myself to be fatalistic any longer in considering the right use of women's artistic creativity, and I began reading your life account as a kind of cautionary tale of yet another Shakespeare's sister. (You remember that horror story in Woolf's *A Room of One's Own?*) The first letters, especially those to your painter friend Mark Gertler, described the dilemma of the young woman artist in classic terms: "If only I had any money I should not be obliged to stick at home like this. And to earn money every day, and paint what one wants to, seems almost impossible." (p. 23)

Carrington

But once you had a room of your own, that studio whose pictur-
esque squalor you described with some relish to Lytton in a 1916
letter, your problems weren't over, were they? (I myself sum up
the three major limitations of the "room of one's own" myth as
Loneliness, Laziness, and Lust.) Then, once entranced by Lytton,
you set about becoming essential to him, and soon you are writing,
as it happens in a letter to Virginia Woolf, that arch-debunker of
the "angel in the house" syndrome: "How can I do woodblocks
when for the last month, ever since in fact we left Northumberland,
I've been a ministering angel, hewer of wood and drawer of water."
(p. 106) Later you complain that your "useful grimy hands" empty-
ing chamber pots and making beds were all that made the elegant
talk of some weekend guests possible and "I couldn't for a whole
weekend do any painting." (p. 152)

Obviously, however, domestic duties, the care of even such a
household as Tidmarsh, would not be enough to deflect a true
painting fervor. The process was rather more subtle than that, as
I chart it in your letters and diaries, keeping my eyes open for the
obstacles women find in becoming committed artists described in
Linda Nochlin's recent *Art News* article; I only have the space here
to summarize my interpretation of what may have happened to you,
the prizewinning Slade student. One difficulty you did *not* encounter anyway was finding nude models—your husband and editor
Garnett himself were glad to oblige—but in more insidious ways the
old patterns enforced themselves even in liberated Bloomsbury.

Lytton always needed a good deal of looking after, of course,
but aside from his ill-health, an atmosphere of expectation prevailed around him (the general feeling being perhaps that so great
an eccentricity must needs be justified by some great "work");
everything was arranged so that the future great man could produce, and produce he finally did. No one seems to have these sorts
of expectations for you, Carrington; indeed all the expectations still
seem to be that if you could just have gotten your sex life straight-
ened out, you'd have been fine. . . . And with a quality as fragile as
creative confidence, these elements of support, expectation, belief
are crucial. In a *ménage* where Lytton Strachey is accepted by all
as The Creator, where Ralph Partridge's difficulties in finding a
suitable career absorbed everyone's energies, a kind of credibility
gap grew up around your image of yourself as a painter.

Garnett, in his preface, takes the men in your life to task for not
encouraging you in your painting: ". . . and she became discouraged." (p. 13) Holroyd, on the other hand, writes in a footnote that
"Lytton always encouraged Carrington with her painting . . ." and
gives it as his opinion that your inviolable shyness kept you from

The Massachusetts Review

exhibiting. (*Lytton Strachey*, II, p. 478) What do you say? Various revealing statements, such as: "R[alph] P[artridge] is so busy tying up these books and typewriting *that I get rather merged into it* and find it interrupts my painting." (p. 173; underlining mine) And even more ominous: "The alternative is to try to be a serious artist." (p. 323) No "serious artist" sees that kind of a commitment as an alternative, but women often do, of course. As Nancy Milford asks: "In the end is it so difficult to understand that as long as we continue to maintain the dichotomy of male as generative and female as gestative that the creative woman (as well, I believe, as the creative man) must face exceptional conflicts in her development?" (*New York Times Book Review*, Sept. 19, 1971.)

The effect of these conflicts on you, all this merging with others, this feeling the primacy of other commitments and roles, this painting of signboards and trunks and cups and dining room walls which Holroyd makes so much of (cf. *Lytton Strachey*, II, p. 478), was that your art did not develop. You did not give your painting the continuous plumbing, reaching, experimenting, and just time in front of the easel necessary to make it grow along with you. You begin to make decisions based on this diminished vision, as in a December 1922 entry when you choose not to start anything too big and difficult "or I know I shall then despair and give up the composition before it is finished." (p. 237) And then later:

> I feel slightly depressed as I can't do any painting. *There is no reason* except that I feel I know what the result will be before I start on the picture and the result is so dull always it hardly seems worth beginning. [p. 369; underlining J.J.W.]

Your painting had begun to bore you. In order to keep interested yourself, and I suspect, dear Carrington, to get some attention from your friends, to surprise and delight them, you began to use your superb technique in *tour de force* works such as the painting of the cook and the cat of the Biddesden wall which you refer to near the end: ". . . perhaps one of the only pictures I have ever 'brought off'. I am glad Lytton saw it and liked it." (p. 496) In this the last reference you made to your art we have its epitaph. "Lytton saw it and liked it" is not motivation enough for being a serious painter; it is all too often the motivation behind much of women's creative activity—to dress so that someone will see and like them, to fix a meal that some will eat and like, to iron a shirt that can be worn and liked—but that kind of motivation is a limitation. Van Gogh or Kathe Kollwitz did not paint so that someone might see it and like it. . . . Well, I hope my point is made, Carrington. I do not

294

condemn the interior decorating even, except insofar as it was a sign of the deflection. After all, Vanessa Bell painted doors and walls all over her house, but the situation at Charleston was quite different and the results were different too—babies were raised, lives lived, parties held, but everybody who wanted to paint, painted.

The deflecting factors are complex but they worked on you, you who were "never quite so happy as when I paint." (p. 258) You would never blame the gradual falling away from your art on anyone else, of course, and come closest to expressing the dilemma as you saw it in the following letter to Lytton:

> And yet do you know, this morning I felt these conflicting emotions are destroying my purpose for painting. That perhaps that feeling which I have had ever since I came to London years ago now, that I am not strong enough to live in this world of people, and paint, is a feeling which has complete truth in it. And yet when I envision leaving you and going like Gerald into isolation, I feel I should be so wretched that I should never have the spirit to work. (pp. 170-1)

Fortunately, the nice, the capping irony, is that out of your very need to "live in the world of people" has come this volume of letters, not a sublimation but a substitution perhaps for the art you did not do. To me, there seem interesting analogies to Anaïs Nin's now famous diaries. Both of you invested much of your creativity in your lives, where it was needed by others (perhaps seeking to evade the demands of your own artistic selves), but then "all the works and days of hands" became your love song; your lives, through your letters and diaries, became your art.

As Gerald Brenan rather ingenuously exclaims in his review of the letters: "Who could ever have supposed that these rapidly scrawled, badly spelled sheets that she was continuously sending off to her friends could look so well in print?" He goes on to claim them among the best letters to have been published in England in this century, however, and long ago writing to Carrington herself, he caught this essence and their importance well:

> . . . gesture, speech, walk, expression, seen through a medium of words; like the rustling of leaves, the voices of birds, the arrangement of natural forms. Education has not deadened in you this mode of expression, has not, as it has for nearly all of us, reduced speech and writing to the level of a vulgar formula, through which we can barely let our own natures be recognized. (quoted by Holroyd, *Lytton Strachey*, II, p. 231)

While fine poetic examples of your unique style and visual imagination leap to the eye when reading the letters (such as: ". . . with only the half-sucked acid drop of a moon for company," (p. 281) or "They [sensations] rush through my head like flames up a chimney" (p. 275), the example which sticks in my memory, neither poetic nor very visual, certainly demonstrates your originality and escape from vulgar formula: "The yellow cat has passed away. Dead as a ducat." (p. 237) To follow the pious euphemism of "passed away" with the abrupt phrasing and startling analogy "Dead as a du*cat*." simply would not occur to someone who saw himself as a "serious writer." And yet it works. My daughter! My ducats!

So I am writing to congratulate you and to thank you, Carrington, and even here we are making literary history—think how few letters written by one woman to another have been preserved in literature (always excepting Clarissa's, which were hardly of the sisterhood is powerful variety). Would you, now at some Yegen where letters are slow arriving if at all, be surprised to know that your life has become allegory for many of us, that we know you better than we know our own friends, ourselves, that we recognize your own nature though we still wonder just who you really are. . . .

love,

J. J. Wilson

SOJOURNER TRUTH CALLS UPON THE PRESIDENT: AN 1864 LETTER

Sojourner Truth was born a slave in Ulster, Ulster County, New York probably in 1797.

In the following letter she tells of her interview on October 25, 1864 with President Lincoln from whom she sought commendation for work among the thousands of freedmen who were living in deplorable conditions in a camp, known as Freedman's Village located in Arlington Heights, Virginia. A month later, she received a commission to serve as Counselor to the freed people living in Freedman's Village. This letter was first published in the Anti-Slavery Reporter *for March 1, 1865. [Dorothy Porter]*

" 'Freedman's Village, Va.,
Nov. 17, 1864.

" 'Dear Friend,—I am at Freedman's village. After my visit to the President, I went to Mrs. Swisshelm's,[1] and remained there three weeks, and held two meetings in Washington, in Mr. Garnet's[2] Presbyterian church, for the benefit of the *Coloured Soldier's Aid Society,* both of which were largely attended. I then spent a week on Mason's Island with the freedmen there; held several meetings, and was present at the celebration of the emancipation of the slaves in Maryland, and spoke upon that occasion.

" 'It was about eight o'clock in the morning when I called upon the President, in company with Mrs. C.[3] On entering his reception room, we found about a dozen persons waiting to see him; amongst them were two coloured women, some white women also. One of the gentlemen present knew me, and I was introduced to several others, and had a pleasant time while waiting, and enjoyed the conversation between the President and

---

[1] Jane Swisshelm, an abolitionist and feminist was a friend of Sojourner Truth with whom she stopped while visiting Washington.

[2] Henry Highland Garnet, Negro abolitionist and Presbyterian pastor.

[3] Mrs. George B. Carse.

his auditors very much. He showed as much respect and kindness to the coloured persons present as to the whites. One case was a coloured woman who was sick, and likely to be turned out of her house, on account of her inability to pay her rent. The President listened to her with much attention, and replied with kindness and tenderness that he had given so much, he could give no more, but told her where she could get the needed aid, and asked Mrs. C. to direct and assist her, which she did.

" 'He was seated at his desk. Mrs. C. and myself walked up to him, Mrs. C. said to him. 'This is Sojourner Truth, who has come all the way from Michigan to see you.' He then arose, gave me his hand, and said, 'I am glad to see you.' I said to him. 'Mr. President, when you first took your seat, I feared you would be torn to pieces: for I likened you unto Daniel, who was thrown into the lion's den; for if the lions did not tear you to pieces, I knew it would be God that had saved you; and I said if He spared me, I would see you before the four years had expired. And He has done so, and I am now here to see you for myself.' He congratulated me on my having been spared. I then said, 'I appreciate you, for you are the best President who has ever taken seat.' He replied thus: 'I expect you have reference to my having emancipated the slaves in my Proclamation; but,' said he, mentioning the names of several of his predecessors, and particularly Washington, 'they were just as good, and would have done just as I have, if the time had come. And if the people over the river,' pointing across the Potomac, 'had behaved themselves, I could not have done what I have.' I replied, 'I thank God you were the instrument selected by Him and the people to do these things.' I presented him with one of my shadows and songs, for which he thanked me, and said he would keep them as a remembrance. He then showed me the splendid Bible presented to him by the coloured people.[4] You doubtless

---

[4] For a description of the Bible and an account of the presentation by the coloured people of Baltimore—See Benjamin Quarles, *The Negro in the Civil War* (Boston: Little, Brown and Co., 1953), pp. 254–255.

Sojourner Truth

have seen a description of it. I have seen it for myself, and can say it is beautiful beyond description. After I looked it over, I said to him, 'This is beautiful; and to think that the coloured people have given this to the head of the Government, and to think that Government ones [once] sanctioned laws that would not permit its people to learn enough to be able to read that book.' And for what? Let them answer who can.' I am proud to say that I never was treated with more kindness and cordiality that I was by the great and good man Abraham Lincoln, by the grace of God President of the United States for four years more. He took my little book, and with the same hand that signed the death-warrant of Slavery, he wrote in her autograph book as follows:

'For Auntie Sojourner Truth.'
'October 29, 1864.   'A. Lincoln.'

" 'I then took my leave of him, and thanked God from the bottom of my heart that I always have advocated this cause, and done it openly and boldly; and now I shall feel more in duty bound to do so. May God assist me! I have obtained a little house here, through the kindness of the Captain of the Guard, and think I will remain, and do all I can in the way of instructing the people in habits of industry and economy. Many of them are entirely ignorant of housekeeping. Any favours in the way of nourishment, and some sheets and pillows, will be very acceptable, and may be forwarded to Washington, addressed to me, care of Captain George B. Carse, Freedman's Village, V. Give my love to all who inquire after me.

" 'Sammy and I are both well and happy, and feel that we are in good employment, and find plenty of friends.

"Your friend,
"Sojourner Truth.' "[5]

---

[5] Sojourner Truth spent a year in the camp teaching the freed women all kinds of domestic work, habits of cleanliness and how best to make use of their new state of liberty.

Sojourner Truth

299

Sojourner Truth, Sophia Smith Collection